Can't We All Just Get Along?

Improving the Law Enforcement-Intelligence Community Relationship

CENTER FOR STRATEGIC INTELLIGENCE RESEARCH

NDIC PRESS

National Defense Intelligence College
Washington, DC
June 2007

The views expressed in this book are those of the authors and
do not reflect the official policy or position of the Department of
Defense of the U.S. Government

The National Defense Intelligence College supports and encourages research on intelligence issues that distills lessons and improves Intelligence Community capabilities for policy-level and operational consumers.

Can't We All Just Get Along: Improving the Law Enforcement-Intelligence Community Relationship

The FBI vs. CIA turf battles of the Cold War are the stuff of Washington legend. Things are much better now. They were getting better anyway, and then 9/11 accelerated the process. But...there is room for improvement.

The first essays here lay out some of the intelligence techniques that have proven effective in either Law Enforcement (LE) or the Intelligence Community (IC) and that might be useful to exchange and apply. They are followed by essays that point out some of the difficulties inherent in integrating the two communities. We conclude with a few abstracts of recent work done at the National Defense Intelligence College on other aspects of this topic. The bibliography is a compilation of key sources from the authors' works but is by no means exhaustive.

The writers, whether faculty, fellows, or students, are professionals with years of experience to inform their scholarship. In addition to the first-hand knowledge they bring to their subjects, they are also well connected, with rolodexes that have opened doors for them into wardrooms and squad bays, as well as office suites, where few academics have access. The writers' own resources are supplemented by the College, which funds travel and makes introductions for visits both with the top brass and to the remotest outposts.

The result, we hope, is a set of articles that is rich in detail. While some "big ideas" have made the cut, the real treasures here are the details of law enforcement analytic technique, the tradecraft of DEA's counter-narcotic intelligence in Bangkok, the HUMINT collection procedures on the streets of Mogadishu or Chicago, and the like. While maintaining high academic standards, this work aims to be more than academic.

This product has been reviewed by senior experts from academia, industry, and government and has been approved for unrestricted distribution by the Office of Security Review, U.S. Department of Defense. It is available to the public through the National Technical Information Service (*www.ntis.gov*).

Timothy.Christenson@dia.mil, Editor
Center for Strategic Intelligence Research

CONTENTS

FOREWORD

Intelligence—vital information about persons and phenomena that would do us harm—has been used to great effect by the Law Enforcement community for many years to support operations and ensure public safety. Human source development tradecraft, technical collection techniques, analytic methodologies and tools, and information sharing policies and systems have been a mainstay of law enforcement operations for many years. Globalization and the decline of the nation state have given rise to new adversaries, many of which resemble shadowy criminal-like networks that use technology to operate across national boundaries and threaten both national security and public safety. *Can't We All Just Get Along? Improving the Law Enforcement-Intelligence Community Relationship* is a powerful and thoughtful compendium that explores law enforcement intelligence techniques and their utility for the National Intelligence Community, as well as proven Intelligence Community methodologies and their potential application for law enforcement intelligence operations. Most importantly, the compendium eloquently reminds us that it is the "soft stuff"—culture, training, trust—that presents the greatest challenge to achieving a partnership between Law Enforcement and the Intelligence Community that the threat demands and our citizens deserve.

Much has been said about Law Enforcement not "getting" intelligence and about the Intelligence Community not "getting" law enforcement operations. Those of us who have had the privilege of serving in both communities know from experience that neither assertion is true and have urged a thoughtful analysis of facts to tamp down the emotion that surrounds this debate. This work succeeds in moving us beyond surface judgments and emotions, exploring law enforcement intelligence tools and techniques in some depth and pointing to their utility in fighting and prevailing over today's adversaries. Just as importantly, it points to extant Intelligence Community practices that if applied broadly will help Law Enforcement make the transition from prosecution to prevention.

There has always been a rather healthy tension between the producers of intelligence and the users of intelligence. *Can't We All Just Get Along?* reminds us that intelligence operations are not conducted for their own sake, but rather to inform the decisions of those who must act in defense of national security/public safety. The value of intelligence is in the eyes of its users, not its producers; intelligence is at its best when it is fully integrated with its users. These simple truths led to the development of intelligence methodologies and techniques as a function of support to specific instruments of national power such as diplomacy, law enforcement, and war fighting. The nature of today's threats has blurred the lines between traditional diplomatic, military, and law enforcement concerns, requiring all instruments of national power to work as a seamless network to defeat our adversaries. The rise of joint task forces, intelligence operations centers, and fusion centers has brought together professionals from across the law enforcement, military, and intelligence communities, offering them a unique opportunity to share tools and techniques in defense of the nation. *Can't We All Just Get Along?* provides an important foundation for understanding the strengths that each community brings to the joint environment and is a must read for all intelligence professionals.

Maureen Baginski
Former FBI Executive Assistant Director
Intelligence
Former NSA Signals Intelligence Director

COMMENTARY

In the five years since 9/11, Law Enforcement has been re-inventing itself, and intelligence agencies have been making changes that run contrary to years of established policy, tradecraft, and procedure. However, old habits die hard and many traditional structures remain firmly in place. Whether the ongoing efforts at restructuring are actually effecting change or are mostly window dressing remains an open question.

We face an enemy who plans operations strategically and exploits our vulnerabilities creatively. This enemy functions in a manner our institutions are not designed to address. To win, it is imperative that we fight more creatively and strategically than our adversaries. That means taking full advantage of ALL the resources at our disposal and wielding them as effectively as possible.

As a criminal investigator for the past 20 years and as chief of a transnational criminal investigative section, I have seen the best and the worst of the relationship between the law enforcement and intelligence communities. I have witnessed how acrimonious that relationship can be; to be honest, I've contributed to the problem myself. But when the relationship works, it works *very* well. These two distinct communities can cooperate to great effect without violating privacy rights or precluding criminal prosecution. There is plenty of common ground that is overt, legal, and proper.

A few years ago, I investigated an anonymous letter that warned there was a visa fraud operation targeting a U.S. consulate in a large Muslim country. The letter alleged that the operation was being run out of an unnamed textile company that was facilitating Al Qaeda's travel by sponsoring several terrorists to attend a U.S. trade show. Working with our intelligence agencies, we were able to identify the textile company in question. Then my investigators and the local police located and interviewed the writer of the letter. Both sides contributed their particular expertise and the situation was quickly resolved.

On other occasions, however, U.S. intelligence gave me information about a threat to a U.S. diplomatic mission but prohibited me from acting on the information; "sources and methods" and all. I had to appeal to higher authorities before I could take necessary precautions—which we did without disclosing the sources or methods.

Out of undue regard for certain concerns, Law Enforcement and the IC have repeatedly stymied one another. Law enforcement invokes privacy concerns and investigative case secrecy to protect its information. The IC invokes "sources and methods" to protect its capabilities. Sure, there are good reasons to maintain case control and protect sources; but there are many occasions when cooperation can work around these issues. In the past, there was less reason to do so. There is more now.

Can't We All Just Get Along? provides ideas that will help law enforcement and the IC realize some strategic advantage from greater mutual awareness. This compilation is an ideal vehicle for an ongoing dialogue between intelligence and law enforcement. I hope it will serve as a catalyst for discussion at the grassroots, operational, and executive levels of both communities. Most of us in Law Enforcement are not formally part of the IC, but we produce and consume intelligence every day. The ideas that follow can help us do better at both.

Mike Bayer, Branch Chief
Transnational Criminal Investigations
Diplomatic Security Service
U.S. Department of State

BEST PRACTICES IN LAW ENFORCEMENT AND THE INTELLIGENCE COMMUNITY

The essays that make up this compendium envision a future with an ideal, seamless relationship between and among law enforcement (LE) and intelligence agencies. The first essays suggest lessons the Intelligence Community (IC) can learn from law enforcement, as well as some IC "teaching points." In each case, years of experience in LE, the IC, or both complement the author's scholarship.

These practitioners focus on specific innovations in a particular area of intelligence or law enforcement that may have application elsewhere. There are no suggestions for overall restructuring of either community, and even the mechanisms for introducing a desirable change are not discussed in any detail. Whatever the benefits of greater integration at the national level, these essays illustrate the value of more transparency among those "in the trenches."

DEVELOPMENTS IN LAW ENFORCEMENT INTELLIGENCE ANALYSIS

Marilyn B. Peterson, MA
Certified Criminal Analyst, Certified Fraud Examiner

This article suggests that it would be beneficial for the Intelligence Community (IC) and Law Enforcement (LE) to cross-train and collaborate in the application of analytic methods. All-source analysis is the norm in both law enforcement and the Intelligence Community, although for different purposes: investigation and prosecution or warning and prevention. The distinctions between the two blur in cases where international actors undertake criminal acts (terrorism or narcotics distribution, for instance) or where investigative techniques support intelligence as well as police work (nuclear proliferation or counterintelligence, for example).

LAW ENFORCEMENT AND INTELLIGENCE

Intelligence, in law enforcement, is defined as information that has been collected, evaluated, collated, and analyzed, with hypotheses drawn from it and potential courses of action noted. This differs from the IC's view of intelligence, which has traditionally emphasized its being secret information. Intelligence in law enforcement is drawn from information subpoenaed from its owner; received through a judicially-approved search of a person's residence, business, or vehicle; obtained from physical or court-authorized electronic surveillance; or found in open records such as deeds, licenses, business filings, or trusted media.

Analysis of materials is needed to achieve the "intelligence" state. Analytic methods and techniques have developed from rudimentary to complex in the 35 years since formal analysis was introduced to law enforcement. Informal sharing of techniques between the IC and LE occurs primarily through literature and professional organizations. The current shared missions of counterterrorism and counter-narcotics work may institutionalize further exchanges of methods, techniques, and intelligence. Recent laws that allow some sharing of the IC's "foreign" intelligence and LE's domestic data support these exchanges.

Early History of LE Intelligence Analysis and Its Relations with the IC

There were intelligence units in larger city departments (like NYPD) in the 1930s and 1940s, targeting primarily anarchists and the Cosa Nostra. Some members of the "Mafia" migrated to the U.S. in the 1890s and, by Prohibition, were firmly established in Chicago, New York, and other major cities. In the 1950s, the Congressional Kefauver Commission investigated organized crime and found that it was involved in bookmaking, prostitution, and the sale and distribution of narcotics. The Commission named 15 cities, from coast to coast, that had organized crime activity and the resultant police corruption.[1] State and local law enforcement authorities were aware of their problems with organized crime, but the FBI would not share data with them at that time, fearing that the locals would give information to the criminals. Thus, the Law Enforcement Intelligence Unit (LEIU) was developed in 1956, begun by the California Department of Justice and others to improve the sharing of organized crime intelligence among state and local law enforcement agencies.[2]

The LE focus on traditional organized crime continued through the 1950s and 1960s. The police raided the Appalachian meeting in upstate New York of the Cosa Nostra family leaders in 1957. Attorney General Robert F. Kennedy tried to prosecute organized crime until he left office in 1964.

The 1967 President's Organized Crime Commission recognized the need for stronger intelligence in law enforcement. In 1970, major state agencies, including the California Department of Justice, the Florida Department of Law Enforcement, the Arizona Department of Public Safety, and the New Jersey State Police, began to hire intelligence analysts.

Law enforcement intelligence analysis owes its formal beginnings in the early 1970s to the IC. The Justice Department's Law Enforcement Assistance Administration contracted with two former IC professionals, E. Drexel Godfrey and Don R. Harris, to write *The Basic Elements of Intelligence*. This book and its revised edition (by Mr. Harris and others in 1976) became the "bible" of LE intelligence units in the United States.[3] It discussed factors from reporting chains and floor plans to analysts' experience levels and data evaluation. It called analysis "the heart of the intelligence process," without which the effort was only a filing function.[4]

As law enforcement analysis capabilities grew in the 1970s and 1980s, they were increasingly used in investigations of organized crime and narcotics trafficking. Initiatives to identify and detail the structure of the major traditional organized crime (Cosa Nostra) syndicates took precedence.

---

[1] Special Committee to Investigate Organized Crime (Kefauver Commission), *Third Interim Report* (New York: ARCO Publishing Co., 1951). One of the components of defining organized crime is the corruption of the criminal justice system.

[2] LEIU continues today and now allows federal membership. More information can be obtained on-line at URL: <www.leiu-homepage.org>.

[3] The book was out of print by the 1990s. In 2001, *Intelligence 2000: Revising the Basic Elements*, ed. Marilyn B. Peterson and others (Sacramento, CA: LEIU and IALEIA, 2000) took its place as the seminal work. It is used as a primary text in training academies, colleges, and universities for classes on intelligence and is available on-line at URL: <www.ialeia.org>. A dozen intelligence professionals contributed to the text.

[4] E. Drexel Godfrey and Don R. Harris, *The Basic Elements of Intelligence* (Washington: Government Printing Office, 1971), 4.

The primary source of analytic training was Anacapa Sciences of Santa Barbara, California.[5] Federal, state, and local law enforcement analysts took its courses; only in the past decade or two have some agencies developed internal training capabilities.

The first professional association for analysts, the International Association of Law Enforcement Intelligence Analysts (IALEIA), was established in 1980.[6] This organization, begun by members of federal and state LE agencies (including ATF, DEA, the California Department of Justice, and the Florida Department of Law Enforcement, as well as some Canadian and Australian agencies), advanced the use and understanding of law enforcement intelligence analysis. By the mid-1980s, it had initiated a newsletter and a professional journal. These, combined with an expanding membership, went a long way toward sharing analytic methods and techniques. IALEIA also developed an awards program that honored analysts, executives, authors, and agencies for exceptional intelligence writing and products.

Some cross-pollination between the IC and law enforcement occurred. In 1986, the *International Journal of Intelligence and Counterintelligence* printed "Law Enforcement Intelligence: A New Look."[7] The article discussed the importance of strategic intelligence in law enforcement and gave examples of collection plans and models for developing strategic products. These were based on models in *Intelligence for the 1980s* published by Roy Godson and his colleagues. A course developed by the author three years later on strategic intelligence in law enforcement was given twice, but it attracted no further students. Law enforcement was primarily still reactive rather than proactive.[8]

There was more evidence of cross-pollination between local law enforcement and members of the IC. Many state and local law enforcement agencies opened their intelligence training to military intelligence, military police's Criminal Investigation Division, and other federal analysts and officers. This was beneficial to all from the standpoint of both current assignments and future employment. Personnel leaving the armed services or retiring from federal employment found second careers in state or local law enforcement and made the transition more easily for having learned law enforcement terminology and methods. When the end of the Cold War

---

[5] More information on Anacapa Sciences is available on-line at URL: <www.anacapatraining.com>.

[6] IALEIA currently has about 1,800 members in over 50 countries. Memberships are individual and are held by intelligence officers and analysts in law enforcement, the military, the intelligence community, and the corporate sector.

[7] Marilyn B. Sommers (Peterson), "Law Enforcement Intelligence: A New Look," *International Journal of Intelligence and Counterintelligence* 1, no. 3 (1986): 25-40.

[8] The course was resurrected in 1999 and given for state and federal agencies over the ensuing three years. Following 9/11, it was re-designed to focus on counterterrorism.

reduced the size of the armed services, law enforcement snapped up people trained in a variety of specialties, including military intelligence.

The priority of the late 1980s in many LE agencies was the rapidly expanding sale and use of narcotics by the public. In a notable cooperative effort that continues today, the National Guard assisted state and local agencies in their counter-drug efforts. Creating regional agencies for communication, cooperation, and coordination, the federal government provided assistance to state and local law enforcement. These included the Regional Information Sharing System (RISS) projects (primarily begun around 1980) and the High Intensity Drug Trafficking Area (HIDTA) projects (begun around 1990). Both these efforts brought together federal, state, and local law enforcement to attack criminal syndicates in particular areas. The RISS involved multiple states, whereas the HIDTAs covered metropolitan areas or specific borders, such as the southwestern U.S. border.[9]

The 1990s

The role of intelligence expanded in the 1990s to support the investigation and prosecution of white-collar crime, internal affairs, street crime, counterterrorism, and money laundering. Intelligence was not limited to an intelligence unit. Most information gathered in an investigation benefits from analytic formats and techniques. Increasing technological sophistication gave criminals more tools to evade detection but also provided similar tools to law enforcement. The traditional "3 by 5 card" method of sorting data, used into the 1980s, gave way to specialized databases that supported various information protocols. Computers became commonplace on the desktops of analysts and investigators.

Professional associations created standards for analysts. A certification body founded in 1990, the Society of Certified Criminal Analysts (SCCA), established educational, training, testing, and experiential standards for criminal analysts.[10] It provides both three-year and lifetime certification and has certified analysts in several countries.

Toward the end of the 1990s, more proactive targeting was done on investigative subjects by text-mining large databases. One example was the use in New Jersey, Massachusetts, and other states of data held by the Treasury Department's Financial Crimes Enforcement Network (FinCEN). These data allowed analysts to identify and track large sums of money moving through banks, casinos, and non-bank financial institutions (check cashers and wire

---

[9] More information on the RISS projects can be found on-line at URL: <www.iir.com/riss>; and information on the HIDTAs is available at URL: <www.whitehousedrugpolicy.gov/hidta/index.html>.

[10] "Purpose," *The Society of Certified Criminal Analysts,* URL: <www.certifiedanalysts.net>, accessed 1 November 2006.

1. Collect the material and mark it for reliability of the source and validity of the data.
2. Number each page or use its pre-numbering for tracking.
3. Organize the case information.
4. Extract the association material.
5. Place the data into an association database.
6. Prepare an association matrix.
7. Count the associations of each person or entity.
8. Create a diagram based on the association matrix or database.
9. Complete background research on entities to fill in knowledge gaps.
10. Produce biographic summaries of each entity on the chart.
11. Review the relationships shown for density, between-ness, closeness, information bottlenecks, degree of centralization, peripheral players, and so forth.
12. Ask critical questions of the data in the chart.
13. Summarize the chart.
14. Establish what necessary information is present and what is absent.
15. Draw interim hypotheses and analyze them for the best hypothesis.
16. Make recommendations for further actions.
17. Present findings and written report to management.

Figure 1. Link Analysis Process
Source: Marilyn B. Peterson, "Association Analysis,"
unpublished research paper, September 2006.

remitters). That allowed investigators to trace the funds back to their illegal sources. These sources often involved fraud of some kind, from large-scale investment fraud to fraudulent documents. This data mining is frequently done in the insurance industry, where "flagging" systems identify care providers or end users with unusual patterns of claims, ailments, or treatments, allowing investigators to identify insurance fraud rings and repeat offenders.

Another shift in LE analysis in the 1990s was distinguishing between analytic products and the analytic process. In earlier days, people focused on the charts and visual products of analysis rather than on the meaning of the visuals. Charting was accepted in place of analysis in many agencies. Then training and practice were revised to focus on link analysis, for example, rather than link charting.[11] Link analysis was a several-step process, while link charting was one of several products within the process (see Figure 1).

The need for critical thinking and cogent questioning of the data was also recognized. Further, LE managers believed that analysis without conclusions and recommendations was incomplete.

LE-IC Collaboration After 9/11

After 11 September 2001, law enforcement agencies expanded their previous commitment to collaborate more with each other and with the IC. In March 2002, the International Association of Chiefs of Police's Intelligence Sharing Summit called for a national intelligence plan. A Global Intelligence Working Group was formed, funded by the Bureau of Justice Assistance. The Working Group included over 30 state and local intelligence personnel who met quarterly with representatives from the FBI, DEA, Homeland Security, and others. The result was the *National Criminal Intelligence Sharing Plan (NCISP)*.[12] The Plan mandated that IALEIA create standards for analysts and analytic products. Completed in 2004, IALEIA and the Bureau of Justice Assistance published a booklet detailing those standards.[13] The Global group also created standards for the fusion centers that were being established across the nation.[14] Fusion centers are supported by the Department of Homeland Security and generally include representatives from federal, state, and local LE agencies, as well as the IC, working together with an all-crimes focus.

Another outgrowth of the terrorists' attacks is the increased training of state and local law enforcement officers on terrorist indicators, the role of intelligence, and the importance of reporting all suspicious activity. The fusion centers, state-level counterterrorism centers, and Joint Terrorism Task Forces sponsored by the FBI sharpen police officers on the street to notice all potentially dangerous behavior and report it to municipal or county counter-terrorism coordinators, who then push the information up the chain to the FBI and other members of the IC. Clearly, homeland security rests increasingly in the hands of police officers on their beats.

One joint LE/IC training effort, the Research and Intelligence Analysis Program (RI/AP), started at Mercyhurst College in Erie, Pennsylvania. A resulting textbook, *The Community Model: A Basic Training Curriculum*

---

[11] Marilyn B. Peterson, "Product vs. Process," *IALEIA Journal* 11, no. 1 (Winter 1998): 1-13.

[12] Global Intelligence Working Group, *The National Criminal Intelligence Sharing Plan*, October 2003, URL: <it.ojp.gov/documents/NCISP_Plan.pdf>, accessed 1 November 2006.

[13] "Law Enforcement Intelligence Analysis Standards," *Information Technology Initiatives*, URL: <it.ojp.gov/documents/law_enforcement_analytic_standards.pdf>, accessed 1 November 2006.

[14] "Fusion Center Guidelines," *Information Technology Initiatives*, URL: <it.ojp.gov/documents/ fusion_center_guidelines.pdf>, accessed 1 November 2006.

for Law Enforcement Analysts, included inputs from DoD, the National Guard, the Navy and Marine Corps Intelligence Training Center, the Coast Guard, and several federal and local law enforcement agencies (see Figure 2). Participating centers included the National Drug Intelligence Center, the National White Collar Crime Center, the RISS projects, the HIDTAs, and the Federal Law Enforcement Training Center (FLETC). As its initial name (Generic Intelligence Training Initiative) implied, it was designed for export across the boundaries of LE and the IC.

- Introduction to Intelligence
- Intelligence Analysis as a Thought Process
- The Planning Process in Intelligence Production
- Basic Intelligence Collection and Evaluation
- Introduction to Analysis
- Data Management
- Crime Pattern Analysis
- Association Analysis
- Flow Analysis
- Telephone Record Analysis
- Financial Analysis
- Developing Indicators
- Practical Approaches to Producing Strategic Intelligence
- Managing Investigations through Managing Information
- Intelligence Report Writing
- Effective Briefing Techniques
- Effective Presentations Using Microsoft Powerpoint

Figure 2. Law Enforcement Analysts' Curriculum
Source: *The Community Model: A Basic Training Curriculum for Law Enforcement Analysts* (Washington: Counterdrug Intelligence Executive Secretariat, March 2003), 1.

Law Enforcement continues to learn from the IC. A presentation on warning analysis at the IALEIA 2005 Annual Training Conference in Alexandria, Virginia, was inspired by the work of Cynthia Grabo (CIA) and John Bodnar (DIA, now with Science Applications International Corporation). Some of the graphics from the presentation are seen later in this paper (Figures 4, 7, and 8).

Several initiatives have combined analytical techniques from both sides of the intelligence aisle (see Figure 3). These include setting up the Counter Narcotics Trafficking office; funding and supporting Office of National Drug

Control Policy and HIDTA projects; working on counter-narcotics with the El Paso Information Center; and establishing Joint Action Task Force locations with law enforcement officers embedded.

Intelligence Community	Used by Both	Law Enforcement
Denial and Deception	Link Analysis	Communication Analysis
Indications and Warning	Matrix Analysis	Discourse Analysis
Cultural Awareness	Indicator Analysis	Crime Analysis/Forecasting
Multi-Dimensional Analysis	Timelines	Financial Analysis
Imagery Analysis	Critical Thinking	Commodity Flow Analysis
Structured Analytic Thinking Techniques	Analysis of Competing Hypotheses	Activity Flow Analysis
	Geographic Analysis	
	Document Exploitation	
	Visual Investigative Analysis	
	Psychological Profiling	

Figure 3. LE-IC Analytical Techniques
Source: Author.

One final example of collaboration between LE and IC was the post-9/11 Realities series organized by the International Association of Chiefs of Police (IACP) and funded by the Bureau of Justice Assistance. The resulting booklets included topics like *Intelligence-Led Policing: The New Intelligence Architecture*;[15] *Multi-Jurisdictional Partnerships for Meeting Regional Threats; Engaging the Private Sector to Promote Homeland Security*; and *Assessing and Managing the Terrorist Threat*. The terrorist threat booklet was written by a Department of Defense staffer on loan to IACP.[16]

LAW ENFORCEMENT INTELLIGENCE ANALYSIS PRODUCTS

The primary products developed by law enforcement analysts in the 1970s and 1980s included telephone record analysis, link analysis, and an occasional overview of a crime group.

---

[15] Marilyn B. Peterson, *Intelligence-Led Policing: The New Intelligence Architecture,* URL: <www. ncjrs.gov/pdffiles1/bja/210681.pdf>, accessed 1 November 2006.

[16] Joel Leson, *Assessing and Managing the Terrorist Threat,* URL: <www.ncjrs.gov/pdffiles1/bja/210680.pdf>, accessed 2 November 2006.

Telephone record analyses

Analyses of telephone records were once the most common product in LE analysis and included information on dates, times, and locations of mostly long-distance telephone calls, with patterns highlighted. An electronic device called a "dialed number recorder" or "pen register" captured outgoing calls as well, with the times the phone was taken "off the hook" and placed back noted. The times and dates of incoming calls could also be captured, but not the number making the incoming call. (Today, caller ID makes more information available, as do cell phones, which give the phone numbers of calls made and received. Text and e-mail messages can be analyzed using similar techniques. This field has grown to the point where hundreds of thousands of call records in large databases can be analyzed to determine links, patterns, and anomalies.)

A follow-up technique to telephone record analysis, *discourse* or *statement analysis,* is performed on written documents or transcripts of conversations. This provides signposts to determine (in some cases) if the statements being made are true, who the dominant participant in the conversation is, and what that may mean. When law enforcement performs electronic surveillance, it records conversations pertinent to criminal activity. It is the transcripts of these conversations that are analyzed to glean further insights into the nature and structure of networks and syndicates.

Link analysis

Link analysis consists of link charts showing who is connected to whom. These charts are based on physical surveillance reports, as well as telephone, payment, and business records (incorporation papers or bank account data). Charts make effective courtroom graphics and can help persuade a prosecutor to bring a case into court. In the world of hierarchical crime (organized crime and outlaw motorcycle gangs, for instance), who is where in the hierarchy can be very important.

By the 1990s, law enforcement intelligence analysis was used in a plethora of police units. As criminals became more sophisticated, so too did law enforcement's incorporation of new techniques and products. *Event flow charts* and *timelines* showed events leading up to or occurring during criminal acts (see Figure 4). *Visual investigative analysis* (VIA) was used after its success in the court case on the Robert F. Kennedy assassination. It allows task forces and other multi-jurisdictional groups to track the progress made in varied investigative efforts. The resulting charts, highly detailed, may take up several large walls of a room.

Other flow charts included timelines to show events leading up to or through a particular activity. *Commodity flow charts* showed how stolen cars, laundered money, or smuggled weapons moved. *Activity flow charts* allowed

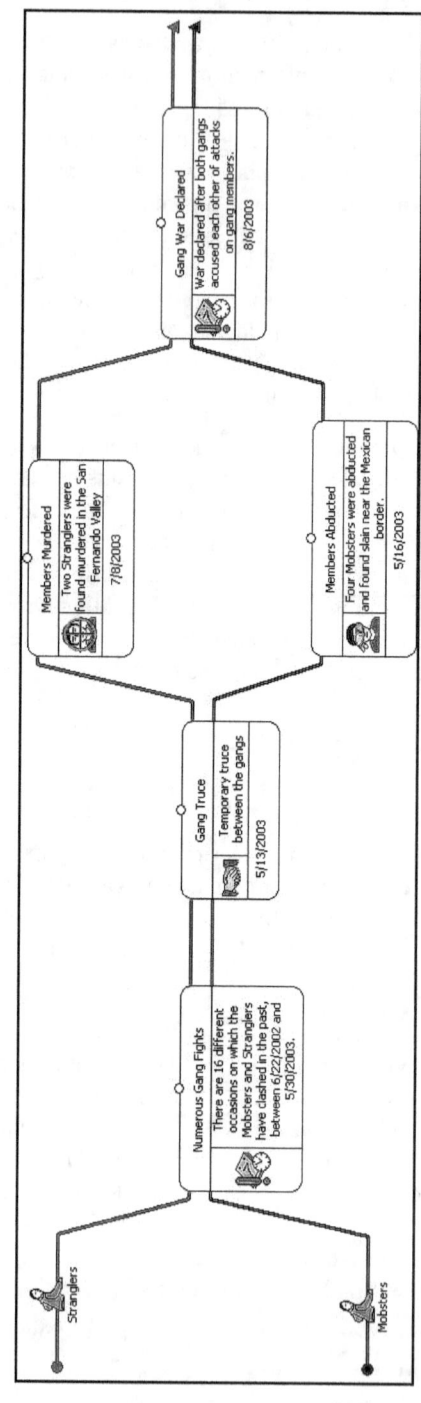

Figure 4. Time Line Flow Chart
Source: Author.

the overall scheme to be seen and gave a macro view of the criminal activity. Trends could be spotted in these graphics, as well as anomalies.

The *financial analysis of bank and business records* is necessary as businesses are often used as "fronts" for criminal activity or are purchased with criminal proceeds. *Net worth analysis* and *source and applications of funds analysis* were introduced by the Internal Revenue Service and adopted by LE agencies. These techniques allowed investigators and analysts to show unidentified sources of income that were not reported to authorities and thus might be illegal. *Bank record analysis* techniques were developed by federal and state agencies to look at criminal assets and the techniques used by money launderers.

Logic and inference development were part of law enforcement intelligence analysis since its beginnings. Probability has also been taught since early days. *Critical thinking* came onto the radar screen of law enforcement in the mid-1990s when it was seen that inference development cannot be done in a vacuum. The questioning aspect of critical thinking is now taught in most analytic courses. So, too, is the *Analysis of Competing Hypotheses,* as advanced by Richards J. Heuer Jr. His book, *The Psychology of Intelligence Analysis,* won an IALEIA award in 2000 for the most significant literature in the field of intelligence analysis. However, the method of critical thinking adopted by several IC agencies (NSA and DIA, for instance), based on the work of Richard W. Paul and Linda Elder and developed further by NSA analyst David Moore,[17] has not yet been fully explored by law enforcement.

Geographic analysis is a mainstay of local police departments, which use pin maps to track homicides, burglaries, and auto thefts. Geographic information systems can now overlay various activities, uncovering criminal "hot spots" for directed enforcement by officers (see Figure 5). This has not generally included imagery analysis, but with the advent of pole surveillance cameras that capture activity at specific locations, imagery analysis will likely develop a more important role, at least in municipal law enforcement agencies.

---

[17] David T. Moore, *Critical Thinking and Intelligence Analysis* (Washington: JMIC Press, 2006).

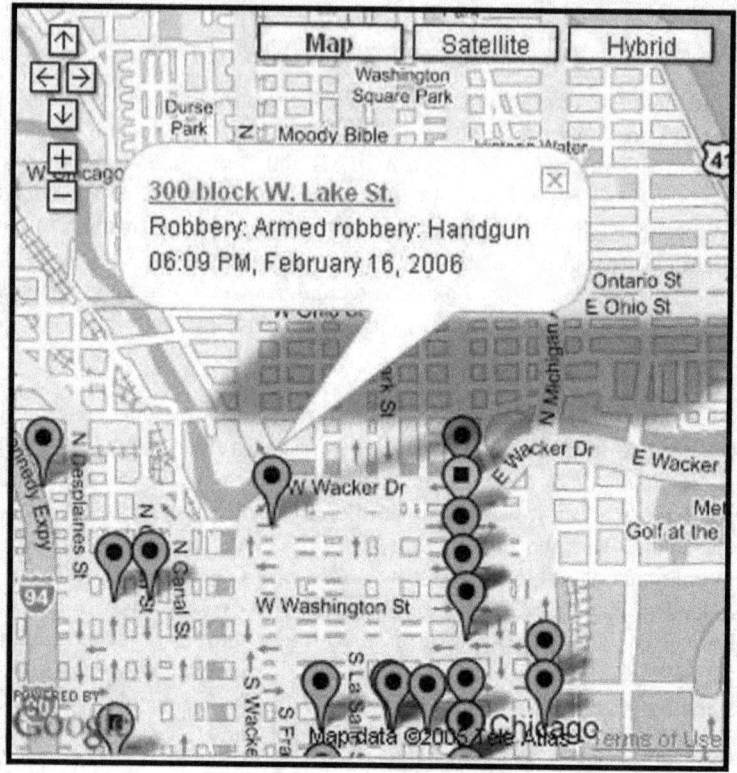

Figure 5. Crime Map Example
Source: "Robbery," *Chicago Crime.org*,
URL:<www.chicagocrime.org/types/robbery>, accessed 7 November 2006,
used by permission.

Additional techniques of crime analysis—*time series analysis, crime factor analysis, predicting* when and where the next crime will occur—may have some validity in the IC as well. For example, looking at the times, dates, and locations of IED or suicide bomber attacks might help prevent further attacks.

Crime Group Analysis

Law enforcement uses *matrix analysis* to develop link charts but also to summarize data for ease of comparison. At the crime analysis level, the dates and times of crimes are put into matrices to complete pattern analysis and compare the components of *modus operandi*. It also helps target limited resources on investigative priorities. One example of this is seen in Figure 6, a matrix used by the Royal Canadian Mounted Police to summarize categories of data (the Y axis) on various organized crime groups (represented by letters along the X axis). This produces a rank-ordering for enforcement priority, with four priority targets in this case.

Another matrix combines the attributes of a street gang, over time, to measure changes in its level of threat (see Figure 7).

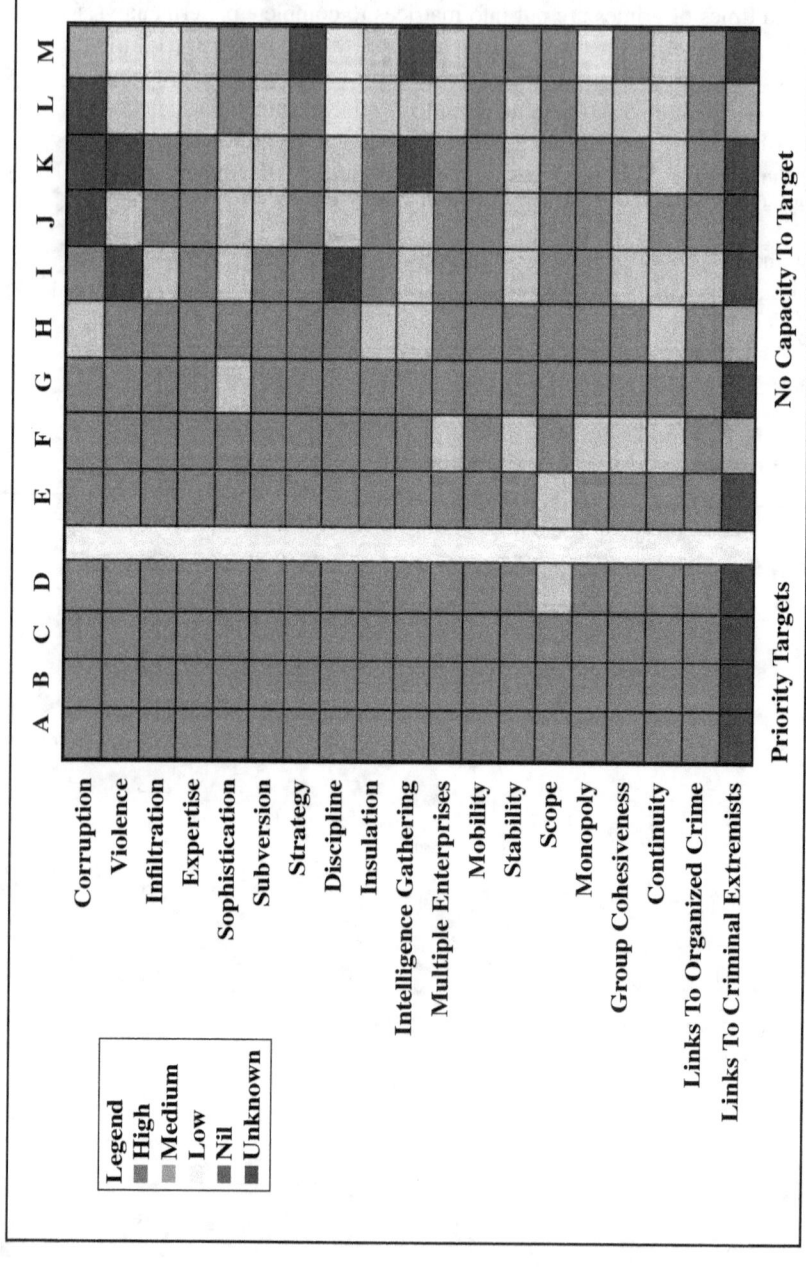

Figure 6. RCMP Organized Crime Prioritization Matrix
Source: RCMP, used by permission.

Gang Threat Level Over Time ______________ Gang

	Expanding Territory	Level of Violence	Membership Levels	Commission of Crimes	Use of Weapons	Narcotics	Gang Related Homicides	Cooperation with other Gangs	Leadership Change	Finances
2001			✔			✔		✔		
2002			✔			✔		✔		
2003	✔		✔	✔		✔			✔	
2004	✔	✔		✔	✔	✔				✔
2005	✔	✔			✔	✔	✔			✔

Figure 7. Gang Threat Matrix
Source: Author.

Law enforcement intelligence also exploits very large databases (*data* or *text mining*). As noted above, financial records maintained by the Treasury's FinCEN are reviewed to find suspicious transactions that can reflect the proceeds of criminal acts. Police then initiate investigations into potential criminal activity. In order to complete these analyses, *indicators* must be developed that flag anomalies or patterns consistent with criminal activity.

Combinations of methods are used to portray the criminal activity more thoroughly. Bodnar referred in his book to "multi-dimensional analysis" where one format is overlaid upon another. Thus, mapping has been used with link chart overlays, as have time sequences (see Figure 8).

Additional products are used in strategic analysis within law enforcement. *Threat assessments, vulnerability assessments,* and other long-range products are completed most often by state, federal, or regional agencies; municipal agencies are more concerned with current crime. The HIDTA projects, for example, prepare annual threat assessments on narcotics trafficking in their respective areas. Fusion centers assess the threat posed by domestic or international terrorist groups. Financial intelligence units look at vulnerabilities in the financial systems. Many of these rely on open source data, as well as police files. Timelines, link charts, and financial analyses are used in the assessment, along with products such as *trend analysis* and *statistical analysis.*

Another type of analysis done in law enforcement is *post-seizure analysis.* This is often part of a *document exploitation* process to derive all possible information from materials collected during an arrest, seizure, or search. One agency in the forefront of this activity in LE is the National Drug Intelligence Center, which uses the Access™-based software called RAID to organize and store the data.

A final method used in law enforcement analysis is *psychological profiling,* also called *criminal investigative analysis.* This is used when looking at serial killers, rapists, arsonists, and other serial criminals. A listing of sociological and psychological traits common to this type of crime is compiled and the listing then compared to a list of suspects to see who fits the profile. The number of possibilities, often in the thousands, is then narrowed.

OPPORTUNITIES FOR SHARING AND COLLABORATION

This review of analysis methods and products used in Law Enforcement provides a reference point for IC members to compare these methods and products with those used in the IC. From the perspective of an individual who has spent a long time in LE and has been in the IC less than a year, several areas of potential IC use of LE techniques seem possible.

Some of the LE techniques listed are highlighted in the Analytic Competency Framework forwarded by the Office of the Director of National Intelligence (ODNI) in the fall of 2006. These include Network/Link Analysis,

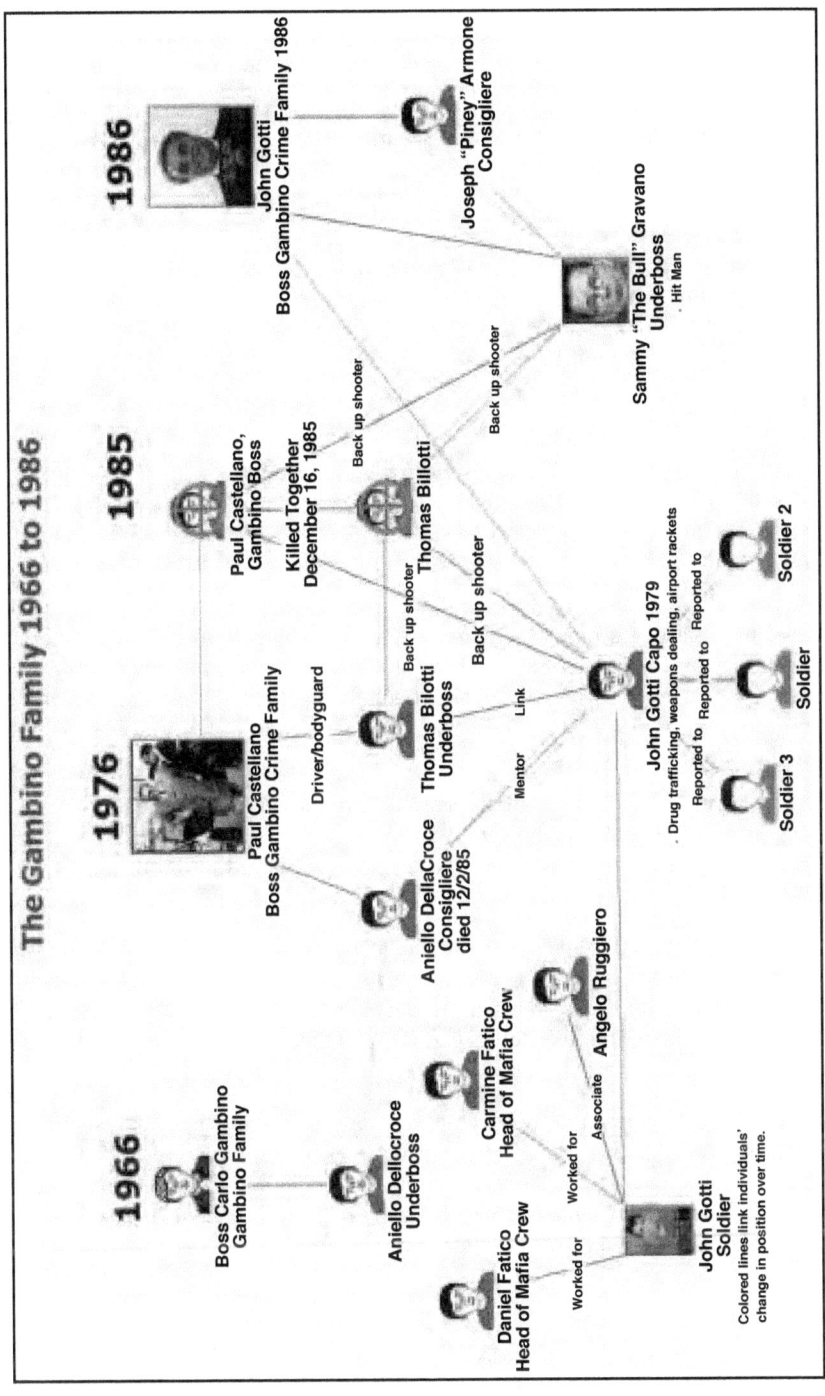

Figure 8. Link Chart in Time Order Setting—Multi-Dimensional Analysis
Source: Author.

Open Source Intelligence, Visual Investigative Analysis, and Indicator Analysis as analytic techniques used within the Intelligence Community. Timelines, the Analysis of Competing Hypotheses, and matrices are also topics recommended for inclusion in new analyst training.

Financial intelligence analysis may also be helpful to at least the counter-drug, counter-terror, and homeland security aspects of the IC. The previous emphasis on economics and macro views is also important, but terrorists need money to buy weapons, travel, and train, for example. Thus, being able to "follow the money" may be key.[18]

Flow analysis (commodity, event, and activity) can help the IC track the movement of people, weapons, nuclear materials, human cargoes, drugs, and terror paraphernalia. While these techniques are, presumably, used to some degree already, they are not taught in current classes and are not evident in the ODNI core competencies.

It might be worthwhile for the IC to focus its training more on the analytic *process* (as LE has done in the area of link analysis, for example) instead of on products that support briefings. As it is, the training and core competencies seem to emphasize shorter-term products (reporting and tactical developments, for example) rather than strategic products dealing with long-term implications.

The IC also has many techniques that could be helpful to LE. Warning analysis, including denial and deception techniques, is as applicable to law enforcement as it is to the IC. Cultural intelligence appreciation is a critical skill in many police departments, since the United States reflects many cultures.

Law enforcement needs to expand its understanding of critical thinking and structured analytic thinking techniques. While law enforcement has been moving in this direction, its classes still lack the depth available within the IC.[19]

More joint conferences and training between the IC and LE would be advantageous. It should not be left to analysts with interests outside their particular assignment to discover that there are methods available that could help them. Open Source Intelligence (OSINT) makes many documents and methods available that could instruct both sets of analysts.

Law Enforcement intelligence analysis and IC intelligence analysis have coexisted with little formal interplay between them and have nonetheless arrived independently at some of the same places. Further sharing of methodologies will strengthen their individual work and also make them better collaborators in defense of the nation.

---

[18] A new Financial Intelligence Seminar is currently offered at DIA's Joint Military Intelligence Training Center on a quarterly basis.

[19] Specifically, a course similar to the NSA/DIA course on Critical Thinking and Structured Analysis should be made available to law enforcement analysts.

UNMASKING NETWORKS: DRUG ENFORCEMENT ADMINISTRATION TRADECRAFT FOR THE INTELLIGENCE COMMUNITY

Gloria Freund
Fellow, Center for Strategic Intelligence Research

The IC never signed on enthusiastically to the counter-drug mission. Counter-drug intelligence analysis has evolved separately from more traditional IC problem sets. Counter-drug analysts in DIA, for example, have long been housed across town from other analysts, who were working order of battle, force capability, infrastructure, and other conventional foreign intelligence problems. Over the years, these CD analysts had little if any interaction or cross-feed with their counterparts—either about potentially overlapping subject matter or about analytical tools and techniques.

The Department of Justice's Drug Enforcement Administration (DEA) is even further removed. A small group at DEA has recently been re-admitted to the IC. It is even more distinct in its mission, focus, and institutional culture. Compared to conventional IC analysis, DEA counter-drug analysis, especially at the field office level, is akin to unique animal species that have evolved in isolation on the Galapagos Islands: It uses distinct analytical tradecraft that few IC analysts working traditional problem sets would recognize.

Yet some asymmetric problems with which the IC now struggles have more in common with asymmetric drug networks than with foreign states or armies. For cracking drug networks, DEA counter-drug analysts have been plank owners of unique models and techniques that confer "survival value" and that they have continued to refine. Insights from their models and tradecraft can assist in solving a broader set of intelligence problems.

DEA's structure and tradecraft illuminate three particular areas of interest to the IC:

- the tailoring of counter-drug intelligence to explicit and clearly-understood user purposes;
- the HUMINT focus of its strategies and proactive source-development for generating new information; and
- the recognition of illegal service providers as a key for unlocking the networks of those using them—whether for the narcotics trade, other criminal activity, or terrorism.

DISTINCT MISSIONS, BUT SIMILAR PROBLEMS

Formed within the Department of Justice in 1973, DEA has more experience than the IC in counter-drug work. As a component of the Department of Justice, DEA also has different purposes for its counter-drug intelligence analysis. While the IC provides cogent estimates about foreign situations to help decisionmakers determine a course of action, DEA assembles evidence that will lead to arrest and conviction. DEA evidence is useful only if unclassified, accurate, relevant, specific, factual, and admissible in court.

DEA field offices are distinct in having defined their intelligence problems wholly through the lens of enforcement purpose and criteria. These offices have shaped the structure and tradecraft of intelligence to support that end. In other words, the "mission" of DEA field office intelligence has shaped the "means" to achieve it. This basic mission approach is distinct from the traditional intelligence "capabilities-based" approach to structure and problem-solving. Accordingly, DEA field offices offer an alternative approach that can perhaps illuminate current IC moves to generate more relevant, actionable intelligence through user-driven Joint Intelligence Operations Centers (JIOCs).

NEW IC PROBLEMS NEED NEW SOLUTIONS

In years past, DEA's counter-drug mission seemed worlds apart from IC missions like monitoring and warning of threats from foreign states, militaries, weapons systems, infrastructures, arms transfers, and so forth. Consistent with a mechanistic view of the world, the IC has long programmed and structured much of its largely technical collections and analytic elements around places, objects, masses, movements, and other "observable" phenomena associated with those traditional problems. A disadvantage of that structuring is a pigeon-holing effect: most analysts do not get to see the bigger picture. In addition, few analysts interact directly with the users of their product.

Events of 11 September 2001 demonstrated that traditional procedures can miss critical threats. Although the details may be murky, the importance of networks among groups, small cells, and individuals who organize to act against us without leaving "observable signatures" is clear. These networks have adeptly exploited our mindsets, structures, and technologies—whose advantages are no longer uniquely our own. These threats confound further by remaining below the level of traditional nation-state governments, armies, and the other familiar constructs around which America's conventional intelligence collection and analysis infrastructure is designed. Indeed, our enemies have formed networks among themselves for achieving their objectives—whether their affiliation is for convenience or shared grievance. Many of these networks are invisible to Cold War-legacy collection systems and analytic tradecraft. Groups and individuals have also prospered by exploiting the walls and disconnects between these legacy systems, structures, and tradecraft.

The relational essence of many critical intelligence challenges, and the need to develop actionable intelligence, commends a closer look at the user-focused, HUMINT-centric intelligence model that DEA field offices use. These offices have refined intelligence tradecraft to expose and explain relationships that enable them to find and apprehend drug criminals. This is not to force problems like terrorism or insurgency into a DEA-style law enforcement paradigm. Rather, it is to recognize and harvest useful new ideas for intelligence, even if they come from outside the IC.

BCO MODEL: CONNECTING DOTS BEARS FRUIT

DEA's Bangkok Country Office (BCO) in Thailand offers a rich case study for seeing more of the whole of an "asymmetric" problem built upon relationships and network behaviors. A major center for international trade, Thailand is also a base of operations for several drug trafficking networks. And Thailand's four southern provinces (see Figure 1) are beset with the problem—tangential, for drug-enforcers—of rising Muslim terrorism that so far has resulted in more than 800 deaths in less than two years.

Figure 1. Southern Thailand Coastline
Source: Author.

BCO's development of cases for prosecution thus offers a useful glimpse into an alternative structure and process for solving a complex, difficult intelligence problem—a relational problem whose true scope would be all but invisible were analysts using only national technical means and other conventional IC methodologies.

BCO has refined its intelligence tradecraft especially for discerning relationships within shadowy networks, for teasing out and proving the activities of individuals involved in the drug trade. The big business of making money through narcotics trade requires access to reliable, professional-grade illegal support services. These services include smuggling and couriering goods and people, transferring and laundering money, and forging documents—including stealing or generating fake passports, visas, drivers' licenses, birth certificates, identity cards, SSNs, and other credentials. Such services enable the business to operate profitably and the network to move its products efficiently beneath official radar. BCO has found that discerning the specific relationships among drug traffickers and such illegal service providers has been one of the best ways to discover the scope, activities, and behaviors of the drug network itself, as well as a means of identifying higher-level operatives.

Hound Dog: A Short Foray across Mission Boundaries

In the course of assembling the puzzle pieces of narcotics trade networks, BCO has seen that, just like drug dealers, terror networks need to move resources invisibly across national borders. They often do so using international or underground financial systems, including Chinese Underground Banking Systems (CUBs) or Hawala, an informal South Asian financial transfer system. Other techniques involve debit/credit cards and Western Union, methods through which guest-workers worldwide have transferred roughly $48 billion in a single year, according to BCO's estimates. Through studying these behaviors, methods, and linkages, BCO analysts have realized that terror networks are using many of the same professional providers for false identity papers, money laundering, and courier services.

Thus, through Special Field Intelligence Program initiatives such as Operation Hound Dog,[20] BCO analysts have discovered in the course of their CD work a critical and identifiable nexus of professional, shared "service" contacts. Because these same contacts are exploited both by drug traders and terror organizations, BCO analysts daring to peek over the walls of their prescribed mission can suggest to the IC that the details of these shared contacts offer a window into both types of networks. Developing a full picture of service industry contacts and relationships like those in Thailand could illuminate a good deal more—not only about drug networks and trafficking, but also terror organizations and activities. BCO has been investigating African and South Asian illicit service providers based in Thailand because of their support to drug smuggling. But BCO's findings that individuals linked to the Middle East and to terrorism are also using these services have drawn high interest from Thai law enforcement and military authorities, including those concerned about the unstable, Muslim-dominated southern provinces. Thai military authorities believe that the terror problem in the south is being

---

[20] DEA Intelligence Officer, Bangkok Country Office, Bangkok, Thailand, interview by author, May 2006.

enabled and exacerbated by drug networks that push drugs to embolden youths to commit acts of terrorism.[21]

Although the IC certainly uses forms of link analysis and document exploitation, BCO analysts have not yet attracted much interest from the IC for their particular relational methodologies or for the service provider details and insights that might be relevant to terror networks. BCO speculates that its narrower counter-drug mission may be obscuring its information's other uses from IC analysts. There may also be an assumption, justified or not, that any relevant information is already passed by the FBI to IC counterterrorism centers. However, it does not appear that the IC is harvesting all the potentially relevant information and insights being captured by organizations like the BCO. Illegal service industry connections, and the BCO relationship-focused methodology in general, offer innovative and potentially valuable analytic pathways into any hard target network whose daily functioning requires professional-grade illegal support services.

"Ends" Shape Structure and Means

The clear ends for BCO's counter-drug intelligence analysis define its analytic structure and tradecraft. These ends are obtaining the evidence required to arrest individuals engaged in money laundering, counterfeiting, and other illegal activities related to drug trade, while also gathering additional evidence and exposing higher-order drug-trade criminals and their activities.

According to BCO, the African Criminal Network (ACN) is one of the largest Thai-based narcotics networks. It comprises one of BCO's largest "intelligence problems." ACN is comprised of often-related Ghanaians and other western Africans. This network also has links to other networks and individuals in Southeast Asia, South Asia, Europe, the Middle East, and Latin America. These large networks have tentacles reaching the U.S. They use family, business, religion, or charity cutouts to obtain the gamut of fraudulent document and fund-transfer services they need to function.

BCO has developed tradecraft and analytic techniques to produce insights and gather usable evidence about such networks and their members.

Integration of Intel and Ops for Actionable Intelligence

About two years ago, DEA's need for accurate, specific actionable intelligence led it to restructure its field offices for producing just such insights. At BCO Bangkok, DEA has developed task-force-like teams to build cases. Each team has embedded seasoned intelligence analysts working alongside special agents executing operations and enforcement actions. These analysts and agents have Thai language skills and are immersed

---

[21] Special Colonel Duangkamal S. Makeswat, Director, Division 4, Armed Forces Security Center, Bangkok, interview by author, May 2006.

in Thai culture (see Figure 2). They also work directly with and in support of Thai law enforcement organizations, which in turn can draw from Thai sources of additional information and directly from Thai criminal elements.

The analyst offers "reach-back" capability to various law enforcement databases. The Special Agent brings law enforcement experience, street smarts, and undercover resources and information.

The BCO Special Agent and the rest of the problem-solving team are the intelligence analyst's main product users. However, the agent and other team members also comprise the analyst's most critical intelligence sources. Viewing the user as an intelligence source is an essential aspect of a sustained Intelligence-Operations conversation that produces "actionable intelligence."

Thai law enforcement and military counterparts are also full members of this team, as detailed below. Each member of these close-working BCO-host country teams comes to learn much about the responsibilities, capabilities, and requirements of all the others. This gives all members a more complete picture and context for the particular expertise or resources they bring to solving the problem. In terms of output, BCO intelligence analysts also prepare analysis cables back to HQ, which HQ may then incorporate into strategic assessments. However, BCO intelligence analysts contend their most important output is the routine brainstorming among their team and with their agent ("operations") and providing amplifying insight about the case as it is developing.[22]

The mission and daily risk that DEA special agents confront means that, just like military units preparing for combat, they must have the fullest possible situational awareness. BCO "Intelligence" (analysts) and "Operations" (agents) suffer no blue doors or green doors—the security, cultural, and bureaucratic barriers infamous for preventing intelligence analysts from knowing about operations or operators from knowing about intelligence insights. The needs of the case drive the BCO intelligence strategy, and the agents have immediate access to all insights about the case that the intelligence analysts produce. As such, BCO offers a useful living example of producing actionable intelligence for the user.

Every BCO agent and analyst interviewed by the author emphasized the importance of agents and analysts being physically co-located and teamed on cases. They insist that this enables BCO intelligence analysts and agents to sustain a necessarily continuous, actionable intelligence-oriented conversation about the status of the case on which they are both focused.

---

[22] DEA Counter-drug Analyst, Bangkok Country Office, Bangkok, Thailand, interview by author, May 2006.

**Figure 2. Mendicant Buddhist
monk in Thai market**
Source: Author.

One 20-year special agent,[23] who now runs a training academy for Thai law enforcement officers, elaborated that no regimen of written messages, emails, or VTCs produces better results than people with relevant skills working the problem together, side by side.

Even when under cover, agents provide immediate "tactical" updates to their intelligence analyst as they discover possible clues and new associations during surveillance, confidential interviews, or undercover activities. The means for providing updates and brainstorming entails no arcane technologies, fusion tools, or software; it consists of frequent face-to-face conversations and cell phone calls.

This direct and continuous communication contrasts with the prevailing form of IC analyst-user interface. IC intelligence users at higher echelons typically "task" questions through liaison officers and collection requirement mechanisms. These are passed down through the intelligence bureaucracy's administrative echelons, through supervisors, and finally to analytic elements—with whom the users have little or no working relationship. Isolated and remote from their users, analysts have little exposure to or real grasp of the user's milieu, perspective, or mission. Users in turn have little knowledge of the analysts' capabilities and limitations.

BCO's continuous direct intelligence-user interaction as a form of output also differs from the IC's tendency to "offer" intelligence judgments in

---

[23] Chief, International Law Enforcement Academy, Bangkok, Thailand, interview by author, May 2006.

formal publications or by posting product on web pages for users to find. This is often done unbeknownst to potential users, who may not discover relevant products while web surfing. An actual intelligence conversation between the line IC analyst and the user is rare. Moreover, while much of the IC's user world works on unclassified and secret level systems, IC analytic elements work and post their product on JWICs, a system that most users cannot even access.

BCO intelligence analysts research new leads as they receive them from U.S. and host country contacts, databases, operations, and other inquiries. The analyst and agent collaborate to decide what and how to follow-up. The two often interview confidential sources together so they can share impressions and brainstorm about follow-on plans. New data often add new branches for Operations or Intelligence inquiry to the case; some lead to entirely new cases. Agents and intelligence analysts thus collaborate at every step—forming objectives, conducting interviews, seizing emerging opportunities, evaluating the quality of information from a source, forming hypotheses, determining evidence gaps, and developing follow-on strategies to fill the remaining gaps. [24]Agents do not view themselves as or want to be analysts, or vice versa. Yet over time, close teaming and common focus has tended to build trust while enabling each to know the other's capabilities and perspectives.[25]

Rules of Evidence Define Case-building Criteria

BCO intelligence analysts begin to build a case by defining their intelligence problem against the user requirement that evidence meet the arrest and prosecution threshold. Requirements also guide the sources and methods that BCO analysts use to discern the scope of the network. Requirements also inform the analysts and agents when the evidence they have built is enough to elevate the case to a higher priority (thus receiving increased investigative resources), or to hand over for enforcement action.

The clarity of enforcement criteria and purpose contrasts with the often vague understanding many intelligence analysts have of the ultimate application and consequence of their analytic tradecraft and judgments. BCO counter-drug analysts know in advance that their conclusions and supporting evidence must be accurate, specific, and admissible in court. That is unlike strategic estimates pertaining to foreign political situations, which may bridge evidence gaps by drawing on supposition, logic, or past patterns.[26] Each defendant in counter-drug work is different and every case is judged on its own details and merits. Consequences of success and failure are immediate and palpable. Moreover, if analysts receive information

---

[24] DEA Special Agent, Bangkok, Thailand, interview by author, May 2006.

[25] DEA, interviews.

[26] DEA, interview.

from sources (for example, classified intelligence) or employ methods (for example, extra-legal wiretaps) that led them to conclusions but are not admissible in court, they know they must also have admissible evidence that can support their conclusion. In this way, the end requirement defines nearly everything about counter-drug intelligence sources and analytic tradecraft.

Figure 3. Market in northern Thailand's Golden Triangle
Source: Author.

In getting tip-offs that may lead them to open cases, BCO analysts say they get little help from conventional intelligence sources, methods, or tradecraft. One analyst, who was conversant with the IC from working at DIA for nearly 20 years, said that in four years on station in Bangkok, only one worthwhile lead came from national intelligence sources.[27] Conventional intelligence data tend to be highly classified. Classification greatly complicates sharing with host-country teammates and is not useful for court proceedings.

The limited use of national intelligence for BCO purposes is also due in part to the more strategic, general, or estimative orientation of most national HUMINT or national technical collection requirements and the data they tend to produce. Generally, national means are neither directed against, nor do they produce, the tactical data or detail needed to construct a case. Moreover, where the IC may weave imprecise or inaccurate details from HUMINT into a strategic IC product without having palpable (or at least recognizable) consequences, the same is not true for a BCO agent interfacing directly with

---

[27] DEA, interview.

criminal elements. Inaccurate details in the agent's understanding of his target can put the agent in danger and raise the risk of operational failure. [28]

Host Nation as Full Team Member

For their case-opening leads, the BCO has a multitude of alternative sources. Among the most important are the tip-offs received from partnerships cultivated among local (Thai) police, immigration, military, and other officials. These officials have overlapping or mutually reinforcing objectives with BCO, and understand the BCO's "case building" needs. In this way, "interested users" from the host country become involved in working the "intelligence problem" with BCO from its inception. They are gateways into a multitude of Thai immigration, telephone, police, banking, and other organizations and databases that can offer specific follow-up information about particular cases with a Thai connection. BCO analysts and agents routinely meet and talk directly with host country officials.

Thai organizations suffer their own "stovepipe" syndrome, and BCO teams often act as the hub of the wheel in collating information from disparate organizations. Thai law enforcement and military officials are looking to apprehend drug criminals within Thailand and, from a military perspective, maintain stability where drug activities may be exacerbating violence. Thus, the Royal Thai Police's Narcotic Suppression Bureau, the Thai Office of Narcotics Control Board, and the Justice Ministry's Department of Special Investigations (all law enforcement offices) are, like the Special Agent, intelligence users as well as intelligence sources. In effect, Thai officials are full working partners supplementing the core BCO analyst-agent team. Working almost wholly at the unclassified level enables BCO to sustain a robust and continuous intelligence conversation with Thai officials. This is the type of relationship intended for DoD's new JIOCs: established mechanisms for operators to become intelligence sources as well.

One of the BCO's largest ongoing cases is that of a West African money launderer and suspected drug trafficker. BCO opened that case with a tip-off from the Royal Thai Immigration Service. In early 2006, Immigration apprehended the African male for the seemingly simple problem of his attempting to enter Thailand on a false visa. They then made available to BCO some of the suspect's possessions. These included several bank/debit cards from China and Thailand, several phone numbers, a business card for a firm that does check-cashing and Western Union transfers, and "world citizen" identification. It later surfaced during a BCO interview with the West African suspect that, before he arrived in Thailand, the Japanese had held him for a month for traveling on a false British passport. (The suspect maintained he was waiting for his "real" passport to arrive from his mother.) Although Thai officials subsequently released the suspect and deported him from

---

[28] DEA, interviews.

Thailand, BCO opened a file to follow the suspect's suspicious activities as a money laundering case, although analysts also suspected that other crimes or criminal associates were involved. Those suspicions grew after one of BCO's confidential sources alerted them that the individual subsequently re-entered Thailand. At that point, BCO set out to uncover the truth and scope of this suspect's activities and associations.

Precise and Proactive HUMINT

BCO relies heavily upon HUMINT to get leads and develop follow-on information. However, BCO strategies for developing HUMINT are beyond those of DoD, where few analysts have even indirect access to sources, and where—at best—they may attempt to pull further information from a source through written guidance comments in a formal evaluation. BCO's HUMINT encompasses an entire strategy or menu of searches, direct interviews, surveillance, and proactive operations, any or all of which can be used to build and verify the evidence.

Databases to Amplify Personal Information. Depending on the nature of the tip-off, BCO intelligence analysts begin by querying multiple, sometimes mutually reinforcing sources to fill in the picture of the activity or of the individual suspect and his relationships. They may check FBI, national, and DEA proprietary databases to see what more they might reveal about the piece of identifying data that they have received about a suspect.

Most such criminals cover their tracks by using multiple names, cutouts, SSNs, disposable "one-two" cell phones, addresses, and so forth. This increases the importance of using multiple sources and databases. Only by comparing data received from many sources and databases is it possible to discover common threads pointing to true identity, relationships, location, or nature of activity. Despite the value of its databases, however, filling in the relationship and identity picture usually entails far more.

Toll Analysis. Toll analysis is a basic methodology, versions of which have been adapted to other problems, that drills down on individual suspects and their particular relationships and activities. It does so by identifying calls made and received from a given phone number either found on or contacted by the suspect.

Albeit detailed and tedious, toll analysis is a foundational tool for starting to build the links and key nodes of a network. Toll analysis relies on the ability to track telephone calls, whether landline or mobile, in a way that enables analysis of their patterns of direction, repetition, frequency, and duration. BCO intelligence analysts note common numbers, numbers called by more than one other number. This may offer additional clues and patterns about the subscribers' contacts. Analysts can then use digital dial analysis or a comprehensive toll analysis in the NCIC database to see what other phone numbers had calls to or from any of the numbers in question. This analysis exposes further associations, albeit not yet the associations' content, and it can lead to links with other cases under investigation. Applying their experience and grasp of typical target behavior, BCO intelligence analysts use the patterns to develop tentative working hypotheses about the associations. In some cases, analysts can determine identity of phone subscribers as well as call location.

Despite the significant reference value of toll analysis, BCO intelligence analysts also recognize that their case cannot rest on toll analysis alone.[29] Doing so would entail the same error as a conventional analyst believing that, despite all its value as a reference, overhead reconnaissance can reveal the entire story about a situation. Toll analysis is itself a model with certain built-in assumptions. If accepted without question, these can lead to faulty conclusions. The tolls do not usually directly reveal or prove the identity of a criminal or the nature of his offence. Subscribers subjected to repeated contact may turn out to be completely benign. Instead, BCO analysts consider toll analysis a useful starting point, one of several building blocks that, once established, can be the basis for further network-picture building and case strategizing. BCO analyzes and amplifies on initial link charts by searching additional U.S. and foreign databases and other DEA country field offices and by proactively developing other HUMINT sourcing.

BCO analysts also, as noted earlier, provide their findings from toll analysis to host-country military and law enforcement partners, who can draw on their access to host country telephone, financial, police, and other records to help fill in details—whether it is telephone call content, financial transfers, or other useful information.[30]

In the ongoing West African case, the numbers found in the suspect's possession showed useful patterns. Although there were few domestic (Thai) calls to the suspect's numbers, there were multiple calls from Canada, UK, New York, and Japan. Another of the suspect's Thai numbers listed several contacts with Chicago-area phone numbers. BCO's toll analysis of the suspect's list of numbers showed an indirect link to individuals already being investigated by DEA in the U.S. Repetitive calling among the UK numbers and a very large number of calls with Nigeria raised further suspicion about a triangular calling pattern. Moreover, the organization that issued the suspect

---

[29] DEA Intelligence Group Supervisor, Bangkok Country Office, Bangkok, Thailand, interview by author, May 2006.

[30] Lieutenant Colonel Tuengwiwat Sombat and Colonel Aryawuit Dusadee, Department of Special Investigation, Royal Thai Police, meeting attended by author, Bangkok, Thailand, 9 May 2006.

his "world citizenship" card had contacts with other known drug traffickers that were already the subject of separate investigations.

Toll analysis has not yet linked the suspect directly with drug trafficking, but tolls with other information show him associated with individuals who are involved in those activities. Those associations do not prove guilt, but they are enough to justify elevating the case in order to receive increased U.S. and Thai investigatory resources. Then the challenge for the agent-analyst team will be to uncover direct evidence of his guilt.

Layering on Other Data. Once analysts establish some type of "fingerprint" (a bank account or several phone numbers pointing to the same subscriber, for instance) by which they can track the individual or activity, analysts can combine what toll analysis has suggested about patterns and associations with other gleaned details. These may include answers to queries sent to field offices and databases in areas implicated by the calling/called locations. Analysts also can research suspicious activity reports (SAR) filed by U.S. financial organizations, cull credit bureau reports to see whether the individual has been identified in the past, and check to see if he is part of another ongoing case. BCO analysts additionally broaden their query to the DEA's database and the FBI's consolidated National Crime Information Center database, a clearinghouse combining data from other DEA field offices, Customs, FBI, immigration, and other agencies with a counter-drug mission.

Many criminals increase the challenge of tracking them by using bank ATM cards instead of credit cards to transfer funds. ATM card transfers only require a card and pin, not necessarily a name. This improves anonymity, adding ease, transparency, and safety to money-transfer and laundering deposits and withdrawals. ATMs enable criminals to transfer funds from and to anywhere in the world, with minimal risk that lost cards will be reported. And they can use the same cards for point of sale purchases—to buy legal consumer goods that they can then sell on the black market, thus laundering their proceeds.

Through SARs and/or access to Thai data afforded by the host-nation partnership, BCO analysts can access specific ATM withdrawal and deposit information and history associated with confiscated credit or ATM account numbers. These show the amount, frequency, time, and date data. Thai officials also can help localize individuals making the calls, in turn raising the possibility of gleaning identifying data from automated tellers equipped with video surveillance.[31] All such data can help amplify BCO analysts' insight and working hypotheses.

---

[31] Sombat and Dusadee, meeting.

**Figure 4. Hill country village in northern
Thailand's Golden Triangle**
Source: Author.

In some cases, BCO intelligence analysts, aided by Thai-provided data, can also gain commercial information to determine whether their suspects have converted any of the money into goods such as drugs or electronics for downstream selling as a means of further laundering. Analysts can add more pieces to the puzzle by overlaying the account number transfer activity with telephone activity they have pinned on the same individuals, addresses, or other identifying data. Further, they can link details of money transfers or goods sales with telephone call activity, layering more useful detail onto the link chart. It begins to reveal the larger picture of who is directing the activity, who is servicing the request, and at least working hypotheses about the nature of the working relationship and services one may be providing to or getting from another.

In the case of the West African, BCO analysts' overlaying of call patterns with deposit and withdrawal information showed an indirect link between the suspect's telephone activity and repeated bank transfers of large amounts of money, strongly suggestive of money laundering.

Confidential Source. BCO's confidential source (CS) program is a form of proactive and precisely targeted HUMINT. The BCO analyst-agent team develops a strategy for using CSs from its knowledge of the case. The purpose is to produce more evidence on the target with help from individuals who know the target, the business, and the neighborhood, and who can be induced to cooperate and to provide details about the suspect's ongoing activities and associations. BCO normally cultivates and turns people into confidential sources when it believes a CS can point to more evidence for elevating the case, or for amplifying a case already underway.

Analyzing the links and associations of its target, BCO looks for individuals who would likely have a particular motive—a grudge or an itch that needs scratching with respect to the main suspect or his associates. In part through undercover work, the BCO agent-analyst team becomes familiar enough with its sources to discern and exploit the collection opportunity that such motivations can offer. Candidates may be induced out of greed; they may be spurned lovers or cheated business partners; they may be facing stiff punishment for drug trafficking or related crimes and hoping that cooperation will be a "get out of jail" card. Other source candidates may find cooperation a far better choice than options such as deportation or hand-over to foreign authorities for interrogation. That each case differs means that CSs cannot be "turned" on generalities. The analyst-agent team must be intimately familiar with the details of the case and the personalities involved, must realize what is credible and available for exploitation, and must know what exploitation might yield. BCO compensates CSs to sustain their relationships with the suspect or his associates and to report developments from which the BCO analyst-agent team can formulate relevant actions for gathering additional evidence.

For the West African case, BCO obtained cooperation from a confidential source who travels in the suspect's circles, who needs money, and who appears repentant following a drug charge.[32] The special agent pays the CS to "hang around," socialize, and pick up what he can at locations the suspect and/or his friends and associates frequent. The BCO intelligence analyst and the agent meet frequently with the CS to gain feedback and provide the source continuing guidance. The BCO special agent encourages the CS to continue cooperating through the promise of a large bonus when the case is resolved. The CS has provided valuable information about the suspect and his whereabouts, as well as information on additional associates, at least some of which analysts have been able to verify independently.

Surveillance. Directly monitoring the movements of suspects is another proven and precisely targeted form of HUMINT that BCO uses to flush out more evidence and associations on suspects. BCO agents may observe individuals, residences, places of business travel, or whatever else might yield further facts about people associating with the suspect or the nature of their illegal activities.

In the West African case, BCO built a joint surveillance plan with help from the Thai Department of Special Investigations (DSI). DSI was able to develop key information related to a bankcard in the suspect's possession from the Siam Commercial Bank. DSI had identified the account owner, her address, and her businesses. From that they could, through surveillance, identify people with whom she lived, worked, and socialized, leading to a

---

[32] Confidential Source, Bangkok, Thailand, interview by author May 2006.

BCO hunch that she is the suspect's girlfriend. The suspect subsequently showed his girl friend's picture to an undercover agent, confirming that she and the Siam bank card account holder were the same person. Knowing that, DSI believes that by monitoring her through surveillance it can confirm if and when the suspect returns to Thailand, and his subsequent whereabouts.

Wires. After narrowing telephone numbers to those of greatest interest, BCO intelligence analysts can obtain Title III wiretaps on numbers it believes will yield additional evidence and associations. Wiretaps track all the telephone numbers in contact with the monitored line, along with content of the conversations over that line.

Figure 5. Giving alms at a Buddhist temple outside Bangkok
Source: Author.

Running Operations. Once the agent-analyst team is convinced, but does not yet have irrefutable proof, that the suspect is engaged in drug-related money laundering, document fraud, or other illicit services, it may elevate the case from a "general" file to a full case. Elevation increases the amount of investigative funding and resources, to include support for crafting and running additional operations.

The purpose of running operations is the same as all else for the agent-analyst team: to fill in gaps of evidence that DOJ needs to support arrest and court prosecution of identified criminals engaged in narcotics trade. An operation makes use of almost everything that the analyst and agent have learned about the case. The operation typically inserts an undercover agent or BCO-controlled confidential source as an apparent participant in the narcotics trade flow. This enables BCO to observe and document the suspects' continuing illicit activity and associations. As such, it produces relevant and direct evidence. This means of gaining direct, first-hand evidence also precludes the kind of imprecision or ambiguity that can characterize second- or third-party HUMINT found in much IC reporting.

Even though agents have the principal responsibility of running operations, it is not the agent alone but the agent-analyst team that formulates the operation and its tactics. Both members bring to bear their understanding about the suspect, his personality, activities, relationships, and foreseeable responses to the operation's tactics; how he will react to the "customer" the undercover agent may pretend to be or to services the undercover agent may offer or seek to purchase. The undercover agent may offer to buy and make payments for drugs to stimulate the network to engage in (and thereby expose to BCO) its "normal" activity. An operation's duration and content depend on the individual situation. If an operation continues to expose new activities or associations to higher-order drug trade, the analyst-agent team may run it until convinced they have seen the entirety of the network and/or the highest-order criminal it is likely to bring to the surface.

For the BCO intelligence analyst, the undercover operation often supplies vital new leads for additional suspects and activities related to the case. These may point to other higher-level criminals, and they may also offer their own new set of service-provider relationships. Thus, an operation can as easily lead to an entirely new set of suspects, to the makings of an entirely new case, or to linkages to cases already under investigation elsewhere in a way that reveals their true scope.

Throughout an operation, BCO takes great care to allow a complete unfolding of the full nature and scope of the suspects' activities and associations. If indictments exist against any of the suspects or their associates, they are sealed so that the suspects will discern no reason to refrain from their "normal" activity.

Training. At the International Law Enforcement Academy in Bangkok, BCO has also initiated training to help host-country law enforcement officials learn how to work together through a case.[33] This training helps the host country develop cases properly as well as recognize the kind of insight that is useful to BCO case development.

A seasoned DEA special agent has designed the training regimen to bring together a broad cross-section of law enforcement officials from Thai immigration, police, customs, DSI, military, and other institutions with a stake in the problem. The program director maintains that his courses are an example of how to break down stovepipes at the most essential, person-to-person level. He observed that many officials in his classes have been working aspects of the same problems, some even at the same locations, without realizing it. His courses offer them an opportunity to meet, realize their overlapping objectives, and build useful relationships with institutional counterparts and contacts.

The Academy coaches its mixture of officials to solve hands-on cases from inception through resolution. It provides the outlines of the problem and sets up challenges, including "crimes" such as actual explosions of satchels or vehicles. The course then exercises students in using their many alternative sources of information for acquiring evidence to enable prosecution.

The hands-on experience has been very successful in eroding stovepipes. He believes the class work and practical problem-solving experience increases respective institutional "buy-in" to a more confederated approach to

---

[33] DEA, interview.

problem solving beyond the classroom. Course graduates bring back to their own organizations a fuller grasp of solution options, as well as advocacy for what interagency cooperation can accomplish. The academy chooses the top students within its classes to become instructors of the methodology within their respective home organizations.

SUMMARY: INSIGHTS FOR REMODELING THE IC

DEA field office intelligence tradecraft contrasts sharply with the intelligence model that the IC has evolved over the years for traditional threat analysis and that it is now remodeling. DEA's field intelligence clearly has a different purpose than the IC's. Some of its methodologies carry risk and not every investigation or operation has produced the intended results. Indeed, not all DEA field office tradecraft is applicable or appropriate to IC intelligence problems. Beyond that, resident expertise and fortuitous personality blends at BCO also contribute to the productive working relationships and high morale evident there. And in fairness to the IC, many of its collection or exploitation capabilities could help BCO analysts with their case-building.

All that said, this analyst's short visit to BCO was an eye-opener. This is especially true of the user-mission orientation of BCO's intelligence structuring, the productive give-and-take with host-country officials, and the relationship-discerning attributes of its tradecraft. Beyond factors of personality or expertise among individuals assigned to BCO, the attributes of an enabling intelligence-operations team structure, mission clarity, and a rich host-country working relationship seem to be a magic combination for solving problems.

This analyst left BCO convinced that, first, the IC should find a way to harvest whatever substantive details and insights organizations like the BCO discover in the course of their counter-drug work that might assist with critical problem sets such as terrorism.

Second, the IC should study DEA field offices' alternative structure and tradecraft to see how it might be useful, wholly or in part, in solving IC intelligence problems. DEA field offices have fashioned an effective approach to address the issues they discern. DEA accordingly has been adjusting its own culture to help resolve two huge challenges that similarly confront the IC: 1) user demands that intelligence structure its analysis to be more operations-integrated and relevant to user requirements (as evidenced by the JIOC's Execute Order[34]); and 2) the need to understand intelligence problems

---

[34] Lieutenant General Jerry Boykin, USA, Deputy Under Secretary of Defense for Intelligence and Warfighter Support, "Joint Intelligence Operations Centers," *Defenselink*, 12 April 2006, URL: <www. defenselink.mil/Transcripts/Transcript.aspx?TranscriptID=1243>, accessed 27 November 2006.

in which details about individuals and relationships offer clues to activities of larger networks.[35]

At least as manifested by the team at the Bangkok country office, DEA has insightful and fresh approaches to offer the intelligence community at large, if the IC is innovative and adaptive enough to grasp and adopt them.

Figure 6. The End.
Source: Author.

---

[35] John Bodnar, *Warning Analysis for the Information Age: Rethinking the Intelligence Process* (Washington: Joint Military Intelligence College, December 2003), 85-122.

IMPROVING TACTICAL MILITARY INTELLIGENCE WITH ANTI-GANG TECHNIQUES

Major Edward Gliot, USA
Master of Science of Strategic Intelligence, 1999

As soon as we got to Mogadishu, we were struck by the similarity to L.A.

A colonel involved in the U.S. Marine
deployments to Los Angeles and Somalia in 1992,
as quoted by Thomas E. Ricks in
"The Widening Gap Between the Military and Society,"
The Atlantic Monthly 280, no. 1 (July 1997): 77.

Problems such as ethnic confrontation, "uncivil wars," and tribal upheaval are not new, but the American military's focus on them is. By looking to American law enforcement's experience with street gangs, the military may find some innovative ways of handling those problems close at hand. In the United States, urban street gangs have steadily increased their membership, their violent crimes, and their lethal weaponry. Because of similarities between civil unrest in the Third World and the U.S., HUMINT collection practices and tactical military intelligence analysis during military operations other than war (MOOTW) may benefit from incorporating successful street-level intelligence techniques developed by police anti-gang task forces.[36]

SIMILARITY OF FOREIGN AND U.S. URBAN ENVIRONMENTS

Operations RESTORE HOPE in Somalia, UPHOLD DEMOCRACY in Haiti, and the continuing NATO operations in the former Yugoslavia all challenge the military intelligence community to provide better intelligence support in these chaotic environments. One promising source of untapped intelligence expertise is America's domestic police departments. In 1996, about 4,800 U.S. police jurisdictions were attempting to maintain law and order against nearly 250,000 gang members in more than 31,000 street gangs. To accomplish their law enforcement mission, many of these police departments actively conduct intelligence operations dedicated to gathering

---

[36] James C. Howell, *Youth Gangs: An Overview* (Washington: Department of Justice, 1998), 12-14; and Malcolm W. Klein, *The American Street Gang: Its Nature, Prevalence, and Control* (New York: Oxford University Press, 1995), 118.

and processing tactical level intelligence to "understand patterns of gang behavior and identify trends." [37]

Similarities of Gangs

U.S. military strategic thinkers have recently observed the similarities between America's armed criminal gangs and the warlord-type formations observed in the Third World. From the police perspective, the military nature of U.S. gangs is apparent. Law enforcement publications describe street gangs using armed rooftop lookouts, "contracts" for the assassination of specific police officers, and active deception operations. Domestic gang sociologists have documented the similarities between American street gangs and youth gangs found throughout the world's urban areas.[38] Given these similarities, enforcing law and order against street gangs should require the same intelligence support, whether in Mogadishu or in Los Angeles. If so, then the intelligence methods used by domestic police forces may improve HUMINT collection and tactical intelligence analysis during constabulary-oriented MOOTW.

Street gangs are not a uniquely American phenomenon. The need to belong to a larger social group is not a merely cultural attribute—it is a human characteristic. Street gang sociologists note that the formation of street gangs is a natural human response to certain environmental factors, including urbanization, poverty, and a widespread sense of hopelessness among young adults. The formation of street gangs, then, can be viewed as a human impulse to create social organization in a socially chaotic environment. Numerous modern gang researchers have observed American-style street gangs in such diverse locales such as Western Europe, South East Asia, Russia, India, Brazil, Jamaica, Tanzania, and Yugoslavia.[39] Therefore, it is reasonable to assume that street gangs in Haiti, Somalia, and Bosnia are also similar to U.S. street gangs.

---

[37] "Intel XXI: Mission," 13 January 1999, *Department of Defense, Intel XXI Task Force*, URL: <www.dami.army.pentagon.mil/projects/intel_xxi/mission.html>, accessed 18 February 1999; *Urban Street Gang Enforcement*, Department of Justice, Bureau of Justice Assistance, Monograph No. NCJ 161845 (Washington: Department of Justice, 1997), 4; Howell, 1; and Deborah Weisel and Ellen Painter, *The Police Response to Gangs: Case Studies of Five Cities* (Washington: Police Executive Research Forum, 1997), 85-86.

[38] Paul B. Rich, "Warlords, State Fragmentation and the Dilemma of Humanitarian Intervention," *Small Wars and Insurgencies* 10, no. 1 (Spring 1999): 79; Ralph Peters, *Fighting for the Future: Will America Triumph?* (Mechanicsburg, PA: Stackpole Books, 1999), 41; *Urban Street Gang Enforcement*, 28; Klein, 213; and Michael Langston, "Guidelines for Operating an Effective Gang Unit," *Journal of Gang Research* 5, no. 4 (Summer 1998): 65.

[39] Malcolm Klein lists research conducted by Spergel, Covey, and his own observations of foreign gangs in Klein, 215.

Similarity of Military and Police Operations

There are also similarities between military operations and police operations. Both police and military forces emphasize the use of human intelligence collection using overt methods, in uniform, with informed sources. In many police jurisdictions, the officers are ethnically and linguistically different from the populations they patrol. In a more general sense, police departments are armed para-military organizations. Like the military, they are structured on authoritarian lines and are responsible for establishing order by force, if necessary. These similarities, as well as the research outlined below, indicate that some police intelligence techniques can be used effectively in MOOTW environments.

In Somali and Haiti, U.S. forces operated under a mandate to establish and maintain civil order, making the street gangs found there part of the threat forces. In Bosnia, the constabulary role is part of the military's mission to the degree it is required to implement the Dayton Peace Agreement. Analysis of the Joint and Service Lessons Learned in these three operations, as well as academic studies and interviews with participants, yields seven tactical intelligence lessons, four on the HUMINT collections aspect of the operations and three on the analysis portion (see Figure 1).

Collection

- Every soldier is a HUMINT collector.
- Maintain the balance between security and HUMINT collection.
- "Non-standard" HUMINT information sources are vital.
- Extracting information via HUMINT is time consuming, complicated, and worthwhile.

Analysis

- Analysts must understand the host nation's cultural environment.
- Tracking the situation requires precise resolution of detailed information.
- Conventional analysis of gang order of battle and doctrine is impractical.

Figure 1. Tactical Collection and Analysis Lessons
Source: Author.

According to the author's evaluation of four metropolitan police departments, the HUMINT collection lessons listed in Figure 1 are comparable to the practices developed by police anti-gang units in major U.S. cities. Like the Army and Marine Corps, three of the four police departments surveyed try to use every officer on the street as a HUMINT collector. The police have also developed collection team structures and security measures analogous to the military solutions that evolved in Somalia, Haiti, and Bosnia. The use of unusual information sources was a common aspect of the military and police collection procedures. The police experiences also reinforce the military lesson that, although the expenditure of time, effort, and resources to develop informants is high, it is a worthwhile investment. Finally, the police departments in the larger cities, like the military in Haiti and Bosnia, found surveillance to be effective but cost prohibitive.

In the analysis area, police investigators acknowledge the need to understand the unique street gang "culture" and environment from a broad economic, social, and psychological perspective. Like the military analysts in Somalia and Haiti, the police analyst must maintain a detailed information tracking system on street gang members and their associations. Finally, the police intelligence system is unable, in most instances, to describe the amorphous street gang using organizational charts, map dispositions, and predictive courses of action. As in MOOTW, association networks, gang membership databases, "turf" maps, and pattern analysis are the most effective analysis tools for describing the American street gang environment.[40]

Police Lessons in Stability, Security, and Surveillance

There are three implications of these results, dealing with stability, security, and surveillance. First, the police system demonstrates the benefits of maintaining unit and soldier stability in the constabulary MOOTW environment. One of the keys to the police anti-gang units' successes is the fact that the police officers in the gang environment maintain "beats," investigators work the same gangs for years, and analysts focus on specific gangs. This "community based policing" approach has the potential to enhance intelligence operations in constabulary MOOTW missions.

The second implication suggests that HUMINT collection teams can, under certain conditions, safely perform their collection duties without dedicated security forces. In the gang environment, investigators use a graduated system of security. In low threat situations, the police HUMINT collector relies on on-call reinforcement. If the officer suspects that a mission will be more dangerous, reinforcement can be coordinated to be nearby, ready to respond within seconds. Finally, in extremely hazardous conditions, an

---

[40] Lieutenant Commander Kathleen Hogan, USN, former Head of the Atlantic Command Caribbean Analysis Division, June 1994 to August 1996, interview by author, 24 June 1999.

investigator can move into a gang's territory with multiple security units, including heavily armed police analogous to infantrymen.

The last implication is that selective surveillance can be directed against street gangs. In spite of its cost, the smaller police departments each conduct surveillance on gang hangouts, parties, and inter-gang meetings. Under certain conditions, foreign street gangs should also be placed under surveillance. These surveillance operations often result in large amounts of intelligence regarding the street gang's size, structure, alliances, and leadership.

These three implications illustrate a few of the insights that arise from leveraging the expertise of police intelligence against the military intelligence paradigm.

STREET GANGS

Once street gangs are defined, it becomes clear that those encountered in recent MOOTW operations are not so different from those found in many American cities.

Defining Street Gangs

A "street gang" is defined as a loosely organized group, with a decentralized chain of command, claiming control over specific territory, individually or collectively engaging in a wide variety of violent criminal activities.[41]

While the territorial nature and violent crime aspects of the definition are fairly straightforward, the loose organization and decentralized leadership components require clarification. The organizational structure of the street gang has two key characteristics: membership and leadership.

First, street gang members can be divided into two categories: "core members" and "fringe members." Core members are more active in the gang's criminal and social activities. They are also more dependent on the gang for their social identity. Fringe members are generally less involved in the group, participating intermittently in street gang activities. They tend to be more independent and individualistic than core members.

Second, the street gang leadership is horizontal, usually composed of multiple six to eight person age-variegated "cliques" led by a single charismatic individual of similar age. Clique leaders rarely take orders from other cliques and are motivated by emotion, the desire to make money, build the gang's reputation, and maintain the chaotic, disruptive, status quo. This kind of emotionally based, decentralized decision making results in virtually non-existent planning cycles and little opportunity for traditional activity indicators to develop.

---

[41] *Urban Street Gang Enforcement*, 30.

The membership and leadership characteristics of the street gang have important implications in the comparison between gang police analysis and tactical military intelligence analysis.

Mogadishu, Somalia: 1992-1994

The threat forces in Somalia were composed of two groups: "military and paramilitary forces" and "armed gangs aligned with the factions or operating on their own." These gangs of young male Somalis, called *mooryaan*, were armed by the warlords and paid with women and the drug *khat* to attack the opposing warlords' forces. According to one firsthand account, "rogue gangs" were a priority for HUMINT collection in the early phases of the U.S. operation.[42]

The *mooryaan* clearly behave as street gangs. They have been described as "informal gangs"[43] with "no recognizable chain of command." The clans sponsoring the gangs held distinct regions of "turf" throughout Mogadishu. The violent crimes committed by the gangs ranged from "sniping and harassment" of UN forces to banditry, looting, and thievery. [44]

Thus, the situation in Mogadishu was analogous to the U.S. street gang situation. The U.S. forces were tasked with enforcing the peace, the environmental conditions approximated those that produce gangs in U.S. urban areas, and the *mooryaan* gangs meet the definition of street gang. In addition to the military efforts directed against the warring clans, the UN's fight in Mogadishu resembled a police action against street gangs.

Port-au-Prince, Haiti: 1994-1996

On 19 September 1994, a multi-national force (MNF) sanctioned by the United Nations and led by the United States occupied Haiti. The MNF's mission was to restore the legitimately elected government, led by President Jean-Bertrand Aristide, to power. By the end of October, 70 percent of the Haitian police had deserted their posts, leaving the responsibility for maintaining order with the U.S. 10th Mountain Division. After the

---

[42] Lynn Thomas and Steve Sparato, "Peacekeeping and Policing in Somalia," in *Policing the New World Disorder: Peace Operations and Public Security*, eds. Robert B. Oakley and others (Washington: National Defense University Press, 1998), 177-181; and Robert G. Patman, "The UN Operation in Somalia," in *A Crisis of Expectations: UN Peacekeeping in the 1990s*, eds. Ramesh Thakur and Carlyle A. Thayer (Boulder, CO: Westview Press, 1995), 87.

[43] Paul F. Diehl, "With the Best Intentions: Lessons from UNOSOM I and II," *Studies in Conflict and Terrorism* 19 (April-June 1996): 164.

[44] Martin N. Stanton, "Lessons Learned from Counter-Bandit Operations," *Marine Corps Gazette* 78, no. 2 (February 1994): 30; F. M. Lorenz, "Law and Anarchy in Somalia," *Parameters* 23, no. 3 (Winter 1993-1994): 27-46; Captain Eric Pohlmann, USA, Deputy Intelligence Officer, 13th Corps Support Command, during deployment to Somalia, January 1993-March 1993, interview by author, 2 July 1999; and Fritz J. Barth, "A System of Contradiction," *Marine Corps Gazette* 82, no. 4 (April 1998): 26.

establishment of the Haitian Interim Public Security Force (IPSF), military police and infantrymen continued to walk the streets of Haiti with them. Six months later, after accomplishing their mission, the MNF transitioned out of Haiti, leaving the operation in the hands of the U.S.-led UN Mission in Haiti (UNMIH). UNMIH's ongoing mission, since October 1994, has included helping the Haitian government "maintain security and stability in Haiti." As in Somalia, the American soldiers deployed to Port-au-Prince were serving as constables while carrying out their other responsibilities.[45]

U.S. forces deployed to Port-au-Prince were concerned with two threats: former paramilitary units and groups of unemployed, criminally active Haitian males. The intelligence effort in the capital was evenly divided between these two threats. By the 1990s, decades of oppression and exploitation produced an environment in Haiti similar to the U.S. gang setting. U.S. military intelligence during the deployment recognized at least five rival street gangs in the ghettos of Port-au-Prince. The character of the Haitian street gang was very similar to the American street gang. Their organization was dynamic and hard for the U.S. to track. They ran extremely decentralized operations, with no clear leadership. The Haitian street gangs competed against each other based on their armaments, fighting skills, ruthlessness, and turf, which was delineated with graffiti. Their criminal endeavors included intimidation, drug trafficking, theft, and vigilante homicide.[46]

The combination of these factors makes Haiti the strongest candidate among the three cases for an operation paralleling the American street gang policing experience. The U.S. forces clearly had a constabulary component to their mission, the environment approximated the street gang model, and the characteristics of the known street gangs match the definition of street gang.

Bosnia in the U.S. Sector: 1995-present

Civil War erupted in Bosnia the day after the Europeans and United States recognized its independence. In spite of the efforts of the UN Protection Force (UNPROFOR) and Operation PROVIDE PROMISE (a humanitarian aid airlift), the struggle between Bosnia's Serbs, Croats, and Muslims still displaced more than two million people, killing thousands. Finally, on 16 December 1995, after the signing of the Bosnian Peace Agreement, the NATO-led Implementation Force (IFOR) deployed to Bosnia. One year later, in December 1996, IFOR was replaced by a smaller NATO-led force—the

---

[45] United Nations Department of Peace Keeping Operations, "Completed Missions," October 1998, *UN Department of Public Information*, URL: <www.un.org/Depts/dpko>, accessed 3 November 1998; Walter E. Kretchik, "Fielding the International Police Monitors for Operation Uphold Democracy," *Low Intensity Conflict & Law Enforcement* 7, no. 2 (Autumn 1998): 113-118; and Irwin P. Stotzky, *Silencing the Guns in Haiti: The Promise of Deliberative Democracy* (Chicago: University of Chicago Press, 1997): 43.

[46] Hogan, interview; and Michael W. Schellhammer, "Lessons from Operation Restore Democracy," *Military Intelligence*, January-March 1996, 20.

Stabilization Force (SFOR). The SFOR's primary mission was and continues to be deterring hostilities and stabilizing the peace in Bosnia.

Although the enforcement of law and order in Bosnia is the job of the Bosnian national police, the U.S. forces in Bosnia viewed the maintenance of "law and order" as a key component to their exit strategy. Accordingly, military intelligence soldiers in Bosnia collected information and analyzed Bosnia's criminal problems.

As in the other two cases, the operation in Bosnia was directed against two threats: paramilitary organizations and criminal gangs. Both of these threats operated throughout the U.S. sector.[47]

The Bosnian criminal gangs exhibited a cellular, hierarchical structure that facilitates the execution of sophisticated organized crimes. The gang leadership divided labor within the organization and specified activities to be carried out via an effective, directive chain of command. The Bosnian gang was territorial, operating in specific areas, occupying public gathering places such as bars and cafes. The focus of their criminal activity was profiteering, whether from drugs, stolen cars, political interference, or the protection of suspected war criminals. Violent crimes were committed, such as drive-by shootings and bombings, but they were not common and were generally limited to reprisals and intimidation.[48] Given these factors, the Bosnian criminal gangs were not street gangs. They were corporate gangs with many of the characteristics of organized crime gangs. Based on the environmental conditions in Bosnia, street gangs probably exist or will emerge among the dislocated and the poor. [49]

INTELLIGENCE FORCE STRUCTURE IN SOMALIA, HAITI, AND BOSNIA

In MOOTW, teaming interrogators with counter-intelligence (CI) soldiers makes sense. Human intelligence soldiers—primarily interrogators—use human interactions to determine the situation on the enemy's side of the battlefield. CI soldiers specializing in HUMINT use human sources to assess the threat to U.S. forces on the friendly side of the battlefield. In MOOTW where there is no distinguishable forward line of troops, both of these missions

---

[47] Captain John Charles, USA, Division-level intelligence officer in Bosnia and Commander, C Company, 501st MI in Bosnia, interview by author, 12 July 1999; and Lieutenant Colonel Kevin Johnson, USA, Commander, 501st Military Intelligence Battalion, while deployed to Bosnia-Herzegovina under Task Force Eagle, December 1995 to December 1996, interview by author, 24 June 1999.

[48] This detailed assessment of Bosnian criminal gangs is derived from the first-hand experiences of Captain John Charles, USA, who spent over 17 months conducting intelligence operations under IFOR and SFOR in Bosnia. Charles, interview.

[49] Spergel noted the existence of street gangs in Bosnia before the civil war. Irving A. Spergel, *The Youth Gang Problem* (New York: Oxford University Press, 1995), 3.

can be accomplished by working together, in the same areas, questioning the same people.[50] Furthermore, the combined HUMINT team blends the vital linguistic skills of the tactical interrogator with the investigative and analytical talents of the trained CI agent.[51] The distinct advantages offered by this cooperative arrangement made the CI/interrogator HUMINT team the organization of choice for collection in all three operations.

In addition to HUMINT teams, the other key personnel in the tactical military intelligence system are the "all-source analysts," the soldiers and marines responsible for putting the tactical battlefield picture together for the commander on the ground.

THE INTELLIGENCE LESSONS: TACTICAL COLLECTION AND ANALYSIS

Seven lessons emerged from these three MOOTW operations:

- Every soldier and Marine in the MOOTW "battlefield" should be used as a HUMINT collector.
- Security is a constant challenge during the collection process.
- Unconventional sources of information must be developed.
- Extracting information from the population is time-consuming, complicated—and worthwhile.
- The conventional IPB process should be broadened to include factors such as geography, ecology, history, ethnicity, religion, and politics.
- Doctrinal situation tracking tools lack the level of detail necessary to portray street gang situations accurately.
- It is impractical to determine the order of battle, organizational structure, and the doctrine of loosely organized and led street gangs.[52]

Lesson 1: Everyone Must be a HUMINT Collector

Each of the three operations under consideration reinforced the critical importance of using every available soldier and Marine as a HUMINT collector. This philosophy is also advocated by current Army and Marine Corps intelligence doctrine. First-hand accounts from Mogadishu indicate that

---

[50] Chief Warrant Officer Two Rick Fulgium, USA, Tactical Counterintelligence Officer, telephone interview by author, 27 June 1999.

[51] Johnson, interview.

[52] Jeffery B. White, "Some Thoughts on Irregular Warfare," November 1996, *Studies in Intelligence*, URL: <http://www.cia.gov/csi/studies/96unclas/iregular.htm>, accessed 19 June 1999.

"a massive amount of HUMINT came from foot, motorized and mechanized patrols."[53] Non-combat military units in Somalia were also used as sources of HUMINT collection.[54] In Port-au-Prince, people on the streets would routinely offer soldiers on patrol information about intimidation attempts, illegal weapons caches, and other gang activities.[55] One report noted that in Haiti there was "no substitute for the immediate gathering of tactical information by soldiers on the ground."[56] In Bosnia, dismounted patrols were "critical intelligence collectors" at the Brigade level.[57]

The successful employment of non-intelligence soldiers as HUMINT collectors depends on the soldier's knowing what information is needed before the patrol and a mechanism for reporting that information to the intelligence analyst during or after the patrol. During the IFOR mission in Bosnia, the effectiveness of non-intelligence soldier patrols was hindered by a critical shortage of trained intelligence debriefers.[58] Early in the mission, IFOR's efforts were also stymied by an inadequate system of archiving security patrol debriefings. In the face of the large volume of information being gathered, a great deal of useful information for future pattern analysis was "lost in the paper shuffle."[59]

Lesson 2: The Challenge of Security During Collection

The second intelligence problem focuses on the precarious balance between keeping HUMINT teams safe in the foreign urban environment and the necessity for them to mingle discreetly with the population to do their job. HUMINT teams normally conduct their collection in uniform, travel in soft-

---

[53] David A. Rababy, "Intelligence Support During a Humanitarian Mission," *Marine Corps Gazette* 79, no. 2 (February 1995): 41; and John R. Murphy, "Memories of Somalia," *Marine Corps Gazette* 82, no. 4 (April 1998): 20-25.

[54] Soldiers working as medics, construction engineers, and in psychological operations were specifically cited as good sources of "what was going on" and "who was shooting at whom." See "The 'Big Ten' Lessons Learned from Recent Operations in Somalia, Rwanda, Haiti and Bosnia," January 1996, observations from two BENS-sponsored symposia on peacekeeping, URL: <www.bens.org/pubs/peace. html>, accessed 23 May 1999; and U.S. Army Peacekeeping Institute, *Success in Peacekeeping* (Carlisle Barrack, PA: USAWC, 1996), 9.

[55] Schellhammer, 19.

[56] "Initial Impressions Report: Haiti, volume 2," 27 April 1995, *Center for Army Lessons Learned*, URL: <http://call.army.mil/call.htm>, accessed 1 April 1999.

[57] Major Christopher Payne, USA, Intelligence Officer, 1st Brigade, 1st Armored Division, during deployment in Bosnia and Herzegovina under Task Force Eagle, December 1995 to April 1996, interview by author, 23 June 1999.

[58] "Initial Impressions Report: Task Force Eagle Continuing Operations Issue #5, Intelligence," *Center for Army Lessons Learned*, File Folder: Bosnia-Herzegovina, URL: <call. army.mil/ call.htm>, accessed 21 May 1999.

[59] Payne, interview.

skinned military vehicles, and carry only light sidearms.[60] From the beginning in Somalia, HUMINT teams "often took direct action in seizing targets upon discovering them," including illegal weapons and ammunition caches.[61] The need for HUMINT teams to conduct these constabulary operations was also noted in Haiti.[62] Unfortunately, in Somalia and Bosnia, the perceived threat against U.S. forces became so great that "as force protection became paramount counterintelligence teams [were] restricted to the compounds."[63] In some instances in Somalia, informants were forced to meet with the HUMINT teams in a secure U.S. compound.[64]

One solution to this problem evolved in Bosnia, where HUMINT teams were permitted to travel in two-vehicle convoys rather than four-vehicle convoys during daylight hours. These modified security convoys[65] escorted the team to a village or city and then remained as "overwatch" security in the local area,[66] allowing the HUMINT teams to more discreetly conduct their mission among the population.[67] This type of security arrangement is very closely paralleled by the domestic law enforcement community and will be discussed further below.

Lesson 3: The Importance of "Non-Standard" Sources

HUMINT collection operations in Haiti and Bosnia also highlighted the importance of "seeking information creatively"[68] by exploiting every human-based information source in the MOOTW environment. The Somali culture is orally based.[69] As a result, newspapers, posters, and graffiti have little relevance and HUMINT collectors had very few non-standard sources available to them.

In Haiti, gang graffiti was used to determine street gang territorial boundaries.[70] During IFOR, English translations of Bosnian media (including newspapers, television, and radio) were circulated throughout the command

---

[60] Larger caliber weapons tend to intimidate the local population into silence; Johnson, interview; and Tim Ripley, "Ears to Ground Beat Sky-borne Eyes," *Jane's Intelligence Review Pointer* 5, no. 4 (April 1998) 2.

[61] Rababy, 41.

[62] "Initial Impressions Report: Haiti, volume 2."

[63] Barth, 27; and David D. Perkins, "Counterintelligence and Human Intelligence Operations in Bosnia," *Defense Intelligence Journal* 6, no. 1 (1997): 241.

[64] Pohlmann, interview.

[65] Traveling in two vehicle convoys also distinguished the HUMINT team from ordinary combat patrols in the eyes of the population. This point has interesting parallels in the civil law enforcement arena.

[66] Charles, interview.

[67] Johnson, interview.

[68] Schellhammer, 21.

[69] Pohlmann, interview.

[70] Hogan, interview.

on a daily basis.[71] As stability returned to the Bosnian communities, HUMINT teams began to exploit locally produced posters and flyers, newspapers, and church bulletins in an effort to develop a more acute sense of situational awareness.[72] Any non-military reporters or aid workers visiting Brigade tactical operations centers in Bosnia were also debriefed regarding the situation out in the countryside.[73]

Lesson 4: Extracting HUMINT is Slow and Complex

The final lesson derived from the HUMINT collection experience reflects the immense difficulty inherent in basic HUMINT operations—both low-level source operations (informant networks) and surveillance operations. According to one first-hand account from Somalia, "the establishment of low-level HUMINT sources is a long and often complicated process."[74] Developing effective informant networks can take weeks or even months, requiring a significant investment in translation resources and CI agent stability.[75] In Somalia, U.S. "soldiers could not communicate effectively [with the Somalis], nor did they understand Somali customs and traditions."[76] As a result, Somali interpreters were in high demand, including military linguists, contracted U.S. civilians, and local Somalis—who were often mistrusted because of perceived factional and tribal loyalties.[77]

Once the language barrier was overcome, source operations required that the HUMINT teams remain in one area long enough to build trustworthy contacts.[78] From the Army perspective, it took HUMINT teams three weeks to produce their first CI report.[79] Marine HUMINT teams in Somalia adopted a "cop-on-the-beat" approach to source operations that was reported to be 50-60 percent accurate.[80] In each of the cases, the creation of source networks is based on the individual CI officer's personality and interpersonal skills.[81]

Once established, Somali sources had to be handled carefully to protect their identity. If discovered, "suspected informants among Aideed's faction were assassinated . . . those recruited from rival clans dared not enter south

---

[71] Perkins, 245.

[72] Johnson, interview.

[73] Payne, interview.

[74] Rababy, 41.

[75] Fulgium, interview.

[76] Thomas and Sparato, 187.

[77] Stanton, 31.

[78] Payne, interview; and Johnson, interview.

[79] Pohlmann, interview, 2 July 1999.

[80] Rababy, 41.

[81] Fulgium, interview; and Charles, interview.

Mogadishu for fear of suffering a similar fate."[82] HUMINT teams in Bosnia used the civil telephone system to receive tips as a measure to protect an informant's confidentiality.[83] Overcoming language differences, extensive time and resource commitments, and source protection measures make low-level source operations expensive endeavors. But as the only source of detailed information on the morale, attitude, and intentions of the host nation's community—including street gangs—they were worth the effort.

Human surveillance (observing individuals) was not widespread in Somalia, Haiti, and Bosnia. In Haiti, surveillance against street gangs was conducted intermittently on key sites such as houses, businesses, or street corners, but U.S. forces did not have the manpower for around-the-clock operations.[84] Likewise, in Bosnia, some surveillance was conducted for short periods, usually around key leader meetings, to observe associations, take photos, and secure the meeting site.[85] While surveillance operations proved effective, the manpower requirements for extended operations were prohibitive.

Lesson 5: Understanding the "Cultural Environment"

The final three intelligence lessons were derived from the analysis efforts of the tactical-level intelligence staffs. The requirement to increase the scope of IPB in MOOTW, which has been noted in Army intelligence doctrine, was reaffirmed by observations from Mogadishu and Port-au-Prince. In Somalia, intelligence analysts had to apply a "much broader scope than that found under the more traditional focus" including "political/military affairs, ethnic conflict, non-governmental organizations, UN operations and police operations."[86] In Haiti, soldiers on the ground observed that IPB in the urban MOOTW environment is "vastly different from IPB in conventional warfare" and must include the population's social class, economic distributions, locations of key facilities—such as schools, churches, and businesses—and known black market areas.[87]

In Haiti, to facilitate this broad analytical perspective, tactical analysts were required to "travel out into the operational environment" to get a "feel for the people, activity, and potential problems" in the community. This

---

[82] Robert J. Allen, "Intelligence Theory and Practice in Somalia," in Perry L. Pickert, *Intelligence for Multilateral Decision and Action*, ed. Russell G. Swenson (Washington: Joint Military Intelligence College, 1997), 172.

[83] Payne, interview.

[84] Hogan, interview.

[85] Johnson, interview.

[86] David Shelton, "Intelligence Lessons Known and Revealed During Operation Restore Hope, Somalia," *Marine Corps Gazette* 79, no. 2 (February 1995): 40; Jonathan Stevenson, *Losing Mogadishu: Testing U.S. Policy in Somalia* (Annapolis, MD: Naval Institute Press, 1995), 115-116; and John R. Murphy, "Memories of Somalia," *Marine Corps Gazette* 78, no. 1 (January 1994): 27.

[87] "Initial Impressions Report: Haiti, volume 2."

approach was also used in Somalia, to a more limited extent.[88] This first-hand, infantryman's view of the situation helped tactical analysts understand the impact of the unique "social, economic, political, and cultural geography"[89] in the street gang environment.

Lesson 6: Tracking the Gang Situation Demands Precise Detail

In addition to the requirement to broaden the scope of the intelligence analyst, the MOOTW environment simultaneously demands a much finer resolution in situational tracking. In Haiti, analysts observed that diverse incidents such as demonstrations, enemy collection efforts, intimidation attempts, and criminal activities—including murders, arsons, beatings, and looting—were relevant to the situation and had to be tracked and analyzed.[90]

The commander's need for high-resolution situational tracking in MOOTW demonstrated the ineffectiveness of conventional map symbols. One tactical intelligence officer lamented that "the process used to graphically capture and communicate intelligence in OOTW is not standardized."[91] During Operation Uphold Democracy, forces in Haiti developed their own internal map symbols, which were "used to portray incidents such as civil disturbances, humanitarian assistance organizations, targeted individual civilian cars," and arms caches.[92] This demand for resolution in Mogadishu and Port-au-Prince also demonstrated that standard military "1:50,000 scale maps were almost useless in the city."[93]

---

[88] Pohlmann, interview.

[89] "Initial Impressions Report: Haiti, volume 2."

[90] Schellhammer, 19; and "Initial Impressions Report: Haiti, volume 1."

[91] Robert E. Slaughter, "Operations Other Than War Standard Symbology," *Military Intelligence*, January-March 1994, 35.

[92] "Initial Impressions Report: Haiti, volume 1."

[93] Pohlmann, interview; and Schellhammer, 19.

Lesson 7: The Impracticality of Conventional Description Methods

This intelligence lesson observes that most irregular forces—including street gangs—cannot be clearly described using conventional intelligence methods. According to Jeffrey White, who wrote as Chief of the Middle East/Africa Regional Military Assessment Branch of the Defense Intelligence Agency, "Shifting patterns of family, tribal, religious, economic, and military relations [in OOTW] produce a complex, dynamic, and uncertain analytic environment. Irregular forces do not have highly articulated doctrine. This makes it difficult to display confidently what the enemy's forces look like and how they are deployed."[94] This frustrating effect was confirmed by observations in all three operations in this study. In Somalia, an attempt was made early in the mission to "apply the same techniques used to display Iraqi order of battle" to the Somali factions and gangs. It proved ineffective.

One Marine Corps observer noted that Somalia's street gangs were hard to track and "build intelligence" on.[95] In Haiti, street gangs also showed no doctrine or pattern of activity, making predictive analysis "extremely difficult."[96] U.S. analysts in Haiti developed "turf maps" of the gang areas in the ghettos, but were unable to produce useable organizational charts.[97] The dynamic nature of the threat in MOOTW consistently limited the ability of analysts to describe the enemy. In all three cases, acquaintance and association networks, general predictive assessments, and vaguely defined areas of "turf" had to suffice in place of more "doctrinal" organizational charts, enemy courses of action, and six-digit map coordinate force dispositions.

TACTICAL INTELLIGENCE FROM AMERICA'S STREETS

A police anti-gang unit in the U.S. deals with the same intelligence issues faced by the MOOTW forces. Understanding the domestic police approach to each of the seven intelligence lessons discussed above provides additional insights for the military's tactical intelligence operations.

Evolution of Police Intelligence

The need to protect the community from the disruptive influence of foreign agents, domestic terrorists, and organized crime in the first half of the 20th century spurred the development of the first police intelligence units.[98] The civic disruptions of the 1960s motivated the use of these organized crime

---

94 White, "Some Thoughts."

95 Stanton, 30.

96 Schellhammer, 20.

97 Hogan, interview.

98 Stedman Chandler and Robert W. Robb, *Front-Line Intelligence* (Washington: Infantry Journal Press, 1946), 7-12.

intelligence techniques against loosely organized urban groups such as the street gang.[99]

These centralized intelligence-gathering units are composed of a range of different police personnel, using a combination of military-style and police rank. In the police community, "lieutenants" and "sergeants" manage and administer units. They are normally senior officers with 10 to 20 years of police experience. The "detectives" or "investigators" (depending on the police department) gather information, question witnesses and suspects, run informant networks, conduct surveillance operations, and solve criminal cases. They are comparable to HUMINT collectors such as counterintelligence agents and tactical interrogators (see Figure 2). Police anti-gang analysts maintain databases, review department arrest reports for gang connections, compile statistics, and assist detectives with pattern analysis.

Unlike the military system, the primary responsibility for developing "situational awareness" in the anti-gang intelligence unit lies with the investigator, not the analyst. Accordingly, the assessment of the police analytical process will rely on the experiences of the gang investigator as well as those of the crime analyst. The next section describes the sources and methodologies used to summarize police anti-gang intelligence.

---

[99] Both Chicago and Los Angeles trace the origins of their anti-gang intelligence efforts to violent urban uprisings in the 1960s. For Los Angeles County, it was the Watts riots in 1965 while Chicago was motivated by the 1968 riots on the city's west side. It is interesting to note that both of these civic disruptions required the deployment of the military (National Guard and regular Army) to quell. Police Lieutenant Drake Robles, Operation Safe Streets Bureau, Los Angeles County Sheriff's Department, interview by author, 1 June 1999; and Police Sergeant Steven Caluris, Supervisor of the Gang Analytic Program (GAP), Chicago Police Department, telephone interview by author, 27 May 1999.

	Military in MOOTW	**Police Anti-Gang Forces**
Enforcement Element	Combat patrols, military police, civil affairs teams	Police or deputies on patrol
Specialized HUMINT Collection	HUMINT teams	Gang investigators or detectives
Tactical Intelligence Analysis	Intelligence staff sections and HUMINT teams	Gang analysis sections, crime analysts or gang investigators/detectives
Intelligence Supervision	Captain grade with senior NCO assistance	Police sergeants
Tactical Intelligence Consumer	Unit commanders and other unit staff, subordinate soldiers and Marines	Police and city administrators, other non-gang analysts, police on the streets

Figure 2. Comparing Intelligence Structures
Source: Author.

Comparing intelligence philosophies and missions at the philosophical level, both the police and military leadership strive to achieve similar uses for intelligence. This parallel may come from the fact that, in spite of their independent origins, the two intelligence systems have shared membership based on the military's Reserve and National Guard systems. Both schools of thought also recognize the primacy of information in the operational planning process. The common military adage "intelligence drives maneuver" is comparable to the police philosophy that "obtaining adequate intelligence data on a gang is a prerequisite to any enforcement action."[100]Regardless of whether your uniform is blue or camouflage, the following observation rings true: "As the world becomes increasingly complex, police administrators and planners are finding it more and more necessary to collate seemingly unrelated bits of information into some kind of understandable whole."[101]

Police Approaches to Intelligence Problems

Beyond the philosophical similarities between police and military intelligence, gang police have developed many of the same approaches to the collection and analysis problems inherent in the street gang environment.

Lesson 1: Everyone Must be a HUMINT Collector

As the soldiers and Marines learned in Mogadishu, Port-au-Prince, and Bosnia, gang police know that "highly useful street-level intelligence can

---

[100] *Urban Street Gang Enforcement*, 27.

[101] Michael F. Brown, *Criminal Investigation: Law and Practice* (Newton, MA: Butterworth-Heinemann, 1998), 54.

be generated by aggressive and alert patrol officers."[102] In Chicago, most of the raw data used by the Gang Analytic Program comes from the beat police and investigators in daily contact with gangs on the streets.[103] In Los Angeles County, one sergeant observed that the most accurate picture of what is going on with the gangs comes from gang investigators and the observations of ordinary patrol deputies.[104] The patrolmen in Norfolk "know what's going on" with the gangs and routinely exchange information with the gang squad.[105] These findings indicate strong parallels between the police and military intelligence systems.

In Dallas, most information regarding the gang situation comes from the gang unit itself—from the enforcement officers and detectives.[106] There appear to be two reasons why the Dallas police do not contribute as much gang information as other city's police do. First, Dallas is the only department observed that has not fully implemented the "community based policing" philosophy. Under this approach, police officers spend the majority of their time in one particular neighborhood. Instead, the Dallas police respond wherever they are needed throughout the city based on citizens' calls. According to one Dallas gang detective, stabilizing police and assigning neighborhood responsibility would facilitate better information flow from the patrol officers.[107] Second, Dallas uses a sizeable complement of special gang enforcement officers. One theory is that the existence of these "gang enforcement officers" frees ordinary police to focus on other priorities leaving the gang specialists to handle the street gang problem.[108] The impact of patrol officer stability and specialized enforcement on information gathering has definite implications for the military and will be addressed below.

---

[102] Richard Kieffer-Adrian, "Street Level Intelligence Gathering," *Law and Order*, May 1995, 31.

[103] Caluris, interview.

[104] Police Sergeant Steven Newman, Operation Safe Streets Bureau, Los Angeles County Sheriff's Department, interview by author, 1 June 1999.

[105] Randy Crank, Gang Investigator, Norfolk Police Department, Gang Squad, interview by author, 20 June 1999.

[106] Detective Sam Schiller, Gang Unit, Dallas Police Department, interview by author, 3 June 1999.

[107] When stabilized, police get to know the kids as people and take the time to talk to them when they do not need information from them or want to "bust" them. Schiller, interview.

[108] Caluris, interview.

Figure 3. Overt Interview, Dallas
Source: "Dallas Police Gang Handbook,"
unpublished handbook produced by the
Dallas Police Department Youth and
Family Violence Division Gang Unit,
February 1995, cover.

Another lesson learned from the military was that soldiers need to know the intelligence requirements and have a method of reporting what they have observed. One of the vexing intelligence problems noted in Bosnia was that debriefing each combat patrol with trained intelligence personnel was costly in terms of manpower and generated more information than the intelligence section could effectively catalog and analyze. The anti-gang police have approached this problem from a different perspective.

Figure 4. Overt Interview, Mogadishu
Source: "Checking the identification of two Somalian women at
Modadishu airport," 15 February 1994, DFST9601070,
Defense Visual Information Center,
URL: <www. dodmedia.osd.mil/Assets/1996/
Air_Force/DF-ST-96-01070.JPEG>, accessed 1 December 2006.

First, instead of attempting to pre-brief each patrol with the latest intelligence requirements, the Operation Safe Streets Bureau (OSSB) in Los Angeles County issues gang identification cards to all deputies. While these cards do not solve the entire intelligence information request problem, they serve to help deputies in the field discern what is important to the OSSB and what is not. OSSB also makes great efforts to ensure the front-line leadership in the Sheriff's Department tour the OSSB so they understand what the unit offers and what is done with the information provided by the street deputies. The relationships initiated with these tours help motivate the collection of gang information.[109] Some departments recommend that gang intelligence personnel brief officers at roll-call on a bi-weekly basis to highlight the specific intelligence needs and concerns from the gang unit.[110] These techniques help the ordinary police officer understand how to help in the anti-gang effort.

The second innovation in every one of the four research sites was the extensive use of "field interview cards" to record and report gang contacts. Individual police officers on the streets fill out a card for every gang member contact they make.[111] After the shift, the cards are forwarded to the gang

---

[109] Newman, interview.

[110] Richard Kieffer-Adrian, "Street-level Intelligence Gathering," *Law and Order,* May 1995, 33.

[111] Army CI personnel use similar methods called "personality cards," but their use is not widespread throughout the military force.

intelligence unit for collation and analysis.[112] Each two-man patrol is also required to write a post-patrol incident report, which is reviewed by intelligence personnel.[113] Using these tools, members of the HUMINT collection team selectively debrief patrols that encountered situations of interest to the intelligence effort. These paper systems help overcome limitations in availability of qualified debriefing personnel and support a card-based filing system for record keeping. While this approach reduced the need for numerous intelligence debriefers, it also places a large responsibility for reporting on the individual police officer. This relies heavily on the average cop understanding the importance of the card and taking the time to fill it out. Police experience has shown that the amount of information flowing from the street cops to intelligence personnel through these tools is proportional to the useful analysis and source credit provided by the intelligence section.[114] This lesson, too, has applicability in the military intelligence world.

Lesson 2: The Challenge of Security During HUMINT Collection

The conflicting need to provide security for HUMINT collectors and to get the collection job done is also a concern in the domestic police environment. Like military HUMINT collectors, gang investigators in each of the four cities operate overtly, normally in two-person teams, using identifiable police vehicles, armed only with light sidearms.[115] The police reliance on two-person teams is not, however, a translator-based requirement. In the gang investigative community, a single officer has a hard time controlling the street corner questioning situation. Three-person teams are occasionally used, but consume space in the vehicle that could be used to secure suspects or witnesses for questioning.[116] As noted by the military experience in Haiti and Somali, police HUMINT teams are also expected to execute ordinary police actions, seizures, and arrests as needed during their investigations. These parallels demonstrate that overt police HUMINT collection units have developed the same structure and mission in both the military and police environments.

The police approach to security during collection in dangerous areas is very similar to the "exception to policy" two-vehicle convoy system developed in Bosnia. If gang investigators anticipate a threatening situation, they discreetly pre-position a police backup team in the area to provide reinforcement within

---

[112] The Chicago GAP estimates that they have over 40,000 field interview cards in their system. Hudspeth, interview, 27 May 1999.

[113] David Hudspeth, Gang Specialist, Gang Analytical Program, Chicago Police Department, interview by author, 27 May 1999; Dale Stacey, Gang Investigator, Norfolk Police Department, Gang Squad, interview by author, 20 June 1999; Robles, interview; and Schiller, interview.

[114] Kieffer-Adrian, 33.

[115] Spratte, interview; Newman, interview; and Stacey, interview.

[116] Police Detective Dana Ellison, Gang Investigator, Operation Safe Streets Bureau, Los Angeles County Sheriff's Department, interview by author, 1 June 1999.

seconds if the need arises. However, unlike military operations, this kind of security coordination is the exception rather than the rule.

For ordinary operations, police HUMINT collection teams use a "zone back up" system. Essentially, the police investigators assume they can control the situation with their two man teams. If reinforcement is required, they call for help via radio and nearby police units are dispatched to assist them. The police patrol patterns in the city are tight enough that back up is expected and received within minutes.[117] This approach to security for HUMINT collection has the potential to shift the way the military secures its HUMINT teams.

Investigating police HUMINT collection security yielded one other difference worth noting. Gang police officers wear distinctive clothing so the public can distinguish them from ordinary enforcement police.[118] While the military's two-vehicle convoy and the armaments used by military HUMINT teams may allow the populace to identify them as a non-combat patrol, no efforts have been made to mark them as HUMINT Teams. The police find that, by marking themselves as "gang cops," gang members seek them out thinking that they understand the gangs' lot in life better than ordinary police and will be less likely to have a "suppression attitude."[119] None of the units has been targeted by the street gangs because they were identified as gang cops, in spite of the fact that they put more gang members in jail than traditional police. Although it may prove to be difficult to operationalize in the military culture, the overwhelming use of this approach by police indicates that this idea may have merit.

Lesson 3: The Importance of "Non-Standard" Sources

The anti-gang police also recognize the importance of exploiting every bit of information available in the gang environment, but have fewer media-based resources at their disposal. Neighborhood-level newspapers were not prevalent in the U.S. communities examined and news reporters were generally not used as a source of information, although at least one detective acknowledged that street gang investigative pieces are examined. Each of the four anti-gang units had strict rules against passing gang names and individual gangsters' names to the media to avoid inadvertently increasing the group or individual's notoriety. Social workers, unlike NGOs, need little support from the police and were not viewed by the police interviewed as cooperative sources. In Dallas, gang investigators attend gang prevention seminars produced by social services, usually to assess the agency's perspective and the level of attention they put into their gang research.

---

[117] Spratte, interview; Newman, interview; Schiller, interview; and Stacey, interview, 20 June 1999.

[118] In each case, gang police wear distinctive T-shirts or jackets over their uniforms; they do not identify leaders or other key personnel.

[119] Newman, interview.

Gang communications such as graffiti and party flyers were, however, extensively photographed, translated, and analyzed for the intelligence effort. As in Haiti, street gang graffiti provides a wealth of information on the gang, from the street gang's name and territorial claims to the intricacies of sub-faction alignment and rosters of member's nicknames.[120]

> **Typical gang graffiti in Dallas showing the gang name roll call on the right side. The perspective of the Dallas skyline and the name "Oakcliff" indicate the location of the gang's home turf.**

Figure 5. Junior Homeboys Graffiti, Dallas
Source: "Dallas Police Gang Handbook."

While the media provide police with little information, the police used a number of sources not recognized in military intelligence after-action reviews. Local businessmen can often provide the police with information on the gang situation, particularly those that make custom clothing (T-shirts, hats), print flyers or business cards, or run clubs or halls—that may be rented for gang parties.[121] Hospitals provide information on gang member injuries, usually out of a desire to protect a surviving patient from enemy gang retaliation.[122] The Norfolk Gang Squad in particular has trained public educators—teachers and principals—in the recognition of street gang clothing, graffiti, and hand signs so that they can act as gang informants for the police.[123] This wide range of information sources exploited by the police suggests some non-standard sources for possible use in tactical military intelligence operations.

---

[120] Spratte, interview; Dirks, interview; Stacey, interview; Schiller, interview; and Ellison, interview.

[121] Michael Langston, "Guidelines for Operating an Effective Gang Unit," *Journal of Gang Research* 5, no. 4 (Summer 1998): 51.

[122] Police Sergeant Paul Keough, Gang Unit, Dallas Police Department, interview by author, 3 June 1999.

[123] Stacey, interview, 20 June 1999.

Lesson 4: Extracting HUMINT is Slow and Complex

Surveillance and the development of gang informants are time-consuming and resource-intensive operations for both the police and the military. The gang police units consulted by the author noted concerns about the protection, motivation, and language barriers associated with developing informant networks. As with the military, the development of informant networks depends on the individual police investigator's interpersonal skills, the amount of time he is stabilized in the area, and the level of intimidation exercised by the street gang. If the officer is familiar with the situation, rival gangs, gang members' former girlfriends, and concerned adult family members can all provide information on a particular gang and its future activities. Trust between the community and the collector is key in any informant work.

The key to protecting police informants lies in the investigator's use of discretion.[124] The communications technologies available in America today, such as the telephone, pager, and postal service, facilitate the discreet transmission of information. In Los Angeles County, investigators pass out business cards to everyone around the crime scene so street gangs cannot easily identify who may have provided information by phone to the police. The phone system was used with informants in Bosnia, but was of little use in severely disrupted cities such as Mogadishu and Port-au-Prince.

In Bosnia, counterintelligence officers routinely supply tobacco and other hard-to-find items to informants to offset the risks entailed in cooperating with the U.S. forces.[125] Only one police unit, the Chicago program, registers and pays informants. While these approaches may generate information of questionable validity, it is a way to motivate potential sources to assume some of the risk inherent in being a street gang informant.[126]

Language also restricts the development of human sources. There is no easy solution to the "language problem" problem; both the military and police do the best they can. Motivated police officers (like U.S. soldiers) learn enough of the local language and culture to complete simple tasks while relying on translators to assist with the more complex missions.[127] Small children in non-English speaking American ghettos usually speak rudimentary English and are regularly used by police as translators.[128] In extreme cases, police officers have even used remote translation via cellular phone to overcome the ever-present language barrier.[129]

---

[124] Dirks, interview; Stacey, interview; and Spratte, interview.

[125] Johnson, interview.

[126] Spratte, interview.

[127] Newman, interview.

[128] Ellison, interview.

[129] Keough, interview.

One distinct difference between police requirements and the military's mission is the domestic necessity for informants to testify in court. In the case of Norfolk, the gang intimidation factor is so high that pursuing informants has been all but abandoned in lieu of surveillance. If the police are conducting surveillance, they become the witnesses in court and can move cases to prosecution.[130] In the U.S., an anonymous tip is useful, but rarely gets criminals put in jail; whereas in the MOOTW environment, an anonymous tip can be just as effective as information from a known informant.

The aversion to extensive surveillance operations noted in Haiti and Bosnia is also found among police forces. The larger gang units, working in well-established gang environments, agree with the effectiveness of surveillance but cannot justify the expense in manpower, preparation, and support required to do it often.[131] In Los Angeles County, the sheriff's department has simply been unable to infiltrate the gang-dominated neighborhoods. The gangsters know their streets so well that a new car or van stands out just like a police patrol car.[132] One exception to this resistance to surveillance is the limited reconnaissance conducted before executing search warrants of gang member's homes. To prepare for a coordinated search operation, LASD gang units conduct surveillance of gang members' homes 24-48 hours before the search to identify features such as exits and entrances, windows, and auxiliary buildings.[133]

In smaller police intelligence sections, where the gang's control over the community is less omnipotent and intelligence assets are not stretched as thin, surveillance is used more readily. As in Bosnia, meetings and events where the gang leaders gather are prime targets for short-duration police surveillance. Gang detectives in Dallas routinely observe street gang parties, gangster funerals, and inter-gang fights in order to determine associations, alliances, or to identify and stop violent situations before they become deadly.[134] Investigators in Norfolk regularly observe known gang hangouts from undercover vehicles using video cameras and still photos in order to establish gang member associations and gather evidence for prosecutions.[135] These findings indicate that the anti-gang police's use of informants is comparable to the military's, while surveillance finds greater application against America's street gangs.

---

[130] Crank, interview.

[131] Caluris, interview.

[132] Newman, interview.

[133] Detective Michael Delmuro, Gang Investigator, Operation Safe Streets Bureau, Los Angeles County Sheriff's Department, interview by author, 2 June 1999.

[134] Schiller, interview; and Dirks, interview.

[135] Crank, interview.

Lesson 5: Understanding the Cultural Environment

According to a recent Justice Department report, crucial elements of the U.S. gang environment include the "relevant social, demographic, economic, and legal factors in the community."[136] In 1994, Spergel observed that to combat street gangs, "knowledge from diverse fields must be integrated into the law enforcement mission."[137] This need for a broad, multi-discipline approach to gangs is similar to the calls after the Somalia and Haiti missions to enlarge the scope of the IPB process.

Police analysts invest time patrolling alongside the street officers and HUMINT collectors to gain perspective on the environment. In Chicago, Los Angeles County, and Norfolk, gang analysts are all experienced investigators who have spent years in gang neighborhoods. As in Somalia and Haiti, police crime analysts in Los Angeles accompany patrols at least once a month in order to get into the environment and see the people they are trying to analyze.[138] In Dallas, the civilian gang crime analysts ride with enforcement officers and the gang investigators at least once a quarter for similar reasons.[139] This demonstrates that, while police academics acknowledge the need for a broad approach to gang analysis and civilian analysts seek opportunities to see the gang community from the patrol officer's perspective, the need for a broad, multi-discipline approach to IPB found in the military missions is not observed among gang police. However, this discrepancy results from the more permanent nature of the police mission compared to the dynamic troop movements inherent in military operations.

Lesson 6: Tracking the Gang Situation Demands Detail

Although police do not use military-style IPB, police incident tracking meets or exceeds the level of resolution demanded in constabulary MOOTW. This need for detail is exacerbated by the U.S. court system and the rules of evidence. As a result, details down to the incident-level are a concern for police gang units, just as they were for intelligence analysts in Haiti and Somalia.

Like their military counterparts, gang analysts track incidents on city maps and attempt to infer patterns that can be exploited by the police. Police also use city maps with a much larger scale than military 1:50,000 maps. Police analysts often end up using "ad hoc" map symbols ranging from shapes to colored dots to represent incidents—just like military analysts. Systems using military-style map symbols, which can be used to show directionality, time

---

[136] *Urban Street Gang Enforcement*, 18.

[137] Irving A. Spergel and others, *Gang Suppression and Intervention* (Washington: Department of Justice, 1994): 7.

[138] Cynthia Gatiglio, Crime Analyst, Los Angeles County Sheriff's Department, interview by author, 2 June 1999.

[139] Brandon Sailer, Crime Analyst, Gang Unit, Dallas Police Department, interview by author, 3 June 1999.

of the day, or to "cue" the nature of the incident with the observer,[140] were not used in any of the four police departments. This is an area where the gang police may benefit from military intelligence techniques.

Another significant difference noted in this area is the absence of situational tracking maps in the police gang units. Any map-based analysis or briefing tool required by the police is custom-generated using automated databases and digital street-level maps.[141] Some investigators believe they can track gang crime patterns themselves and only take the time to map them out when the number of incidents "overwhelms" them.[142] The ability to generate digital maps showing the gang situation, to the street address level, has eliminated the police's need to maintain running situation maps. The military intelligence community may experience the same phenomenon if computer screens ever replace map boards in tactical units.

Lesson 7: The Impracticality of Conventional Description Methods

The dynamic structure and loose, personality-based chain of command found in U.S. street gangs confounds police analysts just as it frustrates military analysts overseas.[143] A 1992 national survey of police agencies revealed that administrators and police policymakers were frequently hindered by "the inability of gang information systems to generate big picture reports."[144] Out of four of the cities investigated, only Chicago attempts to chart street gangs' organizational structure.[145]

It is interesting to note that while gang's structures are constantly in a state of flux, their methods of operation tend to remain constant. Therefore, while the exact structure of the street gang may be impossible to describe, knowing the history and origin of the gang clues the officer to how they will behave. In order to develop this level of understanding about a gang's motivations and unique "culture,"[146] larger police departments actually focus one investigator on each gang or gang faction. This kind of intense analytical focus on the gang mentality allows investigators to assess the implications of finding gang members outside their turf or to notice a subtle change in the cultural norms for body language and behavior in a particular neighborhood.[147] This environmental expertise is routinely used to apprehend individuals who are in the process of breaking the law. The effectiveness of this kind of focused

---

[140] Slaughter, 37.

[141] Gatiglio, interview.

[142] Karen Williams, Gang Specialist, Gang Analytical Program, Chicago Police Department, interview by author, 27 May 1999; Dirks, 3 June 1999; and Stacey, 20 June 1999.

[143] Newman, interview.

[144] *Urban Street Gang Enforcement*, 35.

[145] Caluris, interview.

[146] Spratte, interview.

[147] Ellison, interview.

analytical attention provides a new approach in military environments where the enemy displays no easily discernible doctrine.

Each of the threat description techniques developed during the three military operations is found among the anti-gang units. While all agree that exact gang dispositions are hard to determine, most of the anti-gang units found utility in mapping out gang controlled turf. Military and police approaches to mapping out gang turf are remarkably similar. Like the operations in Bosnia, analyzing gang member associations is a time-tested and effective technique for understanding gangs. In all four cities, the association database served as the starting point in the gang investigation process. Pattern analysis was also noted as a profitable technique by both military and police intelligence analysts. In both Los Angeles County and Chicago, time, day, and map pattern analysis were commonly used to show patterns and trends in crime. [148]

The daunting challenge of developing predictive analysis on foreign gangs also plagues anti-gang units. As in Bosnia, it is difficult to develop more than "general expectations and loose predictions"[149] about future street gang activities. According to police experts, the intractability of this problem is a function of the decentralized nature of street gang command and control[150] and the emotional, spontaneous, and unsophisticated character of their target selection and planning process.[151] Detective Brad Dirks of the Dallas Gang Unit summed up the situation well when he noted that most gang actions "are emotional outbursts," supported by "little planning or forethought ... therefore they are all but impossible to 'predict.' "

While these findings illustrate that police gang analysis offers no "silver bullet" solutions to describing or predicting gang behavior, the fact that both analytical environments are limited by the same analytical tools suggests that it is an area for further cooperation.

ENHANCING TACTICAL MILITARY INTELLIGENCE

From the minute they arrive in Kosovo, NATO troops will become the police, town council and public works department.

Dana Priest and Bradley Graham "For Now, NATO To Rule in Kosovo,"
—*Washington Post*, 10 June 1999, A1

---

[148] Patrolman Richard Heinosch, Gang Analytical Program, Chicago Police Department, interview by author, 27 May 1999; Dirks, interview; Newman, interview; Gatiglio, interview; and Stacey, interview.

[149] Newman, interview.

[150] Delmuro, interview.

[151] Los Angeles County Sheriff's Department, " 'L.A. Style': A Street Gang Manual of the Los Angeles County Sheriff's Department," unpublished manual produced by the Safe Streets Bureau Gang Detail, 15 May 1998, 15.

Interesting implications for the military intelligence community arise not from the similarities with gang police intelligence, but from the differences. In the course of this survey of four different police anti-gang units, three significant implications have emerged. The first difference is the anti-gang police unit's emphasis on stability—for patrol officers, collectors, and analysts. The next implication for tactical intelligence is the police's model for guaranteeing the safety of collectors (such as investigators) in the street gang environment. The third significant implication for military intelligence is the reinforcement of the selective use of surveillance in the street gang environment.

Stability Fosters Situational Awareness

The "community based policing" philosophy is an integral component in the domestic struggle against street gangs. Under community based policing, police officers are stabilized in one neighborhood, allowing a relationship to form between the cop and the local community.[152] The benefit for the police is that these "beat cops" become intimately familiar with their small part of the city. They know who the "troublemakers" are and where they work and live. This approach to law enforcement, which was used by three of the four police departments surveyed, also makes each police officer a crucial source of information on street gangs. Under this philosophy, investigators and analysts are also stabilized in one area. For example, in Los Angeles County, detectives are assigned to focus on specific street gangs in order to develop an "in-house" subject matter expert for each of the gangs.[153] This community based policing strategy offers some interesting implications for the military in MOOTW.

This approach implies that tactical situational awareness increases if soldiers and Marines are stabilized in the same area for extended periods. This benefit can be magnified by encouraging contact between soldiers and the population living in their area of operations. Once the soldier on the ground is stabilized and becomes the most situationally aware individual on the local battlefield, the tried and tested police methods for tapping them as intelligence collectors can begin. Instead of debriefing each patrol to pull information from their memories, the tactical intelligence community can develop a system similar to the police model, where information is pushed to the intelligence staff from the troops on the ground. Local security patrols, armed with an understanding of what the tactical intelligence system needs, can proactively conduct tactical questioning ("police field interviews") of suspected gang members and their associates. These "interviews" can then be used to augment the information gathered by HUMINT teams. Using post-patrol reports, trained HUMINT teams and tactical analysts can selectively debrief patrols and further question contacts or witnesses in the community,

---

[152] Caluris, interview.
[153] Ellison, interview.

increasing their efficiency and focus. Furthermore, as the locals begin to identify particular soldiers as "their" Americans, the flow of information will increase as it does for identifiable gang police officers in U.S. cities.

Adopting a community based policing strategy makes the soldier even more responsible for his "territory." With a "cop on the beat" approach to collection, the battalion intelligence staff can increase its directed collection capacity from one scout platoon and a few HUMINT teams to hundreds of individual collectors. Stabilizing analysts and collectors on specific gangs and areas will mitigate problems of producing predictive analysis on "doctrine-less" street gangs. Instead of committing the limited intelligence personnel at the tactical level to an exhausting "pull-based" debriefing system, this strategy facilitates the selective use of debriefings based on information being "pushed" from the infantry squad level. Furthermore, the police system provides a proven method—with both automated and paper examples—to handle the large volume of information generated by making the infantryman a directed HUMINT collector.

Dedicated Security Is Not the Only Answer

The police experience in securing intelligence collectors reinforces the two-vehicle convoy approach that evolved in Somalia, Haiti, and Bosnia. The critical difference in the police system is that this kind of dedicated security is only used when high-threat situations are expected. During an average day interviewing and observing street gang members, police HUMINT collectors rely on ad hoc, on-request reinforcement. Adapted to the military situation, this strategy would permit HUMINT teams (as well as other teams such as civil affairs and psychological operations) to execute their missions in the city by day in two-man teams. Reinforcement, if needed, would be dispatched to assist the team on request, with the expectation of effective response within minutes. If the density of combat patrols is too low to expect assistance in three to six minutes (the average expectation among the four cities surveyed), then multiple HUMINT collectors in a limited area could be secured with one or two mounted security teams.

The example of the domestic gang police demonstrates that culturally oriented officers in the street gang environment can accomplish their mission safely in two-person teams. Based on the police model, HUMINT teams could even reap benefits from marking themselves as "investigators" similar to the way military police identify themselves with "MP" shoulder brassards. The critical information and intelligence gathered by HUMINT teams should not be limited by security concerns exceeding the threat conditions. Furthermore, HUMINT collectors should not be forced to spend their limited planning time building multi-vehicle convoys unless the threat situation warrants it. The police example indicates that a system of variable security ranging from a reinforcement-on-call system for low threat situations, a dedicated security team "just around the corner" for medium or potential threats, and a multi-vehicle cordon and search approach for high threat missions would give commanders the flexibility they need to maximize the precarious balance between HUMINT collection and security concerns.

The Value of Selective Surveillance

The police anti-gang programs observed in this study indicate that street gang activities should be placed under surveillance when the "payoff" in intelligence promises to be worthwhile. U.S. gang members tend to loiter at specific locations within their turf. They also gather for social events, fights, and to commit economic crimes such as the sale of narcotics and the fencing of stolen goods. It is reasonable to assume that foreign street gangs will likewise gather for important collective activities. These meetings, if anticipated by the tactical intelligence system, should be exploited as surveillance opportunities. Like domestic anti-gang police,[154] U.S. military forces should also be prepared to intervene in the targeted street-gang meeting if the situation becomes threatening to U.S. forces or host-nation innocents. U.S. forces in Bosnia have adopted this approach during factional meetings, observing and recording group membership and inter-group associations for intelligence purposes.[155] Some foreign environments may approach the level of gang influence observed in Los Angeles County, where surveillance is impossible because of the street gang's sensitivity to covert and overt police presence. In these cases, collection via surveillance may also be of limited value to the military. Nevertheless, the experiences of U.S. gang police support the use of surveillance against street gangs as another collection tool in the struggle.

---

[154] Schiller, interview; Dirks, interview; and Stacey, interview.

[155] Johnson, interview.

"HOME-GROWN" ISLAMIC EXTREMISTS IN U.S. PRISONS

Technical Sergeant Lloyd E. Dabbs, USAF
Master of Science of Strategic Intelligence, 2006

Until such time as the Federal government begins to effectively monitor this rise of radical Islam amongst the captive populations of our prison system, a dangerous *fifth column* will continue to grow and will over time find its way from our prisons into the cities and streets of America.

—Mark Silverberg, *Silent War*

Domestic terrorism poses perhaps the greatest challenge ever faced by the American criminal justice system and the Intelligence Community (IC). Ironically, the U.S. prison system may be fertile ground for the recruitment and development of domestic terrorists. In recent years, prisons in the United States have experienced terror-related activity, particularly as increased extremist criminal activity has resulted in greater numbers of ideologically extreme inmates. Islamic extremists have also used prisons as a "safe haven" to recruit and train terrorists and plan and launch attacks on civilians.[156] Examining the prevalence and characteristics of Islamic extremist prison groups is useful, then, in order to identify individuals and organizations that may be facilitating a change in criminal motivation to terrorism.

Though nascent terrorist cells are difficult to observe, of course, even in a prison environment, studies of prison gangs over the past 25 years have identified characteristics that any successful group must adopt in order to thrive in a prison environment. These characteristics can be used to assess the state of Islamic extremist groups in American prisons. Comparing the characteristics of these extremist groups with those of "successful" prison gangs provides a means of predicting how radical extremist groups will develop in prison, as well as how they will interact with the outside world.

Penologists have long been aware that the cellblock is a school for criminals.[157] Muslim extremist groups inside the American prison system are apparently in the process of learning new, more effective organizational styles from major prison gangs like the Aryan Brotherhood and Black Guerilla

---

[156] Robert Hanser, "Prison Security Threat Groups and Domestic Terrorism," *Crime and Justice International*, November 2002, URL: <158.135.23.21/cjcweb/college/cji/index.cfm?ID=98>, accessed 11 February 2006; Anti-Defamation League, *Dangerous Convictions: An Introduction to Extremist Activities in Prisons*, March 2002, URL: <www.adl.org/learn/Ext_terr/ Dangerous_ Convictions.pdf>, accessed 8 December 2005. Cited hereafter as ADL, *Dangerous Convictions*.

[157] Ian Cuthbertson, "Prisons and the Education of Terrorists," *World Policy Journal* 21, no. 3 (Fall 2004): 16.

Family. Considering that many of the recent terror attacks around the world, such as the train bombings in Spain and the attempted shoe bombing by Richard Reid, have been perpetrated by men radicalized in foreign prison systems, it is important to understand and deter such radicalization in U.S. prisons. Recent studies from the Federal Bureau of Investigation (FBI), Bureau of Prisons (BOP), and the National Joint Terrorism Task Force (NJTTF) have identified a need to investigate the motives and organizational structure of radical Islamic groups inside U.S. prisons.[158] This study outlines the characteristics of major prison gangs, reviews recent activity of radical Islamic groups in U.S. prisons, and then compares the latter's development to that of major prison gangs to get a clearer picture of the threat posed by Islamic radicals in U.S. prisons.

PRISON GANGS

The problems inherent in the incarceration of ideological extremists are centuries old. While in Tsarist prisons, Stalin and Dzerzhinsky organized murderers and other hardened criminals who would lead the Bolsheviks and their Cheka secret police. Hitler used his time in prison as an opportunity to reflect and write *Mein Kampf*. In the past 30 years, however, the traditional problems of incarceration have been exacerbated by the development to an unprecedented degree of prison gangs.

Development of Prison Gangs

By the 1970s, the traditional white-dominated inmate system had disappeared from many American prisons. Gone as well was the perception that inmates could be protected from one another by correctional officers. Massive overcrowding, combined with budgetary restrictions on the local, state, and federal levels, left inmates with no alternative but to ally with others for protection. For this reason, highly organized "super gangs" such as the Mexican Mafia and the Aryan Brotherhood formed to compete for power in American correctional institutions.

Today, prison gangs flourish nationwide. They reach out from their cells to organize and control crime, internally in America's prisons and externally on the street. As the street gang phenomenon spread throughout America, officials saw a parallel growth in the spread of prison gangs. In 1996, the Federal Bureau of Prisons found that prison disturbances rose by about 400 percent in the early 1990s, indicating that gangs were becoming more active and seemingly more efficient at evading security protocols.[159]

---

[158] Frank Cilluffo, *Out of the Shadows: Getting Ahead of Prisoner Radicalization*, 2006, URL: <hsgac.senate.gov/_files/091906Report.pdf>, accessed 5 October 2006.

[159] Tiffany Danitz, "The Gangs Behind Bars," *Insight in the News*, 28 September 1998, URL:<www.findarticles.com/p/articles/mi_m1571/is_n36_v14/ai_21161641/print>, accessed 14 May 2006.

Due to the secretive nature of a prison gang, prison and law enforcement officials have only a rudimentary understanding of its dynamics. Clearly, such groups have existed in the prisons for many years with steadily growing influence. In 1985, *Prison Gangs: Their Extent, Nature, and Impact on Prisons* identified 13,000 inmates as gang members in the U.S. prison system.[160] By 1991, that number was thought to be more than 100,000 nationwide.[161] A 2004 survey of prison officials established that 10 major prison gangs operated in correctional facilities throughout the U.S. (see Figure 1).

Ten Largest U.S. Prison Gangs

- Crips
- Gangster Disciples
- Bloods
- Latin Kings
- Vice Lords
- Aryan Brotherhood
- Folks
- White Supremacists (generic)
- Surenos (Sur 13)
- Five Percenters

Figure 1. The Top 10 Prison Gangs in American Institutions
Source: Knox, "The Problem of Gangs," 2005.

However, a few prison gangs stood out from their counterparts. If the gang has fairly long tenure, identifiable leadership, and solid organizational structure, it is classified as a "major" prison gang.[162]

Major Prison Gangs

A major gang is "an organized group of inmates who are likely to be racially homogeneous and to have members in more than one prison in a state."[163] They are likely to have strong ties to the outside world, which permit the direction of external criminal activity and internal smuggling of contraband. Successful prison gangs follow a para-military style, with a designated leader

---

[160] Mark S. Fleischer and Scott H. Decker, "An Overview of the Challenge of Prison Gangs," *Corrections Management Quarterly* 5, no. 1 (Winter 2001): 2.

[161] George Knox and Edward Tromhauser, "Gangs and Their Control in Adult Correctional Institutions," *The Prison Journal*, no. 71 (1991): 17.

[162] George Knox, "The Problem of Gangs and Security Threat Groups (STGs) in American Prisons Today: Recent Research Findings From the 2004 Prison Gang Survey," *National Gang Crime Research Center*, online study, URL: <www.ngcrc.com/corr2006.html>, accessed 8 December 2005.

[163] Richard Hawkins and Geoffrey P. Alpert, *American Prison Systems: Punishment and Justice* (Upper Saddle River, NJ: Prentice Hall, 1989), 251.

who oversees a rank-and-file organizational structure. Prison gangs have a creed or motto, unique symbols of membership, and a constitution prescribing accepted group behavior. Gangs ranging from the Mexican Mafia to the Black Guerrilla Family or the Aryan Brotherhood typically unite along racial lines and ultimately develop their own culture, rules of conduct, distinct fashions, and communication practices. In addition, these prison gangs often devise complex organizational structures to recruit or punish members, counter correctional staff, and outline the gang's sphere of activity.[164]

There are four organizations whose characteristics put them in the category of major gangs:

Black Guerrilla Family. The BGF is the oldest and most violent prison gang in the American system. Established in San Quentin in 1966 by George Jackson of the Black Panthers, the BGF believes in "power for the people." It is the most revolutionary of the prison gangs and copies heavily from the tactics and writings of Mao Zedong.

Aryan Brotherhood. The AB is one of the most violent prison gangs and has strong chapters on the streets of many large cities. Established in 1968 from a core group of biker and neo-Nazi groups, it has a distinguishable "upper tier" leadership structure and para-military style organization.

Mexican Mafia. The Mexican Mafia may be the strongest and ultimately the most organized prison gang in the BOP. It has been recognized as a major prison gang for nearly 30 years. The MM organized around large groups of Latino street gang members. It attempts to run all prison rackets, including drugs, murder, mayhem, prostitution, weapons, extortion, and protection.

Nuestra Familia. Spanish for "Our Family," Nuestra Familia has been a California prison gang since the early 1970s. Initially formed by intimidated Latino farm workers, Nuestra Familia began to adopt essential survival practices to gain preeminence in prison: secret communication, self-defense, weapons manufacturing, and tactics of diversion.[165]

---

[164] R.S. Fong and S. Buentello, "The Detection of Prison Gang Development: An Empirical Assessment," *Federal Probation* 55, no. 1 (March 1991): 66-69; Scott H. Decker and others, "Gangs As Organized Crime Groups: A Tale of Two Cities," *Crime and Justice Quarterly* 15, no. 3 (September 1998): 395-423; and Fleisher and Decker, 2.

[165] William Valentine, *Gang Intelligence Manual: Identifying and Understanding Modern Day Violent Gangs in the United States* (Boulder, CO: Paladin Press, 1995), 224; symbols used by permission.

The complex factors making up prison gangs can be found in nearly all penitentiaries. In the early days of prison gangs, racial minorities were the first to organize, followed by whites who organized in response.[166] Inter-racial conflict among the Aryan Brotherhood (a white gang), the Mexican Mafia (a Latino gang), and the Black Guerrilla Family (a black gang) developed as individual groups vied for influence and power. In his book *Prison Guard*, James Jacobs describes the evolution of the prison population from a disorganized conglomerate into more cohesive groups:

> Among the white inmates, no organizational structure existed in 1972, but one could distinguish secure and vulnerable cliques. By the fall of 1974, there were indications of the beginning of formal white organizations. The Ku Klux Klan and the House of Golden Dragon began to develop mainly for the purpose of providing protection.[167]

By the late 1970s, gangs had appeared in prisons all over the United States. For these groups, power dispersed along racial lines and was based on each group's ability to organize in response to the varying threats found in a prison environment. Vast numbers of highly organized gang members crowded large prisons and today represent the dominant sub-culture.

ISLAMIC EXTREMIST GROUPS IN U.S. PRISONS

On Easter Sunday 1993, a group of Islamic inmates started Ohio's deadliest prison riot. Nine days later, nine inmates and one correctional officer were dead. Sunni Muslims Carols Sanders (also known as Siddique Abdullah Hasan) and James Were (also known as Namir Abdul Mateen) were among the five sentenced to death for their leadership of the uprising. This is an extreme example of the growing influence of Islamic gangs and religious groups in American correctional facilities. Concern is growing that Al Qaeda-inspired prison recruitment and organization is already underway in the United States. A survey of prison officials found 18 different Islamic prison gangs existed, including Five Percent Nation, Nation of Islam, Moorish Science Temple of America, Melanic Islamic Palace of the Rising Sun, Fruits of Islam, Ansar El Muhammed Muslims, Black Gangster Disciples, Black P. Stone Nation, Salifi, United Blood Nation, El Rukns, Melanic Nubian Islamic, and Radical Muslim.[168]

---

[166] Hawkins and Alpert, 250-251.

[167] James Jacobs and Harold Retsky, *Prison Guard* (Springfield, IL: Charles C. Thomas, 1980), 53.

[168] Eric Lichtblau, "Report Warns of Infiltration by Al Qaeda in U.S. Prisons," *New York Times*, 5 May 2004, URL: <www.criminology.fsu.edu/penology/news/Report%20Warns%20of%20 Infiltration% 20by%20Al%20Qaeda%20in%20U_S_%20Prisons.htm>, accessed 3 October 2006; and Knox, "Problem of Gangs."

Interviews with BOP representatives suggest Islamic extremist recruitment and organization might be more prevalent than previously thought. According to Les Smith, BOP liaison to the JTTF in McLean, Virginia, specific terrorists may be monitored, but prisoners' religious preferences are not officially tracked at the federal level. This is due in large part to the rights provided to religious organizations; Islamic-affiliated prison groups are shielded by First Amendment provisions that enable many inmates to mask patterns of criminal behavior under the guise of religious freedom. Consequently, experts have difficulty defining the scope and exact nature of Islamic extremist organizations. Several major prison gangs have begun to take on religious overtones as a means of obtaining additional privileges and immunities from strict oversight. For example, Aryan Nation inmates are adopting religions such as Odinism[169] to gain the freedom to congregate that is afforded to religious sects.[170]

Across the United States, thousands of Muslims are practicing their faith behind bars. Islam is the fastest growing religion among young, incarcerated African-Americans, most of whom have previous gang affiliation and training. Estimates place the number of Muslim prisoners at 5-10 percent of the total correctional population. There are therefore reasons for concern due to the high level of interest terror groups such as Al Qaeda have in inspiring "home grown" terrorists who can operate within U.S. borders.[171] These concerns are reflected in comments by FBI director Robert Mueller to the Senate Select Committee on Intelligence in 2005: "Prisons continue to be fertile ground for extremists who exploit both a prisoner's conversion to Islam while still in prison, as well as their socio-economic status and placement in the community upon their release."[172]

The Black P. Stone Nation (BPSN) is an example of an Islamic gang that has decades of experience in criminal enterprise and terrorist affiliation; it was a criminal gang before it took on its current religious hue. BSPN gained notoriety when its leader, Jeff Fort, was convicted of conspiracy to commit terrorism; specifically, contracting with Libya to shoot down American airliners inside the United States.[173] Prior to his conviction, Jeff Fort and his colleagues traveled to Libya to volunteer as domestic terrorists within the United States. While BSPN

---

[169] Odinism is a religious movement that attempts to revive Norse Paganism from the Viking Age. White Supremacist prisoners embraced Odinism in the 1970s and pushed for it to be officially recognized by the United States. Consequently, although it is considered a minor religion, Odinist inmates receive the same religious benefits and congregation privileges as major religions such as Christianity and Islam.

[170] ADL, *Dangerous Convictions*; and Les Smith, Bureau of Prisons liaison to the National Joint Terrorism Task Force, interview by author, 25 May 2006.

[171] Patrik Jonsson, "New Profile of the Home-Grown Terrorist Emerges," *Christian Science Monitor*, 26 June 2006, URL: <www.csm.com/2006/0626/p01s01-ussc.html>, accessed 6 October 2006.

[172] Robert Mueller, 16 February 2005, transcript of testimony before the United States Senate Select Committee on Intelligence, URL: <www.fbi.gov/congress/congress05/ mueller021605>, accessed 22 May 2006.

[173] Knox, "The Problem of Gangs."

members were clearly gang mercenaries, their activities highlighted the close ties between gang activity and terrorist agendas.

More recently, Islamic radicalism has begun to take hold in a larger number of American prisons. In testifying before the Senate Judiciary Committee in October 2003, John Pistole, the FBI's executive assistant director of counterintelligence and counterterrorism, called U.S. correctional institutions a "viable venue for radicalization and recruitment for Al Qaeda."[174] Similarly, Harry Lapin, the director of the Federal Bureau of Prisons, sees the bloated prison population of disgruntled violent inmates as being "particularly vulnerable to recruitment by terrorists."[175] While identifying the recruitment and radicalization of prison inmates by Islamic radicals may be a first step in curbing the practice, numerous intelligence agencies, including the FBI, continue to be perplexed about how best to identify the nature and organization of radical Islamic organizations operating inside the BOP.

The need to develop such identification procedures was emphasized in July 2005 with the arrest of three members of a previously little-known group, *Jam'iyyat Ul-Islam Is-Saheeh* (Arabic for "Assembly of Authentic Islam"), JIS. From behind bars, Kevin Lamar James had secretly created a sophisticated radical Islamic organization based on the principles of Al Qaeda. He recruited other inmates who, upon their release, planned multiple terror operations against military and Jewish targets in California. The group vowed to "target any enemies of Islam, including the United States government and Jewish and non-Jewish supporters of Israel."[176] While James and his followers were thwarted in their efforts as a result of a bungled armed robbery, the group is part of a new breed of prison-born Islamist terror groups that have recruited, organized, and acted out a form of extreme Islamic fundamentalism.[177]

Prisons may be particularly fruitful ground for radicalization and recruitment, because the message of religious and terror-affiliated extremist groups is appealing to an already disenfranchised inmate population. The inmates who respond to calls for violence represent a threat to prison staff and other inmates, as well as the external society. This is especially true for

---

[174] Harley G. Lapin, Director, Federal Bureau of Prisons, "Terrorist Recruitment and Infiltration in the United States: Prisons and Military as Operational Base," statement before the Senate Judiciary Committee, Sub-committee on Terrorism, Technology, and Homeland Security, 14 October 2003, URL: <judiciary.senate.gov/testimony.cfm? id=960&wit_id=2318>, accessed 7 November 2006.

[175] Cuthbertson, 18.

[176] Michelle Gaseau, Managing Editor of *Corrections Online*, "Terrorist Activity Behind Bars Spurs Inmate Monitoring Plans," Web-only essay, 26 September 2005, URL: <www.corrections.com/news/archives/results2_new.asp?ID=14021>, accessed 14 May 2006.

[177] Donald Thompson, "Concern Grows Over Prison Islam Converts," *AP News Service*, 20 August 2005, accessed via High beam research service, 11 February 2006; "Four California Men Indicted in Terror Plot," *Northeast Intelligence Network*, URL: <www.homelandsecurityus.com/site/ modules/news/print.php?storyid=311>, accessed 2 October 2006; and National Alliance of Gang Investigators Associations, *2005 National Gang Threat Assessment* (Washington: N.p., 2005), 5. Cited hereafter as NAGIA, *National Gang Threat Assessment*.

Muslim inmates who feel the strains of being a minority faith in America and in other Western nations where racial tensions are high. In France, for example, more than half of its 45,000 penitentiary inmates are Muslim, over six times the proportion of Muslims in the overall French population. According to one official, "the nation's prisons have become the cradle of the future jihad."[178]

The growth of Islamic radicalism in French prisons has been attributed in part to the control that inmates exercise over most of the institutions' religious practices. This is a problem in U.S. prisons as well. BOP officials are able to provide only one chaplain for every 900 Islamic inmates. Where a "real" chaplain is not available, BOP officials allow prisoner-run services to be conducted. A survey of prison officials found that the overwhelming majority of these prisoner-run services were Islamic in one form or other. Lacking the religious guidance and moderation of qualified Muslim chaplains, the inmates are developing a radical form of Islam, "Prison Islam," instead. According to George Knox in *Gang Profile Update: Black P. Stone Nation*, there are many Islamic converts who

> read a page or two from the Koran, pick and mix a few phrases that can be adapted to their twisted moral code, and they get away passing as a semi-religious group of some kind; when in fact, they are nothing more than criminal [prison] gangs run by adult career criminals. Their expertise is not following the tenets of Islam, nor in any sense trying to live an Islamic lifestyle other than denouncing pork products; their expertise is in illicit violence and drug sales.[179]

Prison Islam results when inmates follow the faith without direction or thoughtful reflection. Inmates distort Islam to integrate gang values and unquestioning loyalty to Islamic radicals within the facility. While most Muslim chaplains oppose Prison Islam, many say it is likely to continue to thrive in institutions that do not have staff chaplains, contractors, or volunteers to guide inmates in properly practicing and interpreting the Koran. The Department of Justice's Inspector General agrees: "Without a sufficient number of Muslim chaplains on staff, inmates are much more likely to lead their own religious services, distort Islam and espouse extremist beliefs."[180]

---

[178] Frank Viviano, "French Prisons 'Cradle of Jihad': Islamic Radicals Spread Revolutionary Tactics," *Seattle Post Intelligencer*, 2 November 2001, accessed via High beam Research service, 11 February 2006; and Christopher Newton, "Prisons May Breed Terrorist Groups," *AP News*, 11 June 2002, accessed via High beam research service, 11 February 2006.

[179] U.S. Department of Justice, "A Review of the Federal Bureau of Prison's Selection of Muslim Religious Service Providers," *Office of the Inspector General*, April 2004, URL: <www.usdoj.gov/oig/ special/0404/>, accessed 1 March 2006; Knox, "Problem of Gangs"; and Knox, "Black P. Stone Nation."

[180] U.S. Department of Justice, "A Review"; and Jerry Seper, "Prisons Breeding Ground for Terror?" *Washington Times*, 6 May 2004, URL: <washingtontimes.com/national/20040505-111705-4604r.htm>, accessed 4 October 2006.

COMPARING ISLAMIC EXTREMIST GROUPS
TO MAJOR PRISON GANGS

This study measured Islamic extremist groups against an established metric for major prison gangs from the Arizona Department of Corrections—a guide to the level of threat posed by various prison groups (see Figure 2). It assesses major prison gangs based on the following criteria: stated constitution, established communication procedures, recruitment methods, rank structure, gang identification and validation, established alliances, and recognized operational procedures. Corrections officials contend that the identification of these characteristics is essential to create a viable suppression strategy against prison gangs. Furthermore, if the characteristics of Islamic extremist groups are found to parallel those of major prison gangs, then a suppression strategy can be created that counters both groups simultaneously.[181]

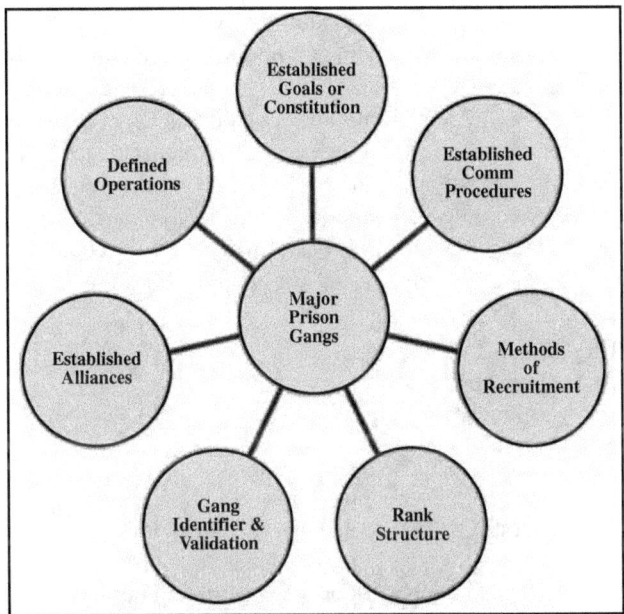

Figure 2. Framework of Major Prison Gangs
Source: "Security Threat Group FAQs."

Established Goals or Constitution

The idealized view that prison gangs have of themselves, whether they be the Aryan Brotherhood or Black Guerilla Family, can be seen most clearly in their stated goals or constitution. Constitutions are so widespread among

---

[181] "Security Threat Group FAQs," *Arizona Department of Corrections*, URL: <www. adc.state.az. us/adc.divisions/support/stg/faq.asp>, accessed 28 November 2006; and ADL, *Dangerous Convictions.*

prison groups that they play an instrumental role in whether federal and state correctional officers define groups as a gang. Analysis of major prison gangs in the United States shows that an organization is only as successful as the ideology it espouses to recruit and organize inmates. Constitutions are important because they formalize the gang's ideology and create a sense of legitimacy, providing new members something with which to identify. Moreover, constitutions lay the groundwork for the entire network of prison gangs and extremist groups that operate behind bars, organizing the power structure within the gang and identifying group goals.[182]

The earliest prison gangs adopted constitutions to outline their strategic objectives. Highly structured documents that outline the basics of gang behavior, constitutions are strictly enforced by all organized prison gangs in American correctional facilities.

Nuestra Familia, which originated in California in the early 1970s, is an example of a prison gang with well-defined constitutional boundaries. It constructed a constitution called the "14 bonds," which ultimately became the rules by which its gang members live. NF's constitution outlined the scope of the organization: to defend migrant farm workers from the violent acts of other gangs that existed in the California correctional system. Shortly after the adoption of its constitution, the gang became increasingly structured, and rigid standards were imposed on its members. Gang members were required to adhere to strict guidelines of dress, hygiene, and conduct.[183] A creed outlined the group's belief in loyalty, leadership, and action:

> If I go forward, follow me
> If I hesitate, push me
> If they kill me, avenge me
> If I am a traitor, kill me.[184]

The Black Guerrilla Family is another example of an ideology-driven prison gang with a strong basis rooted in its goals and written constitution. The BGF was formed as a Marxist/Leninist/Maoist revolutionary organization by Black Panther prisoners in the 1960s. Its constitution outlined three goals:

- Eradicate racism;
- Struggle to maintain dignity while in prison; and
- Overthrow the U.S. government.[185]

The first two objectives are fairly innocuous; however, the overthrow of the United States government is not something to be taken lightly. The written

---

[182] ADL, *Dangerous Convictions.*

[183] Valentine, 220; and Knox, "The Problem of Gangs."

[184] Florida Department of Corrections, "Gang and Security Threat Group Awareness," 1 June 2005, URL: <www.dc.state.fl.us/pub/gangs/prison.html>, accessed 8 December 2005.

[185] Florida Department of Corrections, "Gangs and Security Threat Group Awareness."

constitution of the BGF consists of 16 pages of single-spaced, typed text. It encourages its members to engage in armed conflict with other prisoners. Additionally, the document adopts a revolutionary tone to describe how BGF group members are to achieve their objectives. Guerrilla warfare and terrorism are approved tactics.

Defined Operations

Major prison gangs routinely dominate their competitors through control of "rackets" in correctional facilities: drugs, sex, food, clothing, loan-sharking, and protection, for example. To achieve and retain control, the gangs' operational structures are optimized for efficiency within the prison environment. For example, prospective members of the Aryan Brotherhood must learn physical skills such as unarmed self-defense techniques, knife-fighting, weapons manufacturing, baton takeaway techniques, escaping from handcuffs, key-making, contraband concealment, sign language, complex codes, and a host of other skills needed for survival and secrecy behind prison walls. Also defined in the operations structure of the Aryan Brotherhood are methods by which an inmate might compromise prison staff such as: manipulating where a gang member will be housed, where he will work, and where he will go to school. These methods are used to train new recruits and to place individuals where their skills are needed.[186]

Prison gangs delineate the responsibilities of their group components. Typically found in gangs such as Nuestra Familia, specialized departments oversee aspects of daily operations inside and outside the correctional facility. As in terror organizations, information is highly compartmentalized and known only to a select few in the organization. For instance, one of the departments of Nuestra Familia—the Regimental Security Department (RSD)—provides intelligence and security for the gang. The RSD maintains contacts outside of the prison to compile and disseminate information to gang members. Furthermore, it gathers intelligence on its enemies in order to alert prison gang members. Similar to the Aryan Brotherhood, the security arm of NF teaches self-defense, conditioning, weaponry, killing techniques, interrogation, and related topics to the gang members. Instructors are chosen based on loyalty to the gang, expertise in certain relevant fields, and the ability to teach other inmates. Today, the NF is engaged in drug-trafficking, extortion, murder-for-hire, intimidation, and other violent criminal activity both inside and outside prison walls. The well-defined operational structure put forth by NF leaders aids in all aspects of its criminal activity.[187]

Many Islamic extremist inmates are converts formerly affiliated with gang activity. Thus, the operational patterns of Islamic extremist prison networks

---

[186] Knox, "The Problem of Gangs"; and Valentine, 212.

[187] Smith, interview; and Valentine, 223.

are similar to their gang counterparts. Information is compartmentalized in much the same way as in prison gangs, and both groups have an affinity for covert operations away from the prying eyes of prison staff. JIS, in fact, managed to remain largely unknown to Folsom Prison authorities until some of its members were arrested for armed robbery and conspiracy to commit terrorist acts after being released on parole.[188]

Islamic extremist prison groups operate at a level of dedication and organization similar to a prison gang. They are made up of highly motivated individuals who exhibit a strong sense of loyalty and discipline to the cause. They have an effective operational structure that typically places group members in independent committees in each hall or cellblock to coordinate group activities. For example, JIS defined the requirements and responsibilities of its members, with group leader Kevin James dictating the recruiting, training, and planning of operations and requiring JIS members to contact him regularly for new orders after they left prison.[189]

Established Communications Procedures

The communications apparatus of a prison gang is of utmost importance because it offers "the exchange of information and the transmission of meaning" to members of the group who may be separated geographically or by concrete walls and iron bars.[190]

According to gang investigators, there is fluid communication among gang members both inside and outside the prison environment. Criminal schemes are hatched in prison and carried out on the streets and vice versa. Inmates recognize the need to communicate with gang members on the outside and in other facilities and have learned to utilize multiple methods of transmission. One of the most prevalent methods to organize illicit activity is the use of encrypted messages. Other known techniques to communicate messages and instructions to other gang members include newsletters or "Zines," which often have embedded information; inmate-to-inmate mail; smuggled cell phones; person-to-person message transfer; unmonitored religious services used as a cover for gang meetings; and third-party message transfer using lawyers, clerics, and family.[191]

---

[188] Amy Argetsinger and Sonya Geis, "4 Charged with Terrorist Plot in California," *Washington Post*, 1 September 2005, A2.

[189] Gary Hill, "Gangs Inside Prison Walls Around the World," *Corrections Compendium*, 1 January 2004, accessed via High Beam Research Service, 11 February 2006; and Daniel Pipes, "L.A.'s Thwarted Terror Spree," *Human Events*, 7 September 2005, URL: <www.humanevents. com/article.php? id=8927>, accessed 6 October 2006.

[190] Troy Thomas and William Casebeer, *Violent Systems: Defeating Terrorists, Insurgents and Other Non-State Adversaries* (Colorado Springs: United States Air Force Academy, 2004), 21.

[191] Smith, interview; and Knox, "The Problem of Gangs."

While information on the internal communication of Islamic extremists is fairly limited, the IC and law enforcement have seen multiple methods of communication that parallel gang communication. Known communication methods used by imprisoned Islamic extremists include sending messages in code; using inmate-to-inmate mail service; transmitting extremist rhetoric in unmonitored religious services; and passing messages through lawyers, clerics, family members, and other third parties.[192]

In addition to such communication techniques, terrorists often use the Arabic language as a method to pass instruction covertly to liaisons with the outside world. An example of this was when Sheik Omar Abdel Rahman—incarcerated in a federal penitentiary—was able to get messages to his followers worldwide, despite government efforts to smother his communications. During meetings with his attorney, the "blind Sheik" would exchange messages in Arabic with the accompanying Arabic-speaking paralegal, who would then pass them to the intended recipients.[193]

Religious services are the epicenter of extremist communication in prison facilities. Correctional staff members believe that religious services are used as a front for illicit gang activity. Less than half of those services are monitored by prison staff or video monitoring devices. Jeff Fort, leader of the Black P. Stone Nation, was one of the early Islamic gang leaders to utilize religious ceremonies as a meeting ground. BSPN leaders found that any time a gang can attach itself to a legitimate social institution, such as a church, it increases the gang's power. [194]

Typical of Islamic gang converts, BSPN grossly perverts Islam, using its "quasi-religious" identity as a cover for covert communication and gang organization. The group uses code switching[195] during religious ceremonies. Code switching involves using special terms and phrases that have a "double meaning," allowing indoctrinated gang members to communicate criminal plans by the use of special phrases and terminology. Intelligence relating to the activity of JIS and Brotherhood of Hezbollah activity during religious ceremonies is scarce but suggests they both communicate in a similar fashion.[196]

---

[192] Smith, interview; "4 Charged with Helping 'Blind Sheik' Commit Terrorism," *NewsMax*, 10 April 2002, URL: <www.newsmax.com/archives/articles/2002/4/9/142954.shtml>, accessed 4 October 2006.

[193] "Lynne Steward, Lawyer of Abdel Rahman, Found Guilty of Aiding Terrorists," *Militant Islam Monitor*, URL: <www.militantislammonitor.org/article/id/430>, accessed 6 October 2006.

[194] Knox, "The Problem of Gangs," 2005.

[195] Knox, "Black P. Stone Nation," 2003.

[196] J.R., analyst for the Federal Bureau of Investigation, interview by author, 15 June 2006; and Kenneth O'Reilly, *Racial Matters: The FBI's File on Black America*, 1960-1972 (New York: Simon & Schuster, 1991), 409.

Methods of Recruitment

The recruitment mechanisms for terrorist organizations and prison gangs take multiple forms. A group will employ a variety of incentives to recruit new members to a particular cause, including training, protection, ideology, belonging, power, greed, and eternal life.[197] This section will examine the type of inmates who are recruited and how they are recruited.

Prison gangs routinely recruit according to the racial demographic of a particular institution and evolve according to the particular needs of the group. Black and Hispanic gangs rely on a "strength in numbers" approach to inmate recruitment. Gangs such as the Aryan Brotherhood take a different approach to recruitment by selecting a limited number of members based on strength and willingness to kill. Prison gangs such as Nuestra Familia have begun to take a similarly selective approach to recruitment. Whereas a potential recruit must be of a particular racial demographic (in this case Hispanic), he must also come from a select pool of proven gang members and ex-convicts whose "papers" (prior gang affiliation, criminal involvement, and persons he has killed) can be verified by gang leadership.[198]

Like gangs, extremists use a number of different methods to recruit and indoctrinate inmates, including newsletters and other periodicals. For example, since 1979 the Aryan Brotherhood, a violent white supremacist organization, has been involved in intense prison recruitment and organization. According to John Pistole, Assistant Director of the FBI's Counterterrorism Division, terrorist sympathizers are using many of the AB's recruiting techniques: bringing charismatic visitors in to help recruiting efforts and offering inmates protection, influence, and a network of supporters inside and outside of prison. Religious services in prison can be used as a recruiting forum. Influential inmates sometimes assume unauthorized religious leadership positions in prisons and begin to direct followers, both in and out of the facility. Similarly, some prison chaplains, volunteers, contractors, or staff may be engaged in attempts to radicalize and recruit inmates. [199]

Recruitment of inmates within the prison system continues to be a problem for authorities. Inmates are often ostracized, abandoned, or isolated from their families. Consequently, they naturally seek new forms of socialization. Membership in radicalized groups offers protection, yet ultimately begets more violence in the prison. While Islamic organizations external to the prison may not be recruiting according to a particular terror-related agenda, it

---

[197] Thomas and Casebeer, 25.

[198] Valentine, 211; and Florida Department of Corrections, "Gangs and Security Threat Group Awareness," 2005.

[199] ADL, *Dangerous Convictions*; U.S. Department of Justice, "A Review"; and John S. Pistole, "Terrorist Recruitment in Prisons and the Recent Arrests Related to Guantanamo Bay Detainees," remarks provided in Congressional Testimony, 14 October 2003, URL: <www.fbi.gov/congress/ congress03/ pistole101403.htm>, accessed 15 November 2005.

appears that radicalized inmates are beginning to organize based on "Prison Islam," the only form of Islam to which they have been exposed.

Gang Identifier and Validation

Any gang whose members are required to dress in a certain style, change their name, or tattoo themselves with group symbols is considered a sophisticated prison gang because it exploits the psychology of the human identity. Gang members can be identified by a number of different factors, including distinct style of dress, self-identification as a gang member, or possession of gang-related material. Furthermore, gangs may produce elaborate works of art relating to particular gang themes or may incorporate similar art onto their own bodies in the form of prison tattoos.[200]

Members of white supremacist gangs such as the Aryan Brotherhood will leave prison virtually covered in extremist tattoos and slogans, ranging from portraits of Adolph Hitler or Heinrich Himmler to slogans such as "White Power" or "Rahowa" (an acronym for "racial holy war"). Other tattoos reflecting white supremacist beliefs have become standard. These tattoos are mainly Nazi-style swastikas, eagles, lightning bolts, iron crosses, horned helmets, and anything relating to Nordic mythology (Figure 3).[201]

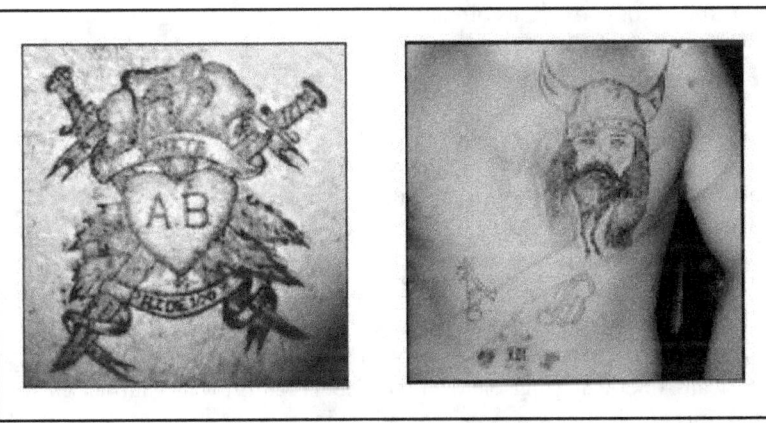

Figure 3. Gang Tattoo Identification
Source: Florida Department of Corrections, "Gangs and Security Threat Group Awareness," 2005.

Islamic extremist prison gangs such as the Black P. Stone Nation follow identification procedures similar to other highly organized gangs, but in a less recognizable manner. Jeff Fort, leader of the BSPN, decided that requiring members to modify their name was important for increasing the solidarity of BSPN members. He had members modify their names to reflect Islamic

---

[200] Knox, "Black P. Stone Nation"; and Florida Department of Corrections, "Gangs and Security Threat Group Awareness," 2005.

[201] ADL, *Dangerous Convictions*; and Valentine, 210.

ties; for example, Jimmy Jones would become Jimmy Jones-el. While not the most sophisticated change, it did provide group identification that set them apart from other African-American inmates.[202]

Many prison officials believe Islamic extremists are in distinct gangs, such as the Black P. Stone Nation. Nonetheless, identifying Islamic terror groups presents particular challenges for law enforcement and corrections officials already overwhelmed by a surplus of inmates. The tracking of religious-based organizations is prohibited according to federal and state laws. Furthermore, since most Islamic converts are former gang members, they still retain the marks of their old affiliation, making it difficult to discern individual loyalties. As Islamic extremist organizations do not require tattoos, identifying those with terrorist objectives is difficult. According to Les Smith, Islamic groups may wear certain hats or neutral colors, but it is nearly impossible to differentiate between the moderate and radically affiliated groups. The only reliable method to identify Islamic extremist prison gangs is through extremist literature, which is often kept hidden. JIS leader Kevin Lamar James kept his group's material well-hidden, even while directing JIS's outside activities from his prison cell. Shia leader Ernest Grandberry of the Brotherhood of Hezbollah similarly kept his group's agenda out of sight. Therefore, identifying Islamic extremists based on outward appearance is difficult for corrections officials.[203]

Established Alliances

In the struggle for control of criminal enterprise, it is quite common for prison gangs to form alliances with other gangs. Profit motive and achievement of group objectives often supersede racism in prison and on the street. In one of the most famous examples, the Aryan Brotherhood forged an alliance with the already well-established Mexican Mafia in the early 1970s. The two work regularly together against MM's chief rival, Nuestra Familia—which allied with BGF in response. Despite their clear belief in racial supremacy, extremist groups like the Aryan Brotherhood are also known to associate with African-American gang elements to encourage prison disturbances and to sell drugs to the black prison population.[204]

Among Islamic extremist groups, such alliances are more difficult to discern, though some apparently exist, often as the result of previous links among members. Black P. Stone Nation, for example, is closely aligned with the Latin Kings, a gang with which BPSN was associated in its earlier, pre-Islamic incarnation. Similarly, there are alliances among some of the various

---

[202] Knox, "Black P. Stone Nation," 2003.

[203] While not officially tracking Islamic inmates, prison officials state that there is most definitely "unofficial" tracking of inmates who attend particular religious services, eat special meals, and frequent Islamic holy events. Smith, interview; Knox, "The Problem of Gangs"; and U.S. Department of Justice, "A Review."

[204] ADL, *Dangerous Convictions.*

Islamic prison gangs (as well as some blood feuds), with groups like Nation of Islam and Fruit of Islam or Melanic Islamic Palace of the Rising Sun and Melanic Nubian Islamic operating so closely at times as to be virtually indistinguishable from one another.[205]

Rank Structure

A 1996 study by the National Gang Crime Research Center (NGCRC) indicates that nearly 62 percent of the individuals in a prison gang carry a titular distinction based on rank. Together with the other elements of prison organization, the application of a rank structure is merely another method of control on the part of the individual prison gangs.

Prison gangs utilize strong peer pressure tactics and a leadership structure that instills fear in its members. The gangs have hierarchical structures based on power and rank, organized to survive the leadership changes that occur quite frequently in a prison environment. The structure is designed to insulate gang leaders from direct involvement, and ultimately to protect them from persecution and prosecution by corrections officials who might be trying to decapitate gang leadership.[206]

Prison gang leaders highlight the structural composition of the group. The Utah-based Silent Area Warriors did so in its manifesto entitled, "Philosophies and SAW Laws and Codes of Conduct," which outlined its leadership and the individual roles and rank of its subordinates. In particular, the gang decrees that it will be headed by Commanders in charge of the group and Generals who act as liaisons with other prison gangs and prison administration. The Silent Area Warriors outline a rank structure from Commander all the way to low-level "Sergeants" and "Enforcers" who do most of the illicit activities, creating plausible deniability on the part of gang leadership.[207]

Major prison gangs, such as Nuestra Familia and the Aryan Brotherhood, adopt a para-military structure. As individuals progress up through the ranks, they may become part of a squad involved in various low-level aspects of gang operations. If the individual shows leadership, then the rank of squad leader, lieutenant, captain, or general may be attained. These structures are likely not followed as closely as the constitution of the particular gang might suggest; however, positions of leadership are coveted within a prison gang and result in numerous benefits for the individual who attains such rank.[208]

Much of the information relating to Islamic extremist groups points to a religious-based leadership structure. Religious beliefs add to the level of

---

[205] Florida Department of Corrections, "Gangs and Security Threat Group Awareness," 2005; Knox, "Problem of Gangs"; and Knox, "Gang Profile Update."

[206] Sandra S. Fortune, *Inmate and Prison Gang Leadership*, Ph.D. Dissertation, advisor Dr. Russell West (East Tennessee State University, 2003), 37; and *2005 Threat Assessment*.

[207] ADL, *Dangerous Convictions*.

[208] Valentine, 222.

social control a particular group exercises over its members, and these beliefs also provide a useful ideology for galvanizing members to commit criminal or even terrorist acts. The Black P. Stone Nation, for example, established religious titles and roles of authority within its gang, with Jeff Fort titling himself Caliph Abdul-Malik. JIS's James required his followers to swear an oath of allegiance to him as their sole religious leader. This oath was to be observed even after leaving prison, with all JIS members required to report to James every three months.

This sort of authority must be exercised surreptitiously in most cases, as modern penology insists that no prisoner occupy a position of authority over other prisoners. In a large majority of American prisons, this extends to a prohibition on use of any religious title by a prisoner.[209]

COUNTERING THE THREAT

Prisons have a variety of other overt and covert strategies to suppress violent group affiliation. These include segregating gang members; monitoring or restricting their phone calls and mail; using inmate informants to obtain information on group members and activities; placing group members in isolation 23 hours a day; moving group leaders to distant prisons ("bus therapy"); and interrupting group communications.

While such tactics may be useful, it is surprising that only about 20 percent of U.S. prisons have an anti-gang program, per se. One such program, Texas' Gang Renouncement and Disassociation Process (GRAD), has 600 inmates on the waiting list for its nine-month course of instruction on living successfully outside the gang. Also, the popularity of free gang tattoo removal services in several communities plagued by gangs suggests that such a program within prisons might be worthwhile.[210]

No prisons, however, report that they have programs aimed specifically at undercutting the appeal of Islamic extremist groups in prisons. In fact, the lack of moderate Islamic chaplains represents a serious challenge for any suppression strategy directed at such religious extremism in the immediate future.[211]

There is, however, an intelligence program aimed at such Islamic radicals within the U.S. prison population. The Correctional Intelligence

---

[209] Jeffrey Cozzens and Ian Conway, "2005 Los Angeles Plot: The New Face of Jihad in the U.S." *Terrorism Monitor* 4, no. 2 (26 January 2006), URL: <Jamestown.org/terrorism/new/article.php? articleid=2369880>, accessed 4 October 2006; Knox, "Gang Profile Update: The Black P. Stone Nation"; and Knox, "Problem of Gangs."

[210] Fleisher and Decker, 4; Robert Riggs, "State Offers Way Out for Violent Prison Gang Members," *CBS 11 News* 26 July 2004, URL: <http://prisonpotpourri.com/PRISON_NEWS/CBS/ members.html>, accessed 11 October 2006; and Knox, "The Problem of Gangs."

[211] Alexandra Marks, "Islamist Radicals in Prison," *Christian Science Monitor*, 20 September 2006, URL: <www.csmonitor.com/2006/0920/p03s02-ussc.html>, accessed 4 October 2006.

Initiative (CII) was established to provide liaison support to the National Joint Terrorism Task Force's efforts to curb radical extremism in the United States. The CII has four general missions: 1) providing general intelligence on extremist activity within the BOP; 2) identifying individuals, especially volunteers and contractors, who may be attempting to recruit inmates into radical organizations; 3) developing inmate sources on terrorism matters; and 4) tracking inmate contacts to the "free" environment. The CII focuses specifically on detecting and deterring the radicalization and recruitment of inmates by extremist organizations or individuals who come into the prisons to provide services directly to the inmates. Additionally, the U.S. Bureau of Justice Administration (BJA) now provides information relating to gangs and internal security threats through a regional information sharing system. The network is evolving into a formal system for sharing gang and terrorist intelligence data throughout the Bureau of Prisons.[212]

In addition to the CII, BOP officials indicate that they will begin to make greater use of the more sophisticated methods of preemption and disruption referenced above, as well as some tactics uniquely designed for dealing with Islamic extremists. Specifically, the BOP plans to preempt terror organization by placing radical leaders in one of six specialized facilities that employ correctional officers more capable of recognizing and disrupting extremist activity. Some of the measures to be used at these special facilities include no private visits for inmates and a more robust intelligence effort. Intelligence and counterterrorism units associated with these facilities would be composed of analysts and linguists who possess a Top Secret clearance, giving them the ability to coordinate with national counterterrorism units such as the NJTTF. An exact time-frame for the initiation of such efforts has not been released, but the information suggests that at least federal correctional facilities will be prepared to mitigate the effects of extremist activity and organization. State and local facilities, however, are likely to remain under-equipped to combat Islamic radicalism in the near future—and they house the vast majority of the nation's prison inmates.[213]

CONCLUSION

It is difficult to identify extremist cells operating behind bars. All too often, terrorist and extremist cadres are not recognized as such by prison authorities. For example, Spanish police had previously identified key members of the terrorist cell that carried out the Madrid bombings as nothing more than drug dealers, failing to uncover their terrorist dealings. Prison extremist groups,

---

[212] Smith, interview; and U.S. Department of Justice, "A Review."

[213] Smith, interview; and Marks, "Islamist Radicals in Prison."

especially when religiously associated, can often operate in a discreet and covert manner, away from the watchful eye of prison security and staff.[214]

Nevertheless, to succeed in prison, extremist groups need to adopt the identifiable organizational elements of major prison gangs. According to Les Smith, this "structure creates powerful networks; inmates could control everything" if they organized in a comprehensive manner. Islamic extremist organizations have begun to grasp this and are organizing along the same lines as the successful prison gangs.[215]

This comparison, then, found the organizational characteristics of major prison gangs being adopted in Islamic extremist prison groups. The elements of successful prison organization, which are found in major prison gangs, can now be found in Islamic extremist groups in prisons. The fusion of gang ideology with religious zeal makes Islamic inmates particularly susceptible to recruitment for acts of terror. This threat will no doubt increase as more gang members are recruited by radical religious extremists.

Groups such as the Black P. Stone Nation represent the gradual incorporation of Islamic extremism into an existing gang organization. As a result, BPSN has generally been driven more by illicit criminal activity than by religious fanaticism. By coupling a fervent belief in the extreme objectives of larger terror organizations with gang organization, groups such as JIS exemplify the next wave of domestic extremist groups. Although JIS lacks the manpower or logistical infrastructure to operate on the same level as more sophisticated prison gangs, it can conduct terrorist activities outside of prison, selecting targets that traditional prison gangs would ignore. While such extremist groups are clearly associated with Islamic radicalism, their gang background and American citizenship set them apart from other Islamists and represent a unique threat to the United States. As corrections officials analyze radical Islamic prison groups using criteria applied to more sophisticated prison gangs, extremist group operations may be more recognizable. Thus, a comprehensive strategy for preempting and disrupting extremist activity may be possible.

---

[214] Dr. George Knox, "Bombs and Arson Crimes Among American Gang Members: A Behavioral Science Profile," *National Gang Crime Research Center*, 2001, online study, URL: <www. ngcrc.com/ bombarso.html>, accessed 14 May 2006; and Cuthbertson, 18-19.

[215] Smith, interview.

PREDICTIVE INTELLIGENCE: WHAT THE DRUG ENFORCEMENT ADMINISTRATION CAN GLEAN FROM THE INTELLIGENCE COMMUNITY

David W. Spencer
Master of Science of Strategic Intelligence, 2005

The Drug Enforcement Administration (DEA) is exploring "predictive intelligence" to identify trends in the evolution of drug organizations and trafficking that should be of concern to law enforcement. Predictive intelligence will enable analysts to warn policymakers of such emerging threats. This will allow policymakers time to set policy and direct assets against a predicted threat before it escalates into a crisis.

How can DEA implement a predictive intelligence program? A prospective answer to that question is that DEA could apply aspects of the strategic warning methodology used by DoD and the Intelligence Community (IC). This study examines the nature and applicability of predictive intelligence for DEA, the particular aspects of strategic warning methodology that DEA might most usefully adopt and adapt, and the means to implement such a program.

PREDICTIVE INTELLIGENCE FOR DEA

In 2004, Karen P. Tandy, Administrator of the Drug Enforcement Administration, expressed an interest in reliable, predictive intelligence on trends in drug trafficking "for planning and programming purposes and to better allocate the resources we have."[216] Thus, there exists a requirement to identify a methodology to fit the drug law-enforcement mind-set, time constraints, and thinly stretched analytical staff of the DEA. A well-developed and functional predictive intelligence program looks 6 to 24 months into the future.[217]

This concept of predictive intelligence is not new to the intelligence world. Sherman Kent's seminal *Strategic Intelligence* addressed the "speculative-evaluative" form of intelligence.[218] The Canadian government has also explored predictive intelligence use for law enforcement. A major conclusion

---

[216] DEA Intelligence Top Down Review Team, *DEA Headquarters Interview: Administrator Karen Tandy*, Washington, 21 April 2004.

[217] Dr. Gregory O'Hayon and Daniel R. Morris, *Creating an Organized Crime SENTINEL: Development and Implementation of a Strategic Early Warning Methodology for Law Enforcement*, Monograph (Ottawa: Criminal Intelligence Service Canada, 30 April 2005), 5.

[218] Sherman Kent, *Strategic Intelligence for American World Policy*, 3d ed. (Hamden, CT: Archon Books, 1965), 39-40.

to their study notes that intelligence must predict future threats to avoid or, at the very least, to mitigate crises. Once a situation has reached the level of crisis management, intelligence is of little utility. Thus, Intelligence must answer the question: what do we need to do today to prepare for tomorrow?[219]

It is this sentiment that has moved DEA toward developing an in-house predictive intelligence capability. Doing so requires an understanding of the relationship between predictive intelligence and warning; a commitment to a predictive intelligence specialty; an acknowledgement of the requirement for predictive intelligence within DEA; an appreciation of predictive intelligence's national security functions; and a resolve to use predictive intelligence in DEA policymaking.

Predictive Intelligence and Warning

The Department of Defense and the Intelligence Community currently use a strategic warning methodology, also called "indications and warning" or simply "warning," as a predictive intelligence tool. Cynthia Grabo's classic definition for warning fits Administrator Tandy's concept of predictive intelligence: intelligence for planning and programming purposes received before local, national, and international phenomena negatively affect the drug situation in the United States.

Grabo states that warning is "the considered judgment of the finest analytic minds available, based on an exhaustive and objective review of all available indications, which is conveyed to the policy official in sufficiently convincing language that he is persuaded of its validity and takes appropriate action to protect the national interest."[220] Grabo's warning methodology so closely mirrors DEA's definition of predictive intelligence that the terms "warning" and "predictive intelligence" are used interchangeably.

The Predictive Intelligence Specialty

DEA can learn many lessons from the Intelligence Community's use of Grabo's strategic warning methodology. The U.S. government created the Intelligence Community to provide strategic warning as a reaction to the surprise attack on Pearl Harbor. In her review of a collection of papers on intelligence warning, Pauletta Otis notes, "The National Security Act of 1947 was, in part, recognition that the United States needs an Intelligence Community that could provide strategic warning by identifying potential threats to national security and communicating that information in a timely

---

[219] O'Hayon and Morris, 5.

[220] Cynthia M. Grabo, *Anticipating Surprise: Analysis for Strategic Warning*, ed. Jan Goldman (Washington: Joint Military Intelligence College, December 2002), 169.

manner."[221] This suggests that to be effective DEA will need to implement its predictive intelligence program with a staff of strategic analysts who will be dedicated solely to the mission of predictive intelligence.

For analysts to provide predictive intelligence to DEA policymakers, they analyze new drugs entering the market, identify trends related to previously identified drugs, and recognize groups trafficking the drugs. Localized events or new technological developments may balloon into the next critical area of concern. DEA might foresee such developments by following Grabo's methodology, modified to DEA's predictive intelligence needs.

These analysts will look beyond U.S. borders, due to the nature of transnational organized crime and economic globalization. Foreign developments often affect the drug markets within the United States; the latest craze in club-drugs from Europe can create domestic demand for the new drug. Alternatively, predictive analysts can also consider how domestic developments can influence global reaction. For example, domestic demand for drugs can stimulate their manufacture in foreign countries for importation into the United States. Therefore, predictive intelligence incorporates information "from other quarters of the Intelligence Community—from sociology, economics, technology, and psychology, as well as from analysis of its relationship to basic, current, and estimative intelligence."[222]

This will involve a big change for intelligence in DEA. DEA produces primarily current intelligence. DEA policymakers and intelligence managers will have to allow some intelligence analysts to transition from their daily crisis-driven routine so they can start to provide decisionmakers with predictive intelligence for future operations.

Current intelligence is not the same as warning. Cynthia Grabo explains, "This opinion will no doubt surprise a lot of people who have come to look on warning as a natural byproduct or handmaiden of current analysis."[223] Grabo elaborates that

> the best warning analysis does not flow inevitably or even usually from the most methodical and diligent review of current information. The best warning analysis is the product of detailed and continuing review of all information, going back for weeks and months which may be relevant to the current situation, and

[221] Defense Intelligence Agency (DIA), *Dangerous Assumption: Preparing the U.S. Intelligence Warning System for the New Millennium, Occasional Paper Number Eight*, ed. Jan Goldman (Washington: Joint Military Intelligence College, June 2000), v.

[222] Defense Intelligence Agency, *Intelligence Warning Terminology*, ed. Jan Goldman (Washington: Joint Military Intelligence College, March 2002), 1.

[223] Grabo, 5.

a solid basic understanding of the potential enemy's objectives, doctrines and organization.[224]

Why DEA Wants Predictive Intelligence

The goal of the DEA Intelligence Division, like any intelligence organization, is to provide decisionmakers with the intelligence they need to make timely and effective decisions. Decisionmakers need such intelligence to employ their limited assets effectively.

DEA's current intelligence program effectively reacts to the needs of drug investigations and defines current threats within the drug arena. However, given the rapidly expanding needs of the organization, a well-developed predictive intelligence program to complement the work done by the inter-agency National Drug Intelligence Center is critical for DEA.[225]

DEA and National Security

The Drug Enforcement Administration was established in 1973. At that time, however, the drug issue was not receiving the level of national attention it later achieved. When the cocaine epidemic of the 1980s elevated drugs from an issue of law enforcement to one of national security, however, the intelligence gathering responsibilities of the Intelligence Community and the law enforcement mission of the DEA became intertwined. DEA looked to the IC to fill intelligence gaps on major international drug trafficking organizations. This created a bond between the IC and DEA. Now that the world situation again compels these agencies to work more closely, DEA and the IC will necessarily adapt to the overlapping areas of responsibility. In doing so, each can gain valuable experience and information from the other—as with predictive intelligence.

Prior to 2001, there was no clear law enforcement or intelligence agency primacy in the area of drug trafficking. DEA, other federal law enforcement agencies, and the Intelligence Community were all working the drug trafficking issue in their normal course of operations, with little regard for what other organizations were doing. However, after 11 September 2001, the Intelligence Community and federal law enforcement agencies other than DEA disengaged from the fight against drugs to focus on terrorism.

Meanwhile, two factors engaged DEA in the war on terrorism. The first was DEA's strength in human intelligence collection and management, which became critical after 11 September 2001. The second factor that brought DEA into the terrorism fight was the nexus between drug trafficking and terrorists, who increasingly fund their operations with drug trafficking proceeds.

---

[224] Grabo, 6.

[225] "Intelligence Division," *National Drug Intelligence Center*, URL: <www.usdoj.gov/ndic/about. htm#The%20Intelligence%20Division>, accessed 13 November 2006.

At the same time, however, DEA also tried to fill the vacuum left as other agencies shifted their focus from drugs to terrorism. DEA re-assumed its role as the single-focus drug law-enforcement agency. Nevertheless, the intermingling of the drug problem, international crime, and terrorism became increasingly more evident. As noted by Mark Lowenthal:

> The conjunction of the narcotics trade with international crime and possibly with terrorism as well adds a new dimension to the intelligence-gathering and policymaking problem. The profits from sales of narcotics, rather than being an end, now become the means to fund a different end. This also puts new and more difficult demands on intelligence, since terrorists and criminals operate clandestinely.[226]

For example, Baz Mohammad, a recently extradited heroin trafficker with links to the Taliban, highlights the connection between drugs and terrorism, and therefore the importance of DEA's relation to the IC. Baz Mohammad provided financial backing to Islamic extremist organizations supporting the Taliban in Afghanistan. He stated that, for Muslims, "selling heroin in the U.S. was a jihad because they took the Americans' money and at the same time the heroin they sold was killing them."[227] These new demands required DEA's intelligence program to take the more proactive, long-range look offered by predictive intelligence.

Predictive Intelligence for Policymakers

DEA policymakers will be able to use predictive intelligence to evaluate allocation of resources and funding on international, national, and regional levels. Policy informed by predictive intelligence products will also initiate localized actions to contain a threat before it can spread to other regions. When DEA policymakers shift resources and funds to an affected region and contain the threat, the fight to eliminate the threat has a higher probability of success.

Predictive intelligence will enhance the role of the intelligence analysts at DEA by demonstrating that their research capabilities can produce high impact outputs. Intelligence analysts at DEA fulfill many roles—including monitoring drug trends, investigating drug trafficking organizations, and conducting specialized projects. Many reports produced by DEA intelligence analysts contain a brief summary of possible future events related to the subject being discussed. However, these summaries rarely contain sufficient substance for policymakers to take action. A predictive intelligence program will open an opportunity for DEA intelligence analysts to provide

---

[226] Mark M. Lowenthal, *Intelligence: From Secrets to Policy* (Washington: CQ Press, 2003), 195.

[227] "Alleged Drug Lord Becomes First Afghan Extradited to US," *Agence France Presse*, 24 October 2005, accessed via LexisNexis, 8 May 2006.

policymakers with information to affect the allocation of limited assets to specific high-impact operations and programs.

WARNING METHODOLOGIES FOR DEA

Among the many methodologies, techniques, and other aspects of predictive intelligence, DEA should identify those that fit its goals. Some methodologies are very academic in nature and have not been proven in a real-world environment. Those that have been applied successfully to live-environment intelligence operations are more relevant. Lessons learned from these methodologies can enable DEA to replicate success.

To adopt such methodologies successfully, DEA needs to understand the difference between predictive and current intelligence; dedicate scarce resources exclusively to predictive intelligence; and allow predictive intelligence analysts time to do exhaustive research and apply appropriate analytic tools.

Predictive Intelligence vs. Current Intelligence

The Intelligence Community has devoted significant resources to the warning process and has refined its methodology. Hard-learned lessons have brought the warning process to its place of prominence in the IC. For example, Robert Clark observes:

> Indications and Warning (I&W) for governments involves detecting and reporting time-sensitive information on foreign developments that threaten the country's military, political or economic interests. Providing Indications and Warning on threats to national security is traditionally an intelligence organization's highest priority.[228]

DEA's emerging national security role will elevate predictive intelligence requirements within the Intelligence Division. This will necessarily move DEA analysts away from the "historically oft-stated responsibility to 'just report the facts.'"[229] An organization that is built to provide current intelligence will be hampered in its ability to provide predictive intelligence—unless it changes.

Mark Lowenthal best summarizes this issue: "Current intelligence focuses on issues that are at the forefront of the policymakers' agenda and are receiving their immediate attention. Long-term intelligence deals with trends and issues that may not be an immediate concern but are important

---

[228] Robert M. Clark, *Intelligence Analysis: Estimation and Prediction* (Baltimore: American Literary Press, 1996), 19.

[229] Dennis D. Stevens, *Between Order and Chaos: An Analytic Method for Warning*, MSSI thesis chaired by Dr. Russell Swenson (Washington: Joint Military Intelligence College, 1995), 14.

and may come to the forefront, especially if they do not receive some current attention."[230]

DEA intelligence analysts traditionally collect and report on current intelligence issues—those that may not extend more than a few weeks into the future or a snapshot of recent information. The daily functions of the intelligence analyst revolve around the current intelligence issues for which the analyst is responsible. This emphasis on current intelligence is an "impediment to recognizing a developing threat"[231] if the analysts lack the time or training to recognize potential trends that require attention now.

The major hurdle for a successful predictive intelligence program is guarding it from consumption by the daily operational needs or crises of the agency. Through Grabo's advocacy, the IC recognized that an effective warning program requires that warning intelligence analysts be sheltered from management's overwhelming requirement for current intelligence. The danger of this voracious current intelligence appetite is great because, as Robert Vickers states, the

> plethora of new US security concerns since the end of the Cold War, including terrorism, crime, narcotics has resulted in analytic resources being stretched thin. Thus, there is more current intelligence reporting and less in-depth analysis, more focus on crisis management and less attention to strategic warning.[232]

Balancing this "urgent" versus "important" tension is difficult because the demand for current intelligence is insatiable. Nevertheless, a small portion of analysts should be segregated to remain on top of strategic warning or predictive intelligence issues. Therefore, predictive intelligence should be established within DEA's Intelligence Division as a specialized field outside the purview of other intelligence activities.

Dedicated Predictive Intelligence

To implement an effective predictive intelligence program requires a dedicated staff of analysts for the predictive intelligence team. Grabo notes that "it has been deemed prudent and desirable to have indications or warning specialists who, hopefully, will not be burdened or distracted by the competing demands placed on current analysts and will be able to focus their attention solely on potential indications and their analysis in depth."[233] This team will focus on building the predictive intelligence program and should have "a balance of true substantive expertise, matched with insightful and curious

---

[230] Lowenthal, 97.

[231] Mary O. McCarthy, "The Mission to Warn: Disaster Looms," *Defense Intelligence Journal* 7, no. 2 (Fall 1998): 17.

[232] Robert D. Vickers Jr., "The State of Warning Today," *Defense Intelligence Journal* 7, no. 2 (Fall 1998): 2.

[233] Grabo, 7.

new analysts to provide the requisite energy to uncover important changes, combined with the expertise to understand their importance."[234]

Due to the ever-increasing demands on intelligence, the team is likely to be very small because "for the most part the work of warning is coordinated by a small group of people who depend on the analytic community's awareness and judgment for their support."[235] This team will analyze potential areas of future crisis and focus on the extensive research necessary to develop predictive tools such as models, scenarios, and indicator lists. These new tools are critical to the methodology of predictive intelligence.

DEA's predictive intelligence program faces the same hurdle that the IC encountered with strategic warning: protecting the predictive intelligence program from consumption by the daily operational needs and crises of the agency. DEA is aware of the critical point the organization is facing. However, with the analytical core focused full-time on current intelligence, it is difficult to allocate scarce resources to predictive analysis. Yet this step is crucial to break the cycle of current intelligence that holds the focus of the analysts on the crisis of the day. Otherwise, "we risk becoming prisoners of our inbox and unable to put daily events in a broader context, which is essential if analysts are to provide timely warning of emerging threats."[236]

Bodnar shows that other organizations that have faced similar challenges needed to shift from a here-and-now mentality in order to develop a forward-reaching predictive intelligence program:

> To provide strategic warning for strategic thinking we need to rebuild ourselves for a strategic war. To do this we must both build new tools to be able to think more effectively and reorient our organizational thinking to provide for strategic warning and planning.[237]

Getting policymakers to commit analytical resources to predictive intelligence is difficult: "The choice is between preparing for some hypothetical future contingency and supporting the current requirements of a real intelligence consumer in the here-and-now."[238] Yet this is the price management has to pay up-front for future gains.

This predictive intelligence group should be separate from current intelligence analysts and report directly to the policymakers it is serving.

---

[234] Stephen Marrin, "Preventing Intelligence Failures by Learning from the Past," *International Journal of Intelligence and CounterIntelligence* 17, no. 3 (2004): 665.

[235] Stevens, 12.

[236] John E. McLaughlin, "New Challenges and Priorities for Analysis," *Defense Intelligence Journal* 6, no. 2 (Fall 1997): 17.

[237] John W. Bodnar, *Warning Analysis for the Information Age: Rethinking the Intelligence Process* (Washington: Joint Military Intelligence College, December 2003), 125.

[238] Bruce D. Berkowitz and Allan E. Goodman, *Strategic Intelligence for American National Security*, 3d ed. (Princeton, NJ: Princeton University Press, 1989), 78.

Layers of management between the policymakers and the predictive intelligence analysts can hinder information flow between the two groups. The policymakers provide guidance to the analysts and the analysts can then be attuned to the needs of the policymaker. The closer the relationship, the more likely the predictive intelligence program will be successful. A close relationship will ensure the analysts are researching the right issues and have direct access to the policymakers they are supporting. The elimination of layers of management between the groups will help ensure the analysts can focus on predictive analysis without being drawn into the daily needs of current intelligence.

Requirement for Exhaustive Research

To provide effective predictive analysis, intelligence analysts integrate new information with previously held intelligence to evaluate how the new information influences the overall situation. This is where current intelligence ends and analysts must be allowed time to start the research process of predictive analysis, because *"it is impossible to overemphasize the importance of exhaustive research for warning."* (emphasis by Grabo)[239]

Clark's methodology for estimation is very clear and useful to the predictive intelligence analyst: "The basic analytic paradigm is *estimation* of the present state of the entity, followed by *prediction* of its future state. An estimation of past state is also useful if an extrapolation is to be made from the present state estimate."[240] Clark's methodology is in line with Grabo's, though she places even greater emphasis on the need for in-depth research of past reporting. As Patrick Henry put it, "I know of no way of judging the future but by the past."

This reveals a problem faced by the IC: there are few historians, librarians, or curators to assemble, catalog, and retrieve its classified data.[241] Here DEA has a distinct advantage over other intelligence organizations: The DEA case file system contains information that has already been collected and cataloged. DEA intelligence analysts can review these files for historical data. With the new perspective of predictive intelligence, and associated indicator lists and models, historical reports will take on new meaning.

The information that exists in DEA's archived case files can complement available open-source information to generate timelines, organizational charts, and maps to document past drug trends that developed into crises. These reviews will require a significant amount of time to complete; however, the products from the reviews will serve as long-term warning files that will be a guide to predicting and countering emerging drug trends. Timelines

---

[239] Grabo, 9.

[240] Clark, 5.

[241] John W. Bodnar, *Warning Analysis for the Information Age: Rethinking the Intelligence Process* (Washington: Joint Military Intelligence College, December 2003), 47-51.

established will allow DEA policymakers to make informed decisions on emerging trends based on decision points developed from indicator lists compiled during the review.

The first critical function of the reviews is "keeping chronologies, maintaining databases and arraying data. . . . These techniques are the heavy lifting of analysis, but this is what analysts are supposed to do."[242] Analysts compile the highlights from the intelligence available and document the information in a chronological timeline. This process will highlight the key points during the expansion of a drug trend. These key points in time will cue the analysts to establish and document the indicators. Analysts can use the indicators extracted during this process to build an indicator list to assist analysts in the field in the early identification of significant drug trends within their areas of responsibility. The improved recognition of emerging trends in the field will lead to earlier notification of DEA Headquarters' predictive intelligence analysts. With earlier notification, they will be able to prepare warning products to alert the decisionmakers in time to take action to curtail or eliminate the identified threat.

APPLICATION OF ANALYTICAL TOOLS

Once the job of research is well along, predictive intelligence analysts have a number of tools they can use to organize and evaluate the information that has been collected. Among these are the Analysis of Competing Hypotheses, Multi-dimensional Analysis, persistence and cyclic forecasting, and—above all—critical thinking.

Analysis of Competing Hypotheses

A key to predictive intelligence production is examining the widest possible range of possibilities. As Grabo rather archly remarks, "The consideration of alternative or multiple hypotheses to explain sets of data is a fundamental of the scientific method which, curiously enough, often is given scant attention in intelligence problems."

Richards J. Heuer Jr. presents hypothesis testing as an analytical tool in *Psychology of Intelligence Analysis*. Heuer's presentation of Analysis of Competing Hypotheses (ACH) applies to the scenario development phase of DEA's predictive analysis program. He describes ACH as "a tool to aid judgment on important issues requiring careful weighing of alternative explanations or conclusions."[243] All reasonable alternative hypotheses compete for validation based on the facts available. Analysts consider all new information received not only to support the current hypotheses, but also to disprove them. Analysts eliminate any hypothesis that they disprove.

---

[242] McCarthy, 21.

[243] Richards J. Heuer Jr., *Psychology of Intelligence Analysis* (Washington: Center for the Study of Intelligence, 1999), 95.

This helps them to narrow the list of reasonable alternatives and to overcome "satisficing"—selecting the first alternative that appears to be "good enough" rather than examining all alternatives to determine which is "best."[244] This methodology also helps ensure that analysts will not selectively fit available information to suit the needs of their "favorite" hypothesis. Instead, it makes them compare the available information to other possibilities before selecting the best-supported hypothesis (see Figure 1).

Heuer also echoes Grabo's point that analysts should carefully review similar situations or scenarios from the past. Heuer infers that sound predictive or forecasting models will be "a generalization based on the study of many examples of some phenomenon."[245]

---

1) Identify the possible hypotheses to be considered. Use a group of analysts with different perspectives to brainstorm the possibilities.

2) Make a list of significant evidence and arguments for and against each hypothesis.

3) Prepare a matrix with hypotheses across the top and evidence down the side. Analyze the "diagnosticity" of the evidence and arguments — that is, identify which items are most helpful in judging the relative likelihood of the hypotheses.

4) Refine the matrix. Reconsider the hypotheses and delete evidence and arguments that have no diagnostic value.

5) Draw tentative conclusions about the relative likelihood of each hypothesis. Proceed by trying to disprove the hypotheses rather than prove them.

6) Analyze how sensitive your conclusion is to a few critical items of evidence. Consider the consequences for your analysis if that evidence were wrong, misleading, or subject to a different interpretation.

7) Report conclusions. Discuss the relative likelihood of all the hypotheses, not just the most likely one.

8) Identify milestones for future observation that may indicate events are taking a different course than expected.

Figure 1. The Analysis of Competing Hypotheses Process
Source: Heuer, 97.

---

[244] Heuer, 43.
[245] Heuer, 34.

With the completion of each review for the various major drug trends of the past, analysts can create a new model. Each of the models can potentially give insights to new or emerging drug trends. Models will display some similar qualities, and some qualities will be unique to a specific model. As the number of available models grows, it will be easier to gauge potential futures for an emerging trend based on parallels drawn from past trends. This brings the predictive intelligence cycle to a point where analysts can develop strategic warning scenarios with some degree of confidence. "One of the most valuable techniques for determining the scale of a threat is to subject the evidence to an 'analysis of competing hypotheses.'" [246] With each established model, intelligence can be collected that will further validate the model's hypothesis, or refute it.

This is an important portion of the process; "as each bit of evidence is obtained, the analysts should try to determine whether it is consistent or inconsistent with each of the hypotheses. Eventually one or two hypotheses will claim a preponderance of evidence."[247] As analysis of the available intelligence narrows the field of viable competing hypotheses, the confidence in a remaining few will increase.

Multidimensional Analysis

Grabo's methodology best fits predictive intelligence on drug trafficking trends, but Bodnar's multidimensional analysis (MDA) bridges the gap to the use of predictive intelligence against drug trafficking organizations. Bodnar's concept of multidimensional analysis addresses the three dimensions in space (often expressed in longitude, latitude, and altitude), one dimension in time (represented with a timeline), and two dimensions in energy (enthalpy and entropy, which he expresses as organizations and the forces that hold them together or tear them apart).

DEA is already very capable of producing graphic representations of the six dimensions addressed by Bodnar. These dimensions can be captured in a meaningful graphic format for analysis with maps (two of three dimensions in space—the third, altitude, usually is unimportant for analysis), a timeline, and organizational charts. These three products "must be used in an integrated manner to track the organization and operation of networks."[248] The products created out of the MDA model's integration of maps, timelines, and organizational charts can provide a clear snapshot and assist in the identification of specific information for targeted intelligence collection.

To produce the most comprehensive models possible, Bodnar recommends taking the bottom-up model approach and combining the results with a top-down approach. The bottom-up model approach will show the structure

---

[246] McCarthy, 21.

[247] McCarthy, 21.

[248] Bodnar, 94.

of the model, which determines the functionality of the organization. The top-down model will show how the functions of the organizational model determine its structure.

Each model has specific positive applications, as well has definite shortcomings. The top-down model helps to develop a clear depiction of the notional network, which is valuable for the planning of intelligence collection. The top-down model tells the analyst where to look and what to look for, but provides no immediate intelligence until the results of the collection tasking are reported. The bottom-up model will reveal the network as it exists at any given point in time. This provides concrete intelligence but does little to define gaps in intelligence for collection planning. The bottom-up model depicts the intelligence contained in the reporting, but cannot provide guidance on where to focus collection efforts next.

Persistence and Cyclic Forecasting

For "continuing situations" like drug use, Carney and Indelicarto's study provides an example of the types of analysis that could be used—persistence forecasting and cyclic forecasting.

> The flow and use of drugs are not static events, but are continuing situations. Understanding of persistence and cycles is the key to seeing the overarching causative factors of the drug problem. This concept is useful in warning, because long-term, persistent threats may not be vulnerable to US counteractions. They may have to be endured as part of predictable cycles. While the core group of users will remain, casual or recreational drug users will vary according to the cycles of abuse.[249]

This type of insight to the inner workings of the drug consumption cycle provides a tool that is valuable to predictive intelligence analysts. Accurate predictions are more probable when the analysts consider all the available information that fits into the context of the situation that they are analyzing, utilizing a number of methodologies.

Critical Thinking

Predictive intelligence analysts will benefit greatly from education and training that enhances critical thinking skills and knowledge of strategic analysis. Management should enhance training programs to instill critical thinking skills in all analysts, but this skill will be particularly valuable to analysts involved in predictive intelligence analysis. Humans have cognitive limitations; therefore, analysts need analytical techniques and methodologies to assemble all the available intelligence and draw accurate conclusions. But

---

[249] Donald J. Carney and Thomas C. Indelicarto, "Indications and Warning and the New World Environment: The Drug War Example," *Defense Intelligence Journal* 3 (1994), 100.

first, intelligence personnel need the skills necessary to use the methodology. Research indicates that analysts need an early introduction to critical thinking skills. The ability to think critically will lead to better analysis and a better mindset to produce predictive analysis reports.

The ideal DEA predictive intelligence analyst will have a balanced background with a mix of strategic intelligence and law-enforcement experience. However, even when the analyst has a strong basis on which to build predictive scenarios, intelligence is often insufficient to give a definitive solution to the issue. "One of an analyst's most difficult tasks is the challenge of identifying the proper analytical framework for interpreting incomplete information."[250] Experienced analysts will have more of a framework to overcome this problem, but novice and experienced analysts alike will benefit from formalized training in this area. Lowenthal states, "Analysts must be trained to develop some inner, deeper knowledge that will enable them to read between the lines, to make educated guesses or intuitive choices when the intelligence is insufficient."[251]

Although intelligence analysts sometimes face situations where information is lacking, they often confront a large volume of conflicting information. When this is the case, analysts should be able to evaluate all the information available to determine its validity and applicability to the situation. "Analysts naturally favor information that fits their well-formed mental models, and often dismiss other information that might support an alternative."[252] Analysts need to develop critical thinking skills to reach correct conclusions in this challenging task. "Expert critical reasoning imposes rigor on the analysis process thereby increasing accuracy in resulting products."[253] For this reason, critical thinking skills are vital, and only training early in the analyst's career allows time for these skills to develop. Without early training in critical thinking skills, analysts develop the tendency of taking reported or printed information at face value, without considering its source or validity. The explosion of available open source information and access to classified intelligence exacerbates this problem.

Training in critical thinking skills early in the predictive analysts' career will foster better analysis. As Moore and Krizan put it:

> The value of successful analysis is evidenced in the rigorous methods analysts employ to guarantee that their judgments push beyond obvious conclusions. Critical thinking skills contribute extensively

---

[250] Roger C. George, "Fixing the Problem of Analytical Mind-Sets: Alternative Analysis," *International Journal of Intelligence and CounterIntelligence* 17, no. 3 (2004): 388.

[251] Lowenthal, 108.

[252] George, 389.

[253] David T. Moore, *Creating Intelligence: Evidence and Inference in the Analysis Process*, MSSI Thesis chaired by Frank J. Hughes (Washington: Joint Military Intelligence College, July 2002), 205.

here to ensure that tendencies toward arrogance are tempered by a questioning of assumptions, thorough examination of evidence, and logically derived inferences. The results of the process are judgments that are as clear, accurate, and precise as analyst skills and available evidence will allow; these judgments stay grounded in reality.[254]

Research indicates that critical thinking skills can greatly enhance sound intelligence analysis. Yet in his study of enlisted military members of the Navy and Marine Corps, Morrow documented that intelligence training provided no significant increase in critical thinking skills.[255] Most basic training courses tend to focus more on the hardware, databases, and basic knowledge needed to become functional at a beginner's skill level. However, students need skills such as analysis, synthesis, and evaluation to conduct effective intelligence. Training courses for intelligence analysts need to incorporate critical thinking skills if intelligence organizations want their analysts to provide methodically evaluated intelligence products.

The good news is that some minor restructuring of the instructional method of courses can significantly increase the critical thinking skills of intelligence analysts. Courses redesigned for analysts to have an open dialog with each other, provide the reasoning for their assessments, exchange ideas, and work solutions in small groups can greatly increase critical thinking skills. Writing exercises also give analysts more time to consider alternatives and think through scenarios and consider different points of view and potential outcomes, which also enhances critical thinking skills.

Analysts and their managers should also be aware of the mind-set developed by the analysts or the agency for which they work. The mind-set of the analyst can be a limiting factor to accurate predictive analysis if critical thinking skills do not override self-censorship of intelligence. Mind-set tends to be counterproductive, especially among senior analysts who have accumulated significant experience and have hardened their positions on the subject matter for which they are responsible. "The more expert one becomes, the more firm become one's set of expectations about the world. While these mind-sets can be very helpful in sorting through incoming data, they become an Achilles heel to a professional strategist or intelligence analyst when they become out of date because of new international dynamics."[256]

For these reasons, a team of junior analysts with the guidance of a senior analyst should conduct analytical reviews for predictive intelligence. This will assist new analysts in building an expert knowledge of the relevant

---

[254] David T. Moore and Lisa Krizan, "Evaluating Intelligence: A Competency-Based Model," *International Journal of Intelligence and Counterintelligence* 18, no. 2 (Summer 2005): 211.

[255] Major Craig D. Morrow, USA, *The Development of Critical Thinking Skills in the Training of Enlisted Intelligence Analysts*, MSSI thesis chaired by Victoria Aud-McCool (Washington: Joint Military Intelligence College, June 2004), 13.

[256] George, 387.

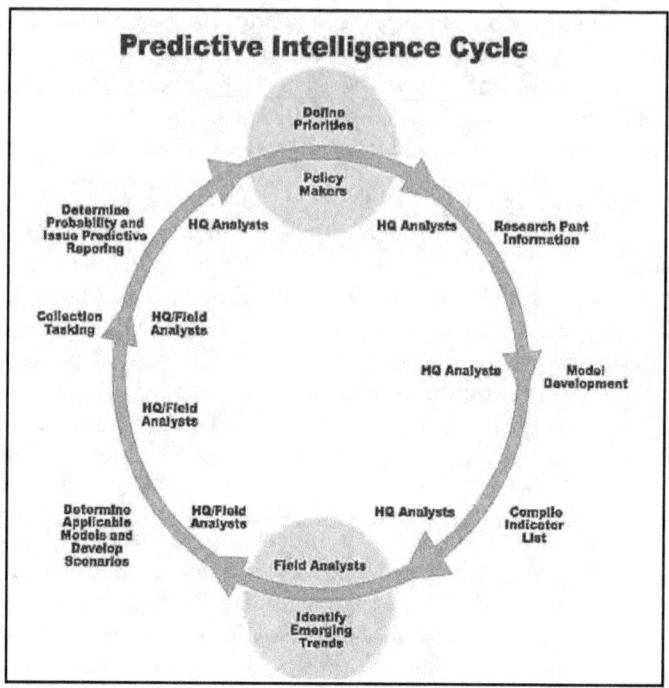

Figure 2. Predictive Intelligence Cycle
Source: Author's conception.

research topics and afford a fresh perspective on historical data. Heuer points out that "an intelligence analyst assigned to work on a topic or country for the first time may generate accurate insights that have been overlooked by experienced analysts who have worked on the same problem for 10 years. A fresh perspective is sometimes useful; past experience can handicap as well as aid analysis."[257]

PREDICTIVE INTELLIGENCE PROGRAM IMPLEMENTATION

To implement a successful predictive intelligence program, DEA has available to it a methodology that is not merely academic in nature, but based on real-world experience. Grabo's methodology for strategic warning has been used by the Intelligence Community and can be adapted to fulfill DEA's requirement for a predictive intelligence program.

Based on research and evaluation of the available literature, this author created the "Predictive Intelligence Cycle" (see Figure 2). This cycle denotes the most practical elements of methodologies described in available

---

[257] Heuer, 11.

literature as they apply to DEA's predictive intelligence needs. The predictive intelligence cycle serves as the systematic guide to DEA's endeavor and represents the synthesis of the best real-world and theoretical applications of warning intelligence for this issue.

Predictive intelligence methodology is a multiple-step process. Intelligence analysts and managers evaluate the current situation to establish a starting point for the research. Analysts and policymakers then work together to start the predictive intelligence cycle, as "the first step in producing intelligence analysis is to determine what information must be analyzed."[258]

Once policymakers establish the direction of the analysis, the analysts delve into the past to uncover all available intelligence on the issue, and related issues, because "in many cases, precedents exist for continuous phenomena, and researchers can infer future events on the basis of analogous antecedents."[259] From this research, the analysts formulate a series of competing hypotheses. These in turn are developed as models that seek to explain and predict current and future trends.

These models will serve the predictive intelligence analysts as well as the field analysts. The models will generate a number of indicators or expected developments if trends move in a particular direction. Analysts can then compile indicator lists based on comparisons of the current drug trend to the models of past trends.

By noting the presence or absence of such indicators, field analysts can compare emerging trends to available models. By doing so, they will both evaluate the usefulness of particular models and report more effectively on those trends.

When analysts identify a model that seems to apply to emerging real-world developments, they can develop predictive scenarios based on timelines generated by past drug trends within the model.

These timelines will drive additional intelligence collection to confirm, refine, or refute the scenarios. As one or more scenarios emerge as having the most confirming intelligence, probabilities can be assigned and predictive intelligence reporting can be issued to the policymaker.

Define Priorities

DEA will address several factors in developing a viable predictive intelligence program. It is apparent that the policymakers of DEA are

---

[258] Bruce D. Berkowitz and Allan E. Goodman, *Strategic Intelligence for American National Security* (Princeton, NJ: Princeton University Press, 1989), 86.

[259] Jerome K. Clauser and Sandra M. Weir, *Intelligence Research Methodology: An Introduction to Techniques and Procedures for Conducting Research in Defense Intelligence* (State College, PA: HRB-Singer, 1976), 297.

supportive of the development of a predictive intelligence program. That being the case, a team of analysts should be selected to start the predictive intelligence program, and all analysts should be trained on the concept of predictive intelligence and its importance to DEA's long-term goals. It is critical for DEA to train all intelligence analysts on basic methods of predictive intelligence to ensure the earliest possible detection of emerging drug trends through such teamwork.

Next, DEA can establish the predictive intelligence team as a separate dedicated unit to work with the policymakers. The policymakers will have to provide guidance and priorities to this predictive intelligence team. An initial step in predictive intelligence is for managers to define the problem on which the predictive intelligence should focus. Goldman states, "Understanding how a problem is defined can enhance the capabilities of the intelligence analyst in comprehending the threat as it may be perceived by the policymaker."[260] This will allow the dedicated analysts to begin their research.

Engage in Research

Based on the guidance received, the predictive intelligence unit will have to relate identified threats to their projected economic and political contexts. At the same time, the team will conduct research to establish a baseline of information so as to compare and contrast emerging models with historical ones.

Analysts assigned to do predictive intelligence need to complete a significant number of file reviews because "predictions based on the assumption that previous events will occur again are usually based on large numbers of observations."[261] In DEA's predictive intelligence program especially, "methodologies that hope to project target intentions into the future must be based on data collection for a longer time period into the past; current intelligence to build warning intelligence."[262]

Prediction of events is less complex when "precedents exist for continuous phenomena, and researchers can infer future events on the basis of analogous antecedents."[263] For example, if drug trend prognosis is called for, the assigned analysts can review significant drug trends that have occurred in the United States in the past involving crack cocaine, methamphetamine, and ecstasy.

Such comprehensive reviews of drug epidemics will accomplish two goals in a predictive intelligence program. First, the reviews will give the analysts

---

[260] Jan Goldman, "Warning and the Policy Process: Problem Definition and Chaos Theory," *Defense Intelligence Journal* 7, no. 2 (Fall 1998): 67.

[261] Clauser and Weir, 298.

[262] Bodnar, 53.

[263] Clauser and Weir, 297.

conducting the research an expert knowledge from which to draw insights and conclusions in their predictive analysis. This process will also address the requirements of Karen Tandy's guidance: "We need to follow-up to learn more information, we need to do After Action Reports/Lessons Learned."[264] It is necessary to delve into previous drug trends to analyze how the organization handled the situations. Lessons learned are frequently forgotten, and it will increase the validity of the analysis to include past successes and failures. "To strengthen the reliability of your prediction you should possess additional packages of knowledge. First, you should know about the courses of action followed in the past."[265] Leaders and analysts rotate out and often the same errors will occur repeatedly. Predictive intelligence that includes the lessons learned from the past will better serve today's policymaker by refreshing institutional knowledge at the time it is most needed.

Develop Models

Analysts conduct a comprehensive review of past drug trends to develop potential models; "predictive model development and validation make up a significant portion of intelligence research activities."[266] These reviews should thoroughly document the history of each of the drug trends. Timelines and organizational charts are appropriately developed and integrated into the models to chronicle the initial appearance of the drug and the trafficking organizations involved.[267]

This type of comprehensive review is essential to produce the variety of baseline models of past trends that can develop future scenarios to map, track, and anticipate developing trends. Clauser and Weir emphasize the importance of this process: "Predictive research attempts to formulate new principles which would enable the researcher to predict, anticipate, or foretell what the results of the interaction of variables will be."[268] As a CIA study noted, the more "potential analogs an analyst has at his or her disposal, the greater the likelihood of selecting an appropriate one."[269]

---

[264] In March 2004, Assistant Administrator for Intelligence Harold D. Wankel, with the support of the Administrator, commissioned Science Applications International Corporation (SAIC) to conduct a "Top Down Review" of the DEA Intelligence Program. This outside review of the Intelligence Program assessed DEA's capabilities and needs based upon new national security imperatives and the Administrator's Vision. The SAIC review did not fully address Predictive Intelligence or Analytical Tools and Methodologies.

[265] Kent, 58-59.

[266] Clauser and Weir, 74.

[267] John T. Picarelli, *Transnational Threat Indications and Warning: The Utility of Network Analysis*, A Military and Intelligence Analysis Group, Pacific-Sierra Research Corporation Report [2004].

[268] Clauser and Weir, 77.

[269] Heuer, 3.

Compile Indicator Lists

During the in-depth analytical review and model development, analysts will identify indicators and compile tailored indicator lists. The retrospective review of these indicators will show when critical decisions were, or could have been, made to influence the development of past trends. This type of after-action review will show what actions policymakers undertook to affect the trend and what opportunities to affect it were missed. This will give the planners a guide with a timeline to revise and implement policy decisions to minimize the threat of the new drug trend.

Depending on the new threat and its similarity to past trends, policymakers may be able to identify when to implement controls on key chemicals or other substances needed to produce the drug, or when to begin an educational program to inform potential users of the dangers the drug poses.

More important for the process of warning, the indicator-based models would reveal indications of the trends as they emerge. These indicator lists will serve as a framework for institutional knowledge, which analysts can update and refine to serve future analysts in predicting future drug trends.

As analysts construct more models of past drug epidemics, they can compare and contrast the results. Analysts can then determine which indicators are common to past trends and which indicators are unique to a certain drug trend.

Identify Emerging Trends

Following the predictive intelligence cycle, predictive intelligence analysts at Headquarters provide field analysts a range of indicator-based models. The models will provide analogies for the field analysts to compare against new or emerging trends.

By finding the best analogies, the field analysts will be better able to identify emerging threats based on the models of previous trends. They in turn can notify the predictive intelligence analysts at Headquarters when they see a new trend in the early stages of development. The predictive intelligence analysts at Headquarters can perform an exhaustive review of intelligence and information to assess the threat on a national or global scale. Early detection of an emerging threat will allow analysts to task additional collection to address intelligence gaps.

Determine Applicable Models and Develop Scenarios

Once analysts have matched their models against reports from the field, they can begin to determine which are the most appropriate. These can be used to extrapolate from past trends as a baseline for prediction. Such a model, "as it describes some of the underlying pressures on crime, can provide a useful baseline for developing forecasts."[270] Nevertheless, the historical perspective is only the starting point for postulating various scenarios. Analysts routinely consider many variables, and some of these variables will not be the same as in previously documented trends.

This caveat notwithstanding, indicator-based scenarios will be largely dependent on baseline information derived from the review of previous drug trends. The predictive intelligence analysts will also use historical models to help fill remaining intelligence gaps until requests for more intelligence are fulfilled. The generation of multiple scenarios is useful to drive intelligence collection. Collection of intelligence on all selected scenarios will enhance their separate validity because in some cases evidence will refute, and therefore eliminate, a scenario. A larger number of scenarios may be expected to give a more reliable set from which to draw information.

Collection Tasking

This review will allow the development of a variety of plausible scenarios on which analysts will be able collect additional intelligence to base their predictions of future emerging trends. These scenarios will be the basis for the additional intelligence collection requirements analysts will levy to focus on the emerging threat before it evolves into a crisis.

Determine Probability and Issue Predictive Reporting

Finally, the predictive intelligence unit will have to communicate its predictions, in the form of a warning product, to the policymakers in time for them to plan for and deploy the necessary assets while allocating the financial resources against the forecast threat.

The intelligence analyst gathers all available information, makes relevant observations, and proposes possible alternative futures. Analysts put these in order based on logic, possibility, and consistency with the available evidence. Analysts can subject all scenarios to further tests as new information becomes available. If new information does not support any of the existing scenarios, the analyst develops new ones and repeats the cycle. When new information fits, analysts reorder the scenarios accordingly. If a scenario is disproved, it is eliminated. The remaining best-supported scenarios become the basis for the predictive reporting.

Analysts should link each prediction with the likelihood or probability that it will occur. As the best-supported hypotheses emerge, the predictive intelligence analyst often makes not just a prediction "but also a rough

---

[270] Dr. Stephen Schneider, *Methodological Design*, 2002, Report Number 2002-7, URL: <www. http://canada.justice.gc.ca/en/ps/rs/rep/2002/rr2002-7/rr2002-7_007.html>, accessed 28 October 2005.

estimate of the probability of the predicted outcome."[271] Without this critical exchange of knowledge, the policymaker may be overconfident in decisions made on incomplete intelligence.

Analysts should then track their predictions to develop a record of accomplishment for each analyst. "Ideally, intelligence managers and analysts will work to record predictions together with confidence levels, then check them after the appropriate amount of time has elapsed."[272] This record will develop confidence in the analysts as well as the policymakers.

The analyst produces a range of predictions based on the available models. Although it is the responsibility of the analyst to present several competing scenarios to take into account the variables that may occur, the "most-likely scenario must be developed, usually with incomplete information, with enough lead time for the policymaker to react."[273] Intelligence is rarely complete, and "every prediction (or predictive model) is based on assumptions. And it is usually the validity of the assumption that determines the accuracy of the prediction."[274] Analysts should clearly define the assumptions derived from this inferred information and make them apparent to the policymakers. The predictive intelligence analyst knows that "the assumptions on which the scenario is based must be made explicit, because of the great potential for misuse."[275] Therefore, the analysts inform the policymaker of the assumptions on which they have based the analysis.

CONCLUSION

It will be difficult to segregate a small number of DEA analysts, remove them from the daily crisis-driven routine, and allow them to engage in the extensive research needed for predictive analysis. If it is done, however, a predictive intelligence program, based on these methodologies, can break the cycle of current intelligence and start to provide strategic warning to DEA policymakers. This will inform and warn decisionmakers and executives in time to implement policy and plan programs to avert threats before they balloon into all-consuming issues.

---

[271] Steven Rieber, "Intelligence Analysis and Judgmental Calibration," *International Journal of Intelligence and CounterIntelligence* 17, no. 1 (2004): 97.

[272] Rieber, 107.

[273] George, 393.

[274] Clauser and Weir, 297.

[275] Clark, 189.

OBSTACLES TO INTEGRATION

The issue of culture comes up repeatedly when we discuss the reasons for a lack of integration between LE and the IC. Each has its own unique culture. True, many aspects of these cultures are shared: duty, honor, country; protect and serve; always prepared; fidelity, bravery, integrity; faithful unto death. Such mottoes resonate within both communities. Nevertheless, in many ways these cultures—customary beliefs, social forms, and traits; shared attitudes, values, goals, and practices—make it difficult for us to work together in the seamless fashion "that the threat demands and our citizens deserve."

As Maureen Baginski also notes in the Foreword, "soft stuff" like culture represents "the greatest challenge to achieving a partnership between Law Enforcement and the Intelligence Community." Part of that challenge is inherent in the nature of the communities. There will always be a certain amount of tension between such organizations, whether the CIA and FBI; GRU and KGB; or British Army intelligence and the Royal Irish Constabulary, as depicted in the essay that follows. Recognizing and taking account of such "where you stand depends on where you sit" issues is critical.

Some tensions, however, are the result of particular circumstances. The second essay in this section argues that this is part of the problem in the United States. Many of the lamented LE-IC practices—undue secrecy, lack of innovation, failure to "connect the dots"—are partly the result of the communities' diligent efforts to obey their political masters. The cultures of both communities were shaped by the revelations and reforms of the 1970s. These final essays suggest some obstacles to implementing any reforms now; namely, the general nature of the institutions and the specifics of their shared history.

BRITISH MILITARY INTELLIGENCE-LAW ENFORCEMENT INTEGRATION IN THE IRISH WAR OF INDEPENDENCE, 1919-1921

Captain Devlin Kostal, USAF
Master of Science of Strategic Intelligence, 2004

The integration of law enforcement and the armed forces is an enduring problem, especially in societies where the two functions are expected to remain separate. Early in the 20th century, this problem bedeviled the British military and police forces involved in the Irish War of Independence. Despite—or perhaps because of—their recent experience in defeating the Central Powers, the British were stymied by the Irish Republican Army (IRA). The British Army and police in Ireland fought the same enemy on different terms and in different fashions. The operational integration of their efforts was usually flawed, at best. The integration of their intelligence capabilities followed much the same pattern. The answer to the question, "How well did the British integrate military and police intelligence efforts during the Irish War for Independence?" is that their integration was significantly hindered, particularly by shortcomings in the areas of training, organization, culture, and personalities. The inability of the British to address these short-comings holds lessons for others who seek to integrate military and police in general and intelligence in particular.

THE IRISH WAR OF INDEPENDENCE

The British were slow to react to the insurgent threat in Ireland after World War I. During the Great War, the Easter Rising of 1916 in Dublin had been put down quickly and brutally. When the war ended in November 1918, there seemed little reason to expect that Ireland would become a problem any time soon. After all, though the Irish had a history of attempted uprisings, all had been suppressed successfully.

The War began on 21 January 1919 when the Dáil Éireann (Irish Parliament) declared war. Fighting an unconventional style of warfare, the IRA attacked the police forces on the island, primarily the Royal Irish Constabulary (RIC), in order to render the island ungovernable. By a campaign of social ostracism, assassination of key personnel, and attacks on isolated police barracks, the IRA was soon able to put the police forces on the defensive. Once the War overwhelmed the resources of the police forces in Ireland, British Army troops stationed on the island were added to the forces fighting the Republicans.

The British military had long been stationed in Ireland, but was not usually used to help maintain public order. When it was ordered to do so in 1919, the military leadership showed little enthusiasm for the task. As stated by Lt.-Col. H. de Watteville in a discussion of military support for the

Major General Sir Henry Hugh Tudor
Source: "Henry Hugh Tudor," *Wikipedia*, URL: <en.wikipedia.org/ wiki/ Image:Henry_Hugh_tudor. jpg>, accessed 5 December 2006.

police, "Civil authorities should, in every possible case, be allowed to deal with the maintenance of public order and security unaided; they must only summon the military power to their assistance when their own capacity has been recognized as inadequate to cope with the forces of disorder."[276] The top British military man in Ireland, the General Officer Commanding-in-Chief (GOCinC), argued the military was not needed to suppress the rebellion. Nevertheless, he was directed to employ the Army in support of the police by the island's civil authorities.

The Republicans initially employed tactics that took advantage of this lack of commitment within the Army. When the War began, the IRA carefully targeted only law enforcement entities. They specifically avoided direct conflict with the British Army. Nevertheless, as the rebellion progressed through 1919, the Army was drawn further and further into the fight.

In May 1920, Major-General Sir Henry H. Tudor was appointed as the chief of police for Ireland. As such, he advised the administration on police matters, but also had coordination authority for military and police operations on the island. The distinction of his being a police commander rather than a military one (although Tudor had been pulled from the military ranks to serve as a policeman) is vital. Because the British government had not declared martial law, the police forces were the supported agency. Although the GOCinC, General Sir Nevil Macready, outranked Tudor, Tudor's civil position gave him considerable authority over Macready's military forces. In fact, as a policeman, Tudor was not answerable to anyone in the military. He

---

[276] Lieutenant-Colonel H. de Watteville, British Army, "The Employment of Troops Under the Emergency Regulations," *The Army Quarterly* 12 (April and July 1926): 283.

reported instead to the civil government in Ireland, headed by the Viceroy. The Viceroy would issue direction to Chief of Police Tudor, who would ask for assistance as the "Civil Authority" from the military. Macready, as the military commander, would then order his forces to assist Tudor's police. The request for assistance from Tudor was not one that Macready could turn down easily; he could refer the matter to London, but not too often.[277]

In many cases, however, Macready, acting in a solely military capacity, did not coordinate his efforts with Tudor. And when the police did not require military help, Tudor did not coordinate his efforts with Macready. This bifurcated arrangement posed one of the major integration obstacles for British forces at the tactical level.

Due in no small part to the ineffective action by the British forces in Ireland through 1919, requests were made for more Army troops by all levels of the police command structure. This request for military troops was augmented by a beefing up of the police forces' own capabilities. Tudor, seeing the huge problems in the RIC, initiated an intensive police recruiting campaign in England, Scotland, and Wales for reinforcements. Most of the candidates had been members of the British Army and each was scrutinized by the police before enlistment. Tudor's deputy maintained that "the re-arming of the RIC, the provision of new equipment and mechanical transport, and the arrival of their reinforcements, rapidly reestablished the morale of the police, and instead of being immobilized in their barracks they took a more active part in patrolling, and helped to open up the well of ordinary police information which had run dry."[278]

In March 1920, the RIC was augmented by the Royal Irish Constabulary Reserve Force, the now-infamous "Black and Tans." The Tans were mostly former British Army enlisted men, specifically recruited for their wartime service. They were not trained as policemen, but assigned directly to the RIC barracks and integrated into the RIC patrols. The name came from the fact that, when this massive influx occurred, the RIC did not have enough police uniforms for all the new men, so they had to wear khaki Army trousers initially. Some wag suggested that the dark blue police uniform blouse and tan trousers recalled the name of a well-known pack of fox hounds in County Limerick. Even after the supply problem was remedied in a few months, the name stuck. The Tans were clearly an attempt by the police to obtain military-like support without having to get it from the Army.

In August 1920, an additional police augmentation force was formed under Brigadier-General Frank P. Crozier as the Auxiliary Division of the RIC (or "Auxies"). Recruited from among demobilized former British Army officers, they were formed into 15 companies of 100 men each. These companies were

---

[277] William Kautt, interview by the author, 21 February 2004.

[278] Brigadier-General Ormonde de L'Epée Winter, *Winter's Tale: An Autobiography* (London: Richards Press, 1955), 293-294.

to be used as mobile strike or raid forces in the south and west, areas of the heaviest IRA activity. Unlike the standard RIC chain of command, which ran from the Divisional Commissioners to the County Commissioners to the District Inspectors, the Auxies reported directly to Tudor.[279]

Although ostensibly part of the RIC, they were not attached to the RIC barracks and performed their own patrols as a police mobile strike force. For the most part, they were identified by the Republicans as Tans, and even today the Tans and Auxies are lumped together, particularly in broader descriptions of the atrocities committed near the end of the war. They immediately began a harsh campaign of interrogations and raids, in effect terrorizing the local populace. The argument can be made, however, that their early success was due in no small part to the fact that they simply lowered themselves to using the violent tactics already being employed by the IRA.

Crozier ultimately resigned as the commander in February 1921, in large part because he was prevented from disciplining his troops' excesses. Indeed, there seemed to be tacit approval for the violent actions of the Auxies from Tudor, Macready, and even Prime Minister David Lloyd George.[280] Macready implied Tudor's complicity in the reprisals when he wrote that "assassination is rife and the G.S. [General Staff] have now adopted it a lá Tudor and Co."[281] Ultimately, however, although the escalated violence and atrocities instilled a certain amount of fear among the Irish, the end result was to strengthen the Republicans' resolve rather than destroy their spirit.

The British proposed a truce in the spring of 1921, which was agreed and implemented in July. Further negotiations continued until the Anglo-Irish Treaty was signed in December of that year. The British conceded the lower two-thirds of Ireland to the Republicans, keeping only six of the nine counties of Ulster as a province of the United Kingdom. This agreement was by no means perfect, but, as Collins stated, it was much more than the Republicans could have expected even three years previously.[282]

BRITISH INTELLIGENCE IN THE WAR

The IRA was quickly able to put the British intelligence effort in the War on the defensive by targeting police officers in general and intelligence officers in particular. This tactic was complemented by intense pressure on the Irish public to cut off all contact with the authorities, drying up the police's

---

[279] Kautt, interview.

[280] Keith Jeffery, *The British Army and the Crisis of Empire* (Manchester: Manchester University Press, 1984), 85.

[281] General Sir Nevil Macready, GOCinC, British Forces Ireland, personal letter to Lt.-Gen. Sir Hugh Jeudwine, Commander of 5th Division, April 1922, Imperial War Museum (IWM), papers of Lt.-Gen. Sir Hugh Jeudwine, 72/82/2.

[282] Hayden Talbot, *Michael Collins' Own Story Told to Hayden Talbot* (London: Hutchinson & Co., 1922), 78.

Michael Collins, IRA Director of Intelligence
Source: "Michael Collins (Irish Leader)," *Wikipedia*, URL: <en. wikipedia.org/ wiki. Image:Portrait_of_Micheal_O_ Coileain.jpg>, accessed 5 December 2006.

traditional sources of information. British attempts to reinforce the police, noted above, included attempts to reinforce their intelligence personnel and sources. Despite some successes, however, they were never able to re-establish the sort of information dominance they had enjoyed before Michael Collins, the head of intelligence for the IRA, launched the IRA's counter-intelligence campaign.

Police Intelligence

The Royal Irish Constabulary (RIC) had been in Ireland since well before the Easter Rising in 1916 as the national police force. As such, they had plenty of experience dealing with Irish dissension. The Dublin Metropolitan Police (DMP) maintained a similar function within the boundaries of Dublin. The relationship and liaison between the two organizations was continuous and extensive. The DMP's G (detective) Division had several officers responsible for "political" work, and the RIC had a few officers for similar duties. The RIC forwarded political reports to a Special Crime Branch in Dublin Castle, staffed by two inspectors and several clerks, which was responsible for maintaining situational awareness of political crime for the Irish Executive.[283]

The police (including Scotland Yard's Secret Service) had a pervasive intelligence gathering network in Ireland, which would presumably give warning of any new rising. This British espionage network in Ireland was renowned as one of the best in the world. Collins said that the British Secret

---

[283] Eunan O'Halpin, "British Intelligence in Ireland, 1914-1921," in *The Missing Dimension: Governments and Intelligence Communities in the Twentieth Century*, eds. Christopher Andrew and David Dilks (Urbana: University of Illinois Press, 1984), 54-55.

Service "had for its cornerstone a historical and unhappy fact about the Irish people, the presence in every generation of a small minority ready to sell their country for English gold."[284]

The "G-men" (a term coined in Ireland from the G Division) had been engaged in espionage since roughly 1850 with the formation of the Fenian movement.[285] According to Collins, there were "spies on every street," representing in his estimation "one-tenth of the actual total of the spy organization. Every street in the city was an open book to the English agents."[286] The Irish Republicans assumed the British had a virtually unlimited budget with which to buy informants.

Attacks on the Police

Collins described his strategy against the British as twofold: shut off the police's sources of information within the Irish population and then attack the police themselves. He announced that "the way to do this was obvious, and it fell naturally into two parts-making it unhealthy for Irishmen to betray their fellows, and making it deadly for Englishmen to exploit them."[287]

"Royal Irish Constabulary Station Badge"
Source: *Wikipedia*, URL: <en. wikipedia.org/wiki/Image:RIC_ station_badge.gif>, accessed 5 December 2006.

[284] Talbot, 75.

[285] David Neligan, *The Spy in the Castle* (London: MacGibbon and Kee, 1968), 44.

[286] Talbot, 76.

[287] Talbot, 81.

He began by attacking the police. After the declaration of independence, members of the RIC and the DMP were ostracized by the communities they patrolled. Shopkeepers began to refuse to do business with them. Key members were assassinated, threatened, or told to resign or transfer out of Ireland. A large portion, especially of the DMP policemen, were married and lived locally with their families. The IRA found it quite easy to use threats and intimidation against them.[288]

By 1920, the RIC was in a shambles both organizationally and mentally. Their ineffectiveness, combined with the IRA's increasing effectiveness, led to serious morale issues. The prisoners from the Easter Rising of 1916 had been released, leading many RIC men to question the value of their efforts. The poor pay and benefits, combined with sub-par living conditions, resulted in many of the RIC and DMP men becoming IRA informants rather than risking their lives as IRA targets.

Attacks on Informers

Collins next went after the sources of information on which the police relied. Initially, these informants were very productive for the British. As the conflict progressed, however, the IRA was so successful at intimidating and targeting informants that the RIC's intelligence network dried up and virtually collapsed.

The Director of Intelligence for the police maintained that "captured IRA orders laid down that 'Anyone, man or woman, found guilty of giving information to the enemy, will be shot.' Many instances occurred in which men were convicted and executed merely for 'the intention to convey information to the enemy.' It was the object of the rebels, by systematized murder, to render the community inarticulate."[289] Collins' violent and coercive strategy worked very effectively. The reluctance of the Irish people to act as informants was reinforced by a strong propaganda campaign in the press. The dilemma of the Irish informant was summed up in an Irish newspaper:

> If they openly declare [to the British] they will not act as spies, they are imprisoned; if they do not so declare, and anything happens in their district, they will be held responsible and punished [by the IRA]. The futility of the scheme is laughable, and, as illustrating the psychology of the military governors of Ireland, most illuminating. The people will not act as spies.[290]

---

[288] *A Record Of The Rebellion In Ireland In 1920-21, And The Part Played By The Army In Dealing With It*, vol. 2, May 1922, 5, PRO WO 141/93. Cited hereafter as ROTR.

[289] Winter, *Winter's Tale*, 300-301.

[290] "General Strickland's New Scheme Futile," Newspaper article [no name or date given], IWM EPS 2/2.

British Intelligence Reinforcements

In addition to the new RIC recruits and the Tans and Auxies who were brought in to reinforce the overall police effort in Ireland in 1920, there were also attempts to reinforce the British intelligence capability in particular.

Tudor brought in Colonel Sir Ormonde Winter as Deputy Chief of Police. According to Winter, the job title served two purposes: it allowed him to stand in for Tudor during his absence, and it covered up his real job: Director of Intelligence, Chief of Police.[291] Although Winter had no real intelligence experience prior to assuming the job, he and Tudor knew each other. That, presumably, was the basis for his selection.

Winter, to his credit, offered and immediately implemented several innovative changes to the stalled intelligence system in Ireland. These included an increased emphasis on collaboration and integration, as well as exploitation of documents and photographic intelligence in ways the British had not previously pursued.

In England, the British Army recruited a group of what would now be called clandestine case officers, primarily from demobilized military officers, and formed them into a "plain clothes branch" in April 1920. The War Office helped establish a school of instruction in England to train them to collect both military and political intelligence.[292] They proved moderately successful at infiltrating agents into low-level laborer-type jobs, and obtained information about Dublin and "about Sinn Fein in England and about Irish secret societies in the U.S.A,"[293] but incurred heavy losses in getting that information.[294]

Winter's police got involved in a competing agent recruitment business shortly thereafter, setting up a recruiting office in London.[295] Winter's efforts were far less successful than those of the Army: "during a period of some eight or nine months, only sixty agents were obtained and sent to Ireland; and even many of these proved unsatisfactory and had to be discarded."[296]

---

[291] Colonel Sir Ormonde de L'Epée Winter, *A Report on the Intelligence Branch of the Chief of Police, Dublin Castle from May 1920 to June 1921*, PRO, Colonial Office (CO) papers, 904/156B.

[292] Winter, *Winter's Tale*, 297; and Keith Jeffery, "British Military Intelligence Following World War I" in *British and American Approaches to Intelligence*, ed. K.G. Robertson (New York: St. Martin's Press, 1987), 71. The school was later shut down, forcing the agents to be trained on the job in Ireland, which led to higher casualties.

[293] *ROTR*, vol. 2, 18-21. Dublin provided a good test bed for trained agents, as it was a large city; in a smaller city, such as Cork, the familiarity between people presented an enormous problem since "everyone knew everyone else [so] of secret service in the strict sense there was none."

[294] Winter, *Winter's Tale*, 297.

[295] Christopher Andrew, *Her Majesty's Secret Service: The Making of the British Intelligence Community* (New York: Elisabeth Sifton Books, 1986), 255.

[296] Winter, *Winter's Tale*, 296.

British Intelligence Sources

In 1920 the IRA increased its violent campaign of rooting out informants, and the police intelligence network the British had maintained for years virtually ceased to exist.[297] When Winter took over as the Head of the Chief of Police Intelligence Division in May 1920, he realized that he would have to start almost from scratch. The HUMINT effort he attempted to resurrect relied to varying degrees on informants and agents; debriefings and interrogations; document and photographic exploitation; and counter-intelligence.

Informants and Agents. Despite the danger, many people did in fact become informants for the British police and military. British headquarters' direction to the tactical level was to increase the efforts at gaining the confidence of the people in order to obtain more information: "Increase and speed up Intelligence activity and encourage people to give information and even to oppose the extremists. If people are safeguarded from the fear of having to be disclosed by giving evidence or otherwise, a lot of valuable information may be got which will lead to other means of getting actual evidence for prosecution."[298]

The hurdle was to assure confidentiality to the source, because Michael Collins' counter-intelligence campaign was extremely effective. Most Irish informants had "the strongest objection to putting anything on paper" and "preferred to tell verbally what they knew, usually to an individual officer in whom they had confidence."[299] Thus, the British intelligence officers, both police and military, had to be extremely creative in their methods of contacting informants: a raid could be carried out on their house, providing a cover during which time the informant could be pulled into a different room and asked for his information; or billeting forms could be served to everyone in a certain area, and on the form given to the agent a series of questions to be answered.

In addition to known informants, anonymous letters were received at most police and military headquarters. While there was a large amount of bogus information in these letters, they "could not be neglected as they occasionally led to results."[300]

---

[297] *ROTR*, vol. 2, 4, 8, 11.

[298] Major Ian MacBean, Brigade Major, Londonderry Brigade, untitled Secret memorandum to O.C. 1st Bn., "The Queen's" Regt., O.C. 1st Bn., Bedfs. and Herts Regt., O.C. 1st Bn. The Dorsetshire Regt., O.C. 2nd Bn., The Rifle Brigade, 6 Dec 1920, PRO WO 35/180A. Of note is the indication of use for evidence at prosecution as opposed to an operational intelligence perspective, this note being from a military organization.

[299] *ROTR*, vol. 2, 25.

[300] *ROTR*, vol. 2, 24.

The Secret Service operation, or the placing of an agent into an organization, "was on the whole a failure in Ireland. For many reasons it was practically impossible to place a man in any inner circle."[301] It proved so difficult because "Irish persons who were prepared to act as genuine secret service agents, i.e., as Sinn Feiners or as I.R.A. were difficult to find, while Englishmen were almost impossible to employ because of their accent."[302] In January 1920, the Viceroy admitted, "Our Secret Service is simply non-existent. What masquerades for such a Service is nothing but a delusion and a snare."[303] In fact, "despite repeated attempts right up to the Truce, British intelligence agents never succeeded in infiltrating the underground."[304]

Nevertheless, Scotland Yard, though seemingly ineffective on this score, did make a concerted effort to get its detectives into Ireland and, while not successful at infiltrating the inner circles, did seem to achieve some success with intercepting letters and other secondary types of HUMINT.[305]

Debriefings and Interrogations. Debriefings (questioning friendly personnel who had gone into a specific area) were not conducted by the British to any significant degree. The presumption can be made that the previously mentioned police mindset, of being experts in an area, contributed to the thought that, even if someone had spent time in a particular area, no one knew better than the police the intricacies of that area and the people in it.

Concerning interrogations, however, it seems that "the best information, i.e., that on which the most successful operations, where the heaviest loss was inflicted on the I.R.A., were based, was that given by I.R.A. deserters and prisoners under interrogation."[306] While both police and military intelligence officers conducted interrogations, the police may have been more suited to the task, at least initially. They had better local knowledge, and "usually the most successful interrogator was the local intelligence officer who knew about the neighbourhood or village of the man he was examining, the names of his friends and of the local I.R.A. officers."[307]

The training and experience of the interrogator had much to do with the success of the interrogation and the methods employed. For instance:

---

[301] *ROTR*, vol. 2, 28.

[302] *ROTR*, vol. 2, 25.

[303] Andrew, 253. Original citation is from the Viceroy to Londonderry, 3 January 1920, IWM, papers of Lord French, MSS 75/46/12.

[304] O'Halpin, "British Intelligence in Ireland," 10.

[305] Carl W. Ackerman, "Ireland from a Scotland Yard Notebook," *Atlantic Monthly*, April 1922, 442

[306] *ROTR*, vol. 2, 26; Keith Jeffery, "Intelligence and Counter-Insurgency Operations: Some Reflections on the British Experience," *Intelligence and National Security* 2, no. 1 (January 1987): 134.

[307] *ROTR*, vol. 2, 27.

Local intelligence in some cases became a failure because intelligence officers often adopted the same method of adducing information from a captured farm hand as that employed to interrogate a man of even better education than the interrogator himself, and there was a total ignorance of the true temperament of the people. ... It was ludicrous to watch an interrogator trying to badger information out of a doctor, or other professional man by means of a two-foot-ruler and a gun; or hanging on to the throat of a crofter, whose only tongue was Gaelic, trying to make him give information in English.[308]

Other specific interrogation methods involving mental stress included giving the "third degree" to a fake prisoner and then insinuating a similar treatment lay in store for the real prisoner.

One place chosen for this process was in an old water mill. A couple of prisoners were led into the outer room of the mill-one being a fake prisoner. The "fake" was taken into the inner room through the floor of which water rushed: a violent interrogation the [sic] ensued during which the "fake" made constant refusals to give information. Finally there was a clanking of chains; the grinding of machinery a dull thud a shriek a splash!!! The interview had ended. With a horse [sic] laugh back came the inquisitors for their "next" victim; usually he would become tractable on seeing [sic] the black rushing water below or on being reminded of it by an application of the cold water. Sometimes this "fake prisoner" routine in the water mill didn't work, however: One night the victim happened to be older than usual and perhaps the shabbiness of his clothes prevented the captors from perceiving that he was a man of some intelligence. The inquisitors watched eagerly for the expected signs of fear as the whole play was acted for his benefit. In the inner room the explanation of his impending fate was given; but the prisoner, instead of becoming overcome by the usual cold fear, drew himself up and looking round scornfully on his captors calmly said—"Drown me in that? There isn't a foot of water in that race—I happen to be the engineer who built this mill!"[309]

One important note is that the lessons learned indicate that "brutal methods" were not effective, that they encouraged a man to admit being IRA even if he was not.[310]

Another technique used was to take a cue from Hamlet ("The play's the thing wherein I'll catch the conscience of the King"), re-enacting a murder scene for the suspected killer.

---

[308] Doctor Mannix," *Under the Shadow of Darkness — Ireland 1920*, 6, KCL, LHCMA, papers of Lt.-Col. Evelyn Lindsay-Young.

[309] Doctor Mannix," 7.

[310] Jeffery, "Intelligence and Counter-Insurgency Operations," 135.

Sometimes, in the case of a killing, information was adduced from prisoners believed to be connected with the event by actually re-acting the killing before them—a most trying ordeal. A room was curtained in two, on one side the prisoner was seated and left sitting for some duration in the uncanny silent darkness; perhaps after a time a cold wet clammy hand would silently embrace him or wander over his face in the gloom ..then suddenly the curtain would drop! And behold before him lay the cold waxen face of the victim in it's [sic] funeral shroud; the very wounds being accurately depicted. Few who had actually had to do with the deed could resist such an appeal.[311]

In addition, Winter mentions the success of "Moutons," a term for fake prisoners used as plants within a prison. An agent would be arrested with "due 'pomp and circumstance' and bearing obvious signs of having 'resisted arrest,'" then be put in prison to elicit information in conversations with other prisoners.[312]

Names and records of the interrogations were kept and sent forward to the Intelligence Branch, but in many cases the prisoners would not reveal their real names, so the usefulness of this record-keeping, while well-intended, was suspect.[313]

Document Exploitation. In contrast to the post-War assessment that the best information came from interrogations, Winter maintained that, "of all sources of information, undoubtedly the most valuable was that derived from the examination of captured documents."[314] And even the assessment noted above did concur that at least in Dublin "both the military and police agreed that their most important sources of information were captured documents," although "the relative importance of the various sources of information varied according to localities."[315]

Winter brought over staff from England to man a Raid Bureau; all of English descent and screened by Scotland Yard.[316] The Bureau immediately proved its worth, analyzing captured documents detailing the inner workings of the IRA, as well as naming informants and sympathizers. In one case, they captured a complete list of all subscribers to the Republican loan, which was a front for protection from IRA targeting. "It was fortunate," Winter said, "that the Irish had an irresistible habit of keeping documents. They would

---

[311] "Doctor Mannix," 7.

[312] Winter, *Report*, 45.

[313] *ROTR*, vol. 2, 27.

[314] Winter, *Report*, 15.

[315] *ROTR*, vol. 2, 24.

[316] Winter, *Winter's Tale*, 302-305; and Andrew, 256-257.

hide them in the most unexpected places, but they seldom evaded discovery by the trained sleuth."[317]

Another example cited by Winter proves the value of analysis in detecting IRA agents. An unsigned letter found in one location was initially discarded for seeming lack of value. Once it was found and sent in, however, it was matched against another letter, which disclosed the identity of the writer, allowing the British to arrest the agent.[318]

One of the difficulties faced by the Raid Bureau was increasing the understanding at the troop level of the importance of these documents. One assessment lamented that, "had the importance of documents been realized in county districts, and had those captured at the time been more carefully scrutinized and analyzed, the source might have proved a fruitful one, but unfortunately, many papers were destroyed, many more were not examined." In some cases, documents were thrown out or kept as souvenirs by the police or soldiers who conducted the raids.[319]

Nevertheless, the importance of the captured documents slowly gained acceptance—even though obtaining them was often dull work: "At other times our quietness was interrupted by a call to arms; sometimes the mails had to be raided—a tedious job as a whole night's entertainment, but many interesting pieces of information were gathered."[320]

The Raid Bureau led to several significant arrests of IRA agents and provocateurs, but the effect was too little, too late. Unfortunately, "this side of intelligence was not developed until the I.R.A. had begun to take what steps they could to safeguard themselves."[321] Because of the limited time frame, the ability of Winter's intelligence network to produce viable results, particularly on the human side, where they had virtually no sources, was significantly hampered at best, and completely ineffectual at worst. Despite the hindrances, however, Winter was able to begin the resurrection of several

---

[317] Winter, *Winter's Tale*, 303. The effectiveness of the British troops at finding hidden documents was corroborated by IRA correspondence, which reinforced operational security measures to ensure the British were not able to exploit their communication: "When you are writing it would be an advantage if you used thin paper, something like the enclosed. It is much easier for putting away in places securely." (Padraig G. O'Daly, personal letter to "P," 8 March 1921, Archives Dept., UCD, papers of General Richard Mulcahy (P7) P7/A/5), and "destroy all letters after the [sic] are answered it would be well to repeat that paragraph." (Neill [NK?], personal letter to "Mick," [Michael Collins], 23 October 1920, Archives Dept., UCD, P7)

[318] Winter, *Winter's Tale*, 304

[319] *ROTR*, vol. 2, 24; Winter reinforces this assessment, saying "it had taken some time to instill into the minds of the police and the military services the importance of sending all captured documents, however apparently irrelevant, to the Central Raid Bureau." (Winter, *Winter's Tale*, 304).

[320] Doctor Mannix," 6.

[321] *ROTR*, vol. 2, 24.

facets of intelligence collection, and as discussed, document exploitation became a significant source of information for the British. Winter cites several examples of document exploitation that resulted in enormous finds for the British, most notably the discovery of correspondence between Mulcahy and Collins in which a proposal was put forward to infect the troops with typhoid and the horses with glanders![322]

Photographic Exploitation. In addition to the Raid Bureau, another of Winter's ideas that slowly came to fruition was a Photographic Bureau, taking pictures of captured IRA suspects. These photographs proved invaluable when, on several occasions, they were matched against IRA members under assumed names.[323] Mark Sturgis mentioned in August 1920, "The gay Ormonde's [Winter's] scheme to photograph the entire population of Ireland back and front is maturing."[324]

The Photographic Bureau's efforts "marked a distinct advance in identification, but their full effects had not had much time to be felt." It is important to remember that pictures were not as easy to take, store, or distribute in 1920 as they are now; a photograph session was not simply a "point-and-shoot" endeavor, it involved significant preparation time and a lengthy development process. It was similarly difficult to make additional copies of each photograph, much less distribute copies to the numerous RIC stations around the city; never mind the enormous problems associated with mass distribution of major personalities around the country. Nevertheless, given the limited equipment and facilities available, the effectiveness of this concept is noteworthy.[325]

Winter was realistic in his expectations of results from the section but understood the psychological impact as well. In August 1920, he told Sturgis, "We must arrest the leaders in thousands and photograph the lot—should convict say 1 in 5, but the photographing will put the wind up the others."[326] Winter's concept did not mature as quickly as he wanted, and it was certainly not perfect—"Michael Collins and Richard Mulcahy are each reported to have been actually in the hands of the Crown Forces on more than one occasion and to have been released unrecognized, because nothing incriminating was found on them"[327]—but the photographic section seemed to have been somewhat effective, at least in Dublin.

---

[322] Winter, *Winter's Tale*, 325.

[323] Winter, *Winter's Tale*, 305. Winter also describes an incident in which he was sent a picture of a man who was shot on a golf course, who he was able to identify by comparison to the photo archive. (Winter, *Winter's Tale*, 306).

[324] Mark Sturgis, unpublished diaries, vol. 1, 12 August 1920, 34, PRO WO 30/59. Cited hereafter as Sturgis Diaries. Michael Hopkinson edited the Sturgis diaries for publication in 1999 under the title *The Last Days of Dublin Castle: The Diaries of Mark Sturgis* (Dublin: Irish Academic Press, 1999). All citations are from the original documents held in the PRO.

[325] *ROTR*, vol. 2, 34.

[326] Sturgis Diaries, vol. 1, 30 August 1920, 56.

[327] *ROTR*, vol. 2, 33.

Counter-Intelligence. The British were clearly aware that Collins' IRA intelligence effort, in addition to cutting off their sources of information, was developing increasingly accurate information on British forces, personalities, and operations. Given the difficulty in finding witnesses to help them detect Irish agents within their organization, however, the British were largely stymied. Indeed, as O'Halpin asserts, the British seem to have put little effort into this task.[328] A post-War assessment stated that "neither military nor police had a contre-espionage, properly speaking. The military depended on the police and the police had no clear conception of the difference between I. (a) and I. (b) [Intelligence and Counter-Intelligence]. Yet never was an efficient system of contre-espionage more needed than in Ireland."[329]

Though they were able to lay their hands on relatively few IRA agents within British ranks, there was a recognition that they were there. The British realized that it "was comparatively easy for the I.R.A. to have agents working among the Crown Forces and even to enlist them in the R.I.C. and D.M.P."[330] One writer recalled being in a bar as a convoy of British raiders drove by.

> With a roar a lorry rushed by! Then another! And another—all loaded with khaki clad figures. The crowd round the club-bar seemed to turn as one, significant looks passed between some. "What's on?" said I, breasting up to one. "They're going to raid this place," said my informant, pointing to an island in one corner of the map on the wall. How quickly things leak out—the raid was supposed to be secret![331]

To mitigate the presumed existence of spies within their ranks, the British tried to strengthen their forces' operational security measures. But these often proved to be less help than hindrance. With a realization that the IRA had successfully penetrated much of the civilian workforce supporting the British forces, the Army directed that "orders for an operation will be issued to the troops taking part in it, immediately before they start out, so as to obviate any chances of conversation with outsiders and consequent leakage."[332] This waiting to disseminate orders would limit the number of people with access to the information, but it would also hinder proper preparation, briefing, and rehearsals for the operation. Such constraints due to operational security contributed further to the ineffectiveness of the military and para-military units, whose operational ineffectiveness was primarily due to their lack of good intelligence on which to operate.

The IRA went to great lengths to keep its enemies in the dark. Colonel Winter, as head of British Intelligence, received death threats through the

---

[328] O'Halpin, *The Missing Dimension*, 75.

[329] *ROTR*, vol. 2, 33.

[330] *ROTR*, vol. 2, 33.

[331] "Doctor Mannix," 2nd section.

[332] "Notes on Guerrilla Warfare in Ireland."

mail at Dublin Castle, as did others.[333] In fact, some of the British personnel employed in Ireland secretly paid off the IRA to get immunity. As Winter recalled in his memoirs, "Later on, when a complete list of all subscribers to the Republican loan was captured in a raid, it was surprising to see the price that had been paid for immunity; and I may say that on the list I discovered the names of several of my personal friends."[334]

Then, in November 1920, Michael Collins' "Squad" (a select group of Republican assassins) targeted a group of British intelligence officers working in headquarters in Dublin. The IRA knew for the most part who and where they were. In fact, a picture of the officers was distributed to the Squad. On "Bloody Sunday" morning, "the Squad entered the civilian houses where the officers were billeted and shot 12 of them."[335] The small semblance of a British intelligence network that remained stumbled along as the Republican attacks intensified until the truce was negotiated in the spring.

DIAGNOSIS: A FAILURE TO INTEGRATE

The failure of British intelligence to integrate the efforts of its constituent parts during the War was due to problems of training, organization, culture, and personalities.

Training

Within the British Army, "One of the great obstacles to intelligence was the almost universal ignorance of all ranks as to what intelligence might be."[336] To the degree that this indictment included commanding officers, and it clearly did, that ignorance would handicap the entire intelligence effort, because commanders drive the intelligence effort.

It is, of course, unrealistic to expect the commanders of the time to have the same appreciation of the intelligence business as today's. Many of the commanders and troops had gained any understanding they may have had of intelligence in the Great War, which in most cases was very limited and of limited applicability to the situation they faced in Ireland. Winter observed that

> a war-time Intelligence Service has little resemblance to one concerned with political crime. In war, information regarding the

---

[333] "IRA," letter to Colonel Winter, PRO CO 904/177(2).

[334] Winter, *Winter's Tale*, 300.

[335] Charles Townshend, *The British Campaign in Ireland 1919-1921: The Development of Political and Military Policies* (London: Oxford University Press, 1975), 129. As an interesting side note, Lt.-Col. Woodcock's wife wrote an article published in *Blackwood's Magazine* entitled "The Experiences of an Officer's Wife in Ireland" and was brought back to Ireland as a witness in the trial of one of his killers (Anderson to Macready, 8 February 1921 and Macready to Anderson, 5 February 1921, PRO CO 904/188/1(2)).

[336] *ROTR*, Vol. II, 33.

passing of troop trains, the mobilization of forces, the estimation of resources, and even the intentions of the enemy are obtainable without much difficulty. But in the complex situation that existed in a country where it was almost impossible to distinguish friend from foe, where an underground organization had so terrorized the ordinary populace as to render them inarticulate, where any stranger in the village was regarded as a potential spy, the difficulties became acute.[337]

As previously mentioned, the British did not even have a formal military intelligence apparatus until the beginning of the Great War. Lacking knowledge of the functions of an intelligence system or the benefits it could provide, relatively little attention was paid to establishing and integrating such a system. The result was that "prior to 1920 there was no intelligence organized on modern lines with complete and up-to-date records and capable of being developed and expanded without dislocation into an effective intelligence organization.[338]

In time the British came to understand this deficiency, but the results of this on-the-job learning were uneven, at best. After the War, the British noted that their intelligence efforts had "depended to a large extent on the good will and support of officers commanding units, and the importance of this was realized only gradually and during the course of operations. In most units this good will was eventually forthcoming, but there were a few in which it never seemed to be understood that much depended on the support and assistance that was given by the Battalion Staff to intelligence officers." The conclusion to which they came was that more training was required:

> It is not probably any exaggeration to state that [with one exception] no course would have been more generally useful than at a school of military intelligence where all ranks, both military and police, could have received instruction in this subject, and could have discussed how best intelligence could be developed in the difficult conditions which prevailed in Ireland.[339]

This lack of intelligence training was particularly noticeable among the police who did not have "any conception as to what intelligence meant" and thought that "a lifetime spent in Ireland and in the R.I.C. more than compensated for lack of training in intelligence duties and organization."[340] This was due in large part to the nature of police work, where decentralized operations at the tactical level are standard: the individual constable generally knows better than a headquarters staff what information he needs to obtain and how best to obtain it when targeting someone for prosecution.

---

[337] Winter, *Winter's Tale*, 293.

[338] *ROTR*, vol. 2, 23.

[339] *ROTR*, vol. 2, 24, 33.

[340] *ROTR*, vol. 2, 12, 21.

In this new relationship, however, where the police were the supported agency, it was vital that they understand the functions and benefits of the military intelligence system supporting them. Because they did not, the direction from the police to military intelligence supporting units was practically non-existent; policemen were not trained in the employment of military intelligence-style assets. The military intelligence officers in Ireland, initially almost completely reliant on the police for their intelligence, discovered themselves partnered to a system that was decentralized and non-communicative:

> The weakness of the system lay in the fact that to a large extent the amount and nature of the information was left to the initiative of the County Inspectors. There was little guidance from above, owing probably to the fact that the headquarters was so small that it was impossible to communicate fully with every County Inspector. The result was that at headquarters information on general subjects was meager and patchy while information concerning individuals was limited to that about comparatively few persons of the most extreme type.[341]

The police were the supported agency throughout the war, except in the few areas put under martial law late in the war. Thus, "one of the principal duties of military intelligence was to collect information which could be used as legal evidence."[342] That being the case, it was incumbent on the police to train military intelligence assets as to procedure, methods, targets, local idiosyncrasies, and rules of evidence.

There was a distinct realization from the military, however, that while the police were becoming more aware of the benefits that military intelligence could provide them, police commanders still did not appreciate the concept of military-police integration: "Senior police officers were all believers in local knowledge and were slow to accept new, and as they considered, military ideas on the subject of intelligence."[343]

The British military realized that it was a problem of training, which had to start at the command level. If the divisional commissioner was the senior police authority in that region, then as the supported commander he should be the first to understand and communicate to lower levels the need to integrate police and military assets.

What the post-War assessment focused on, however, was the lack of training at all levels. Many of the officers appointed as intelligence officers were criticized for lack of any training in intelligence. In fact, the only intelligence training seems to have been for the Auxiliaries' intelligence

---

[341] *ROTR*, vol. 2, 4.
[342] *ROTR*, vol. 2, 9.
[343] *ROTR*, vol. 2, 11.

officers, who went through a course held by the Divisional Headquarters. No other mention is made of training for intelligence officers.[344]

At the end of 1920, each divisional police commissioner was allocated an intelligence staff to "link up police and military intelligence."[345] Thereafter, on an individual basis, some police intelligence officers and commanders began to understand the importance of integrating their intelligence efforts with the military's. Overall, however, this was the exception rather than the rule. Unfortunately for the British, the breakdown in this area began the fundamental collapse of their intelligence in the War.

Training problems for military personnel were exacerbated by unit deployment policies. While policemen might operate in the same area for years, military officers and their units typically rotated out on a regular basis. It took some time for the problems this created for military intelligence functions in Ireland to be recognized: "at first, intelligence officers were changed far too frequently. Once a suitable officer is appointed and knows his area, he should not be changed save in most exceptional circumstances and, even if his battalion is transferred to another station, it may be desirable for him to remain."[346]

Organization

The problem of integration at all levels reflected the problems the British were having at the GHQ level. When the Office of the Chief of Police was established in May 1920, Tudor and Macready decided that, since the military was supporting the police, "it would be natural and logical if the main Intelligence Branch were in the office of the Chief of Police."[347] The idea was that they could then integrate intelligence staffs down to the tactical level, organized along military lines. The implicit assumption was that this odd lash-up (military intelligence section for a police headquarters) would be neatened up once there was a declaration of martial law—something for which Macready was pressing. When that happened, the military would be running the entire operation and this "police" Intelligence Branch would revert to the GOC-in-C's staff. Winter as head of this Branch would, in the event of martial law, presumably have been shifted from the Office of the Chief of Police (where he was the deputy as well as the intelligence chief) to the GOC-in-C's staff as the Director of Intelligence.

What ended up happening, however, was that martial law was not declared, so the Army entered the conflict as a supporting agency of the police instead. Then Winter took too long setting up the system. And when it was set up

---

[344] *ROTR*, vol. 2, 5, 10, 22, 30.

[345] *ROTR*, vol. 2, 11.

[346] *ROTR*, vol. 2, 30.

[347] *ROTR*, vol. 2, 9.

General Macready "did not consider it satisfactory or one on which military intelligence could be grafted."[348]

Macready's staff also, perhaps picking up on their commander's preferences, seemed to think a separation of efforts between themselves and the police was best. Their advice was that, rather than integrating their efforts closely with those of the police, "military intelligence must depend on itself if results were to be obtained."[349] As a result, the police and the military did not exchange information in a regularized fashion for most of the war. This lack of communication between the two gave the Republicans many opportunities they would not have otherwise had.

Debates at the headquarters level tend to be felt at lower levels. In the case of the British, this separation between military and police intelligence headquarters played out at tactical levels for much longer than it should have. If there was this much discussion of whether the intelligence functions of the police and military should be integrated, the actual integration, even after a decision to integrate was finally made, would not go well or quickly.[350]

Tactical intelligence organizations at the time relied to a large extent on direction from the intelligence staff at the next higher level (battalion relies on brigade, brigade relies on division, and so forth). Accordingly, in the organizations proposed for the intelligence networks across the island, all of the "control" emanated from these higher-level intelligence organizations.[351] That control, however, is of a rather nebulous quality. Even when a single individual was placed in charge of intelligence for the Army and the police, his authority was limited. While he received information from all British intelligence entities active in Ireland, he had tasking authority over only one of them. That is not a formula for organizational integration.[352]

The Raid Bureau's procedures provide an illustration of the problems caused by this lack of organizational integration. The process by which documents were forwarded to the Raid Bureau was a convoluted attempt to integrate military and police requirements. The military was responsible for all documents pertaining to order of battle information. These documents

---

[348] *ROTR*, vol. 2, 9-10.

[349] *ROTR*, vol. 2, 8.

[350] The interesting note on this topic is that at the HQ level, the police seem to have been most intent on integrating (Macready paid it lip service, but really did not give it much of a chance). Hart, however, makes the point that while the police in general were supportive of integration at HQ, Winter was in fact a proponent of "competing agencies," because it preserved police autonomy, which in turn kept the morale of the policemen high (see *British Intelligence in Ireland*, 8-9). At the tactical level (where the collection and immediate turnaround of operational intelligence was occurring), the military were the ones trying to force the integration onto the police (much in the same mindset as Winter). The reason for this was largely personal at both levels, for completely different reasons.

[351] *ROTR*, vol. 2, 9, 18.

[352] O'Halpin, *The Missing Dimension*, 55.

were copied and then forwarded to the police for chain of evidence handling. The police were responsible for documents dealing with individuals, addresses, propaganda, and political intelligence. The police had to pass military documents to the military for copying and then get them back for chain of evidence handling. The military documents went up to the Brigade Headquarters, while the police documents went up to the Divisional Commissioner's office.

Additionally, the Raid Bureau itself suffered from bureaucracy of epic proportions. Because it was Winter's focus, he naturally wanted to maintain control of the information flow. As a result, all captured documents were supposed to be sent to the central repository at Dublin Castle. While legitimate from a collection point of view, the vast number of documents precluded appropriate analysis by the limited number of document reviewers.

Furthermore, Raid Bureau's dissemination process was abominable,[353] although even today pushing intelligence down to the lowest levels is still one of the most difficult tasks for which a commander is responsible. The intelligence officers at the lowest levels had to peruse cumbersome and time-consuming disseminated documents to see if there was any operational value to them. Even then, "the weak point about such documentary information was that it arrived almost invariably too late to take action."[354]

So once the documents were sent to the Raid Bureau, they were effectively gone, and timely information was seldom given back to the field units in the area from which the documents came. The idea that a police station could confiscate documents, send some to the military for copying, forward them up to the Raid Bureau for processing, then request a summary, wait for a copy of it to arrive, and then slog through a typically enormous document that might in fact amount to more pages than the original documents themselves, was disheartening to say the least. This sluggish dissemination process further exacerbated the rift between police and military. Finally, "the branch was all so secret that no one was allowed to know anything about it,"[355] a compartmentalization issue that can still prevail in modern intelligence operations.

Despite varying degrees of success enjoyed by both military and police organizations, the lack of organizational integration between the two severely hampered the British effort. A simple example of this involves the case of Liam Tobin, Collins' chief assistant. According to David Neligan, "Tobin ran a secret intelligence office within a stone's throw of [Dublin] castle. It was never discovered by the British." In fact, as Neligan points out, the Army had discovered evidence of Tobin's involvement in the IRA, but the police had not been informed. Due to the lack of interagency cooperation, Tobin was

---

[353] *ROTR*, vol. 2, 13.

[354] *ROTR*, vol. 2, 24.

[355] *ROTR*, vol. 2, 23.

not arrested.[356] The modern diagnosis would probably fault "Stovepipes": the various "intelligence services gathered information and sent it through separate channels, sometimes to the same and sometimes to different destinations; nowhere was it cross-checked or fed back."[357]

Culture

Former U.S. National Security Advisor Brent Scowcroft outlined the cultural differences between law enforcement and military personnel: law enforcement personnel start with an incident, which they investigate with the goal of bringing the people responsible to justice. Therefore, law enforcement personnel have a hard time sharing information because they must protect the evidence and documentation of the investigation. On the other hand, military intelligence personnel begin with a flood of material, looking for patterns to find indications of the incident before it happens. Therefore, they *must* share information to compare ideas.[358] Thus, the nature of the jobs that police and military intelligence personnel perform dictates that integration of their efforts will be difficult.

The RIC intelligence network was tailored to a law enforcement judicial system, as with most democratic societies. The emphasis was on evidence for court rather than military intelligence oriented toward an enemy. The difficulties inherent in intelligence were exacerbated by the competing police and military intelligence priorities. As in other areas of intelligence, the tension between using information in court or for "actionable intelligence" created problems. The military would generally prefer to keep informants' identities secure, while the police were eager to use those informants for identification of IRA members, which in most cases had to be done in person.[359]

The British never found a way to bridge the cultural gap between these two distinct foci of intelligence. For instance, the British Army set up a special Intelligence Fund whereby intelligence sources could be recompensed for losses and relocated to England for their safety, if necessary. The police, however, had no parallel fund for their witnesses who were asked to give evidence in court.[360] Since the fund was established by the military, military regulations apparently precluded its use by the police—who were apparently

---

[356] Neligan, 71-72.

[357] Townshend, *Britain's Civil Wars*, 28.

[358] Lieutenant General Brent Scowcroft, USAF (Ret.), former National Security Advisor, untitled lecture presented in NFI624 class at the Joint Military Intelligence College, Washington, DC, 5 May 2004.

[359] General Headquarters, Ireland, "Notes on the Administration of Martial Law for the Use of Commanding Officers," Confidential/FOUO memorandum, 1921, IWM EPS 2/2. "(a) *INDENTIFICATION* [sic]. It should be made impossible for an arrested man to know the name of, or see, his indentifier [sic]. Arrangements should therefore be made for prisoners who have to be indentified [sic] to file past the indentifier [sic] who should be concealed."

[360] "Draft," Para. 2.

expected to take care of their own informants rather than relying on the military to do so.

Additionally, it was clearly difficult to get the police to share information with the Army, despite a recognition that it was necessary. Recall Scowcroft's explanation of the police mindset: the nature of the job precludes an active dissemination of information. The police in fact punished their men for sharing information with the military. In 1920, one DMP sergeant's promotion was held back because he gave "important information" to the military intelligence liaison officer![361]

As noted, the tactical-level cross-flow of intelligence information depended on the personalities of the military and police commanders. Around the end of 1920 each police division commander was given an intelligence staff to link police and military intelligence, since Winter's efforts at the headquarters level were simply not being felt further down the chain. This innovation, however belated, seems to have helped: "On the whole they were a success [and] did much to improve co-operation between the police and the military."[362]

Instructions to troops in 1920 made the presumption that the police would provide ground-level information to new military units as they moved into the area. Whether this always happened is uncertain, but its inclusion as a standard operating procedure was encouraging. Additionally, Lt.-Col. Evelyn Lindsay-Young described a case where there was evidently discussion, if not full integration of effort, between the police and military intelligence officers in a certain area.[363] While laudable, the ad hoc nature of such arrangements makes them fragile. An institutionalized integration of efforts would have been preferable, had the competing cultures allowed it.

Personalities

The difficulties in implementing a top-down integration of the British intelligence efforts were not solely educational, organizational, or cultural in nature. Personalities were also involved. While some differences may have had a basis in substantive disagreements, there is also a clear sense that personal animus developed as an additional factor.

---

[361] "Re Promotion of Sergt. McCabe 'G' Division," undated but sometime around Feb-Mar 1920 based on surrounding documents in collection, PRO CO 904/24/5. "Major Price at the time was the Military Intelligence Liaison Officer who was in close touch with the Detective Branch of the D.M.P. It appears that on meeting Sergt. McCabe at G.H.Q. he asked him if he had anything of interest to tell him and in reply Sergt. McCabe, having some intelligence which had come to his knowledge, informed Major Price without first having informed Superintendent Brien. That appears to be the only incident. The Superintendent of 'G' Division resented this, and when the Sergt's name came up for consideration in 1920 he remembered it, and made it a reason for refusing to recommend him to the Board."

[362] ROTR, vol. 2, 12.

[363] "Doctor Mannix," 4.

For instance, although General Macready thought that Chief of Police "Tudor is going to be a great success,"[364] he was concerned about Tudor's choice of Winter for the deputy's position. In fact, Macready had put forward his own, competing candidate for the deputy's job. This officer, however, was not selected; Winter was.[365] Not getting his man appointed as the police intelligence chief seems to have played a role in Macready's subsequent attitude toward police intelligence. He gave it lip-service only.

A contributor to the problem seems to have been Winter's failure to maintain a Big Picture view of his responsibilities. Macready felt that Winter devoted too much of his time to the situation in Dublin, where he could indulge "his fondness of cloak and dagger methods" by getting personally involved in arrests and raids. As a result, the actual setup of a combined police-military intelligence organization throughout Ireland did not develop as quickly as his military counterparts thought it should have.[366]

Macready also felt that Winter, once appointed, had been slow to put much effort into his work until his office was relocated to Dublin Castle. Once the move to Dublin Castle occurred, Macready in particular had expected Winter to be up and running. Instead, Winter was just then getting started, leaving a bad taste in Macready's mouth. Macready wrote to colleagues on several occasions, mentioning his dissatisfaction with Winter's methods and abilities. In December 1920, for instance, he indicates his desire to keep the police and military intelligence organizations separate due in large part to Winter's involvement: "the great point will be for O. [Ormonde Winter] to keep his finger off what may be called purely military intelligence and devote himself to the tracking of criminals."[367] When Winter did not cooperate in

---

[364] Macready, personal letter to Field Marshal Sir Henry Wilson, Chief of the Imperial General Staff (C.I.G.S.), 21 May 1920, IWM, papers of Field Marshal Sir Henry H. Wilson (HHW), 2/2A/12.

[365] Macready, personal letter to Wilson, 25 May 1920, IWM HHW 2/2A/15.

[366] Townshend, *The British Campaign in Ireland, 1919-1921: The Development of Political and Military Policies* (London: Oxford University Press, 1973): 126-127; and O'Halpin in The Missing Dimension, 73. See also Sturgis diaries, from roughly mid-September 1920 through 17 December 1920, and ROTR, 18-20. O'Halpin states that Macready was in fact the one who suggested to the cabinet that one person be appointed to supervise all the intelligence agencies in Ireland. Winter's statement was that until the move to Dublin Castle in October 1920, there was not enough room to work in their old accommodations and that once they moved to Dublin Castle he became far more efficient, but Townshend, through an analysis of the Sturgis diaries, demonstrates that Winter did not step up to take control of the organization; he was happier working as the coordinator for intelligence in Dublin rather than in all of Ireland. On 17 December 1920 a Castle conference reduced Winter's responsibilities, but only for a short while; in early 1921, the Dublin District Special Branch was moved under him.

[367] Macready, personal letter to Anderson, 18 December 1920, PRO CO 904/188/1. See also Macready-Anderson correspondence in April 1921.

this diminution of his office, Macready tried to have him removed by their civilian superiors but was unsuccessful in this as well.[368]

EPILOGUE

After the treaty granting Irish independence was implemented, the British realized their mistakes in Ireland and made a concerted effort to reorient their military to handle future counter-insurgency situations. There was "a drive towards the centralization of policing and intelligence on an imperial level which had scarcely existed before."[369] By 1923, the effects of the War were being felt doctrinally within the British military. In reaction to the conflict, the British Army was ordered to prepare "only for small wars during the next few years."[370]

After the embarrassment in Ireland, the powerful British Army was being told—despite its success in the World War—to change the way it did business. It then began a transition, in fact becoming something of an example to the rest of the world on how to conduct limited warfare. Unfortunately, their immediate efforts were short-lived; the inherent inertia in transforming a large organization such as the Army from a cumbersome, monolithic entity capable of major land warfare into a lighter, maneuverable force is considerable, and by the time the British had made some headway on this process the Germans were already posturing for what would become the Second World War. Again the British had to reorient themselves for another major war, and the preparation for small wars was put on hold. While the British succeeded to a point in terms of tactics, techniques, and procedures, the overall result of the timing of wars was that the empire crumbled. Ireland was divided, the counter-insurgencies and emergencies in India, Kenya, and Cyprus failed, and arguably only Malaya could be counted a British success. Mockaitis and Killingray indicate that a model for British counter-insurgency

---

[368] Macready, personal letter to Anderson, 8 April 1921, PRO CO 904/188/1. "I think before C.S. [Chief Secretary] leaves the country it would not be a bad thing to have a conference on the two points of propaganda and Intelligence. As regards the latter I would suggest, although it may not be quite correct, that you should have a heart to heart talk with Boyle and Haldane without Winter knowing anything about it, and get them to really open their hearts to you. I happen to know that they take almost the same view of what is to some extent preventing the machine from becoming as perfect as possible as we hold up at G.H.Q., but of course being only subordinates they cannot put the thing right. If they will speak quite frankly to you and give you their point of view, then I think if you, C.S., myself, and Brind, who knows our point, could have a talk which might be for good. Later it might be advisable for C.S. to call in Winter and hear his side of the question, but everything seems to point to the view that Winter has not got the right method, and we here very much doubt whether he will ever get it. He is, I fancy, a 'born sleuth,' but I doubt his organizing power, and that, so far as I can see, is what is holding up the machine."

[369] Richard Popplewell, " 'Lacking Intelligence': Some Reflections on Recent Approaches to British Counter-Insurgency, 1900-1960," *Intelligence and National Security* 10, no. 2 (April 1995): 348.

[370] Lieutenant Colonel C.E. Vickery, "Small Wars," *Army Quarterly* (April and July 1923): 307.

did finally begin to form by the end of the 1950s. Then, a clear model of British counter-insurgency emerged, based on the coordination of the civil and military authorities in gathering intelligence on insurgents.[371]

---

[371] Popplewell, 348.

THE WALL BETWEEN NATIONAL SECURITY AND LAW ENFORCEMENT

Chief Warrant Officer Five Devin Rollis, USA
Master of Science of Strategic Intelligence, 2003

In the 25 years that preceded 9/11, a wall was created to reduce or eliminate the exchange of intelligence information between law enforcement (LE) agencies and the intelligence community (IC). Some have even suggested that this wall was partially responsible for the terrorists' success. Why had the nation's intelligence and law enforcement agencies not shared information and cooperated to prevent such an attack? Congress conducted an investigation to discover what went wrong; passed the *U.S.A. Patriot Act of 2001*, which expanded the Department of Justice's authority to conduct domestic intelligence collection; and created the Department of Homeland Security to strengthen cooperation between intelligence and law enforcement agencies. But it may take more than reorganizing government agencies and expanding their authorities to dismantle the wall.

The wall developed during the 1970s as a result of investigations and reforms after decades of unsupervised intelligence operations and questionable practices. The wall, however, is now as much cultural as legislative. Even if the policies and laws that helped build the wall are removed, the culture in both communities will have to change before they can cooperate fully.

LE-IC COOPERATION IN THE "GOOD OLD DAYS"

While they were sometimes at odds, there was also a long history of cooperation between the law enforcement and intelligence communities in the United States prior to the 1970s. Throughout most of the 20th century the IC was involved in domestic intelligence activities as it assisted law enforcement agencies' investigations of threats to national security. The subjects of these investigations were generally agents of foreign nations, but at times included Americans who challenged the government through public dissent.

In the years following World War I, the Bureau of Investigation (predecessor to the FBI), Office of Naval Intelligence (ONI), and the Army's Military Intelligence Division (MID) continued their wartime collaboration, conducting domestic surveillance operations against dangers such as those associated with communism and socialism. They also monitored American dissidents, radicals, and labor organizers. This surveillance continued through World War II, with only loose controls or oversight.[372]

---

[372] Jeffery M. Dorwart, *Conflict of Duty: The U.S. Navy's Intelligence Dilemma, 1919-1945* (Annapolis, MD: United States Naval Institute, 1983), 7.

With the passage of the National Security Act of 1947, domestic operations of the IC became more limited, but domestic counterintelligence operations continued throughout the Cold War. During the early years of the Cold War, the fear of Soviet spying and influence in the U.S. led LE and the IC to cooperate on investigations of foreign espionage. Then, beginning in the 1950s and continuing throughout the 1960s, a wave of protests and rioting by increasingly radical groups demanding change spread across the nation. In response to this perceived threat to national security, domestic surveillance activity by law enforcement and intelligence agencies increased.

Civil Rights Movement

The Civil Rights movement accelerated after the Second World War. The Army became directly involved in 1957 when President Eisenhower sent federal troops to Little Rock, Arkansas, to enforce a federal court order to integrate Central High School. Agents from the Army's Counter-Intelligence Corps (CIC) arrived before the troops to gather information on the developing situation.

While the FBI had few black agents available to observe developing racial trouble, the CIC had integrated during the Second World War. The CIC had needed black agents to access populations generally inaccessible to white agents, in the U.S. and around the world. Thus, when the need for undercover sources arose in Arkansas, the CIC agents were sent. The agents in Little Rock observed the situation, identified prominent figures and troublemakers, and filed reports with the 111th Intelligence Corps Group in Atlanta. Similar missions were carried out by military intelligence agents during the desegregation of Ole Miss in September 1962.[373] They collected data on suspected instigators and began building a "black, white, and gray list" of those individuals assessed to be potential problems, potential supporters of the authorities, and those whose inclinations were unclear.

As a result of these experiences, the Army realized that it would need much more information to support planning and deployment of troops in response to future domestic crises. Accordingly, military intelligence agents began collecting information on people and political organizations that might become involved in such situations, to include all political activists and racial extremists in the Southern states. The program was expanded to other areas of the country as civil rights disturbances spread.[374]

---

[373] Paul J. Scheips, *The Role of the Army in the Oxford, Mississippi Incident: 1962-1963*, Monograph no. 73M (Washington: U.S. Army Office of the Chief of Military History, 1965), 2-3.

[374] Joan M. Jensen, *Army Surveillance in America, 1775-1980* (New Haven, CT: Yale University Press, 1991), 237-240.

Protests and Riots

The growing concern about the Civil Rights movement continued under President Lyndon B. Johnson. However, a new threat developed as Johnson committed American troops to the conflict in Vietnam. Army planners began to worry about a war on two fronts, one in Vietnam and one in the American streets. In 1965, the Army began to collect information on radical domestic groups in order to protect military personnel, equipment, and facilities. The following year, civil contingency plans were revised, giving the Intelligence Command a broad scope of civilian surveillance and collection targets.[375]

In 1967, rioting grew to the level of a national crisis. The antiwar movement grew stronger and the Civil Rights movement's extremist groups, such as the Black Panthers, advocated a racial war. Large riots broke out in major cities during July and August 1967. The National Guard was deployed to quell 25 separate incidents. Following these riots, the Army's domestic intelligence priorities changed. Army Intelligence became more interested in information on the increasingly violent antiwar movement and black militants.[376]

The Army's CONUS intelligence operation was expanded to 1,500 agents operating out of 300 detachments. Intelligence agents infiltrated universities and student groups, often becoming involved in demonstrations themselves. They collected information on university radicals, extremists, civil rights marchers, antiwar protesters, and many people who simply crossed paths with them, including local political figures and members of Congress. These agents contributed to a database that eventually contained information on over 150,000 American citizens. The Army maintained copies of the database on three separate computer systems and shared it with the FBI.[377]

National Intelligence Agencies

National intelligence agencies were also involved in domestic spying in support of law enforcement during these years. The center of the CIA's effort in the late 1960s was Operation CHAOS, whose mission was "to gather and evaluate all available information about foreign links to radical, antiwar, and other protest activity in the United States."[378] The project resulted in the collection of a large volume of information on Americans with any suspected connection to radical or antiwar groups.

---

[375] Paul J. Schieps and M. Warner Stark, *Use of Troops in Civil Disturbances Since World War II, Supplement II (1967)*, CMH Study 75 (Washington: Center for Military History, 1974), 507.

[376] John Patrick Finnegan and Romana Danysh, *Military Intelligence of the Army Lineage Series* (Washington: GPO, 1997), 155.

[377] U.S. Congress, Senate, Book 3, *Supplementary Detailed Staff Reports on Intelligence Activities and the Rights of Americans*, 94th Cong., 2d sess., 1976, S. Rept no. 94-755, 800. Cited hereafter as U.S. Congress, Senate, Book 3, *Supplementary Staff Reports*.

[378] U.S. Congress, Senate, Book 3, *Supplementary Staff Reports*, 681-682.

The most serious domestic program in which the CIA became involved was the opening of private mail. From 1953 through 1973 the CIA opened mail sent to and from the USSR. The objective of the project was to identify Soviet agents who might use secret methods to send messages through the mail service. The project was carried out with the approval of the Postmaster General and the knowledge of the FBI, which received copies of all significant information intercepted through the project. Some information was also disseminated to other law enforcement agencies with the source disguised. While not a great success, this project did uncover two agents.[379]

The National Security Agency (NSA) was created in 1952 to bring all interception of foreign electronic communications for intelligence purposes under a central command.[380] NSA was chartered to intercept only foreign communications, those having at least one foreign terminal. Thus, when tasked to monitor communications for evidence of foreign espionage, and later for foreign influence over antiwar or civil rights groups or individuals, the Agency was within its legal authority to do so. Between 1967 and 1973, watch lists were submitted to NSA by the Secret Service, FBI, CIA, DIA, and the Bureau of Narcotics and Dangerous Drugs (predecessor to the Drug Enforcement Administration). The agencies asked for intercepts of foreign communications with domestic groups or individuals who might be under foreign influence. By the time such monitoring was discontinued in 1973, a total of nearly 6,000 foreign and 1,650 U.S. citizens appeared on these watch lists.[381]

REVELATION OF DOMESTIC INTELLIGENCE ACTIVITIES

Beginning in January 1970 and continuing almost non-stop through 1974, many covert government domestic intelligence operations were exposed. The ensuing outcry from the press and the public led to the establishment of Congressional committees in 1975 to study governmental operations with respect to intelligence activities.

---

[379] Richard Helms and William Hood, *A Look Over My Shoulder* (New York: Random House, 2003), 439-440; and U.S. Congress, Senate, Select Committee to Study Governmental Operations with Respect to Intelligence Activities, Volume 4, *Mail Opening*, 94th Cong., 2d sess., S. Report No. 94-755, 1976, 1-2.

[380] U.S. Congress, Senate, Select Committee to Study Governmental Operations with Respect to Intelligence Activities, Book 6, *Supplemental Reports on Intelligence Activities*, 94th Cong., 2d sess., S. Report No. 94-755, 1976, 130-131. Cited hereafter as U.S. Congress, Senate, Book 6, *Supplemental Reports*.

[381] U.S. Congress, Senate, Select Committee to Study Governmental Operations with Respect to Intelligence Activities, Volume 5, *The National Security Agency and Fourth Amendment Rights*, 94th Cong., 2d sess., S. Report No. 94-755, 20-21. Cited hereafter as U.S. Congress, Senate, Volume 5, *National Security Agency*.

Army CONUS Intelligence

In January 1970, Christopher H. Pyle, a former Army captain, published an exposé disclosing the domestic CONUS Intelligence operation conducted by the Army.[382] In February, the ACLU filed a class action lawsuit against the Army on behalf of Arlo Tatum, an activist who was reportedly in the Army's database. The suit asked that the court enjoin the Army to cease the surveillance and destroy all the accumulated records.[383]

The Army argued that the surveillance was justified to support its civil disturbance mission. The Supreme Court found that Tatum had not suffered "cognizable injury"; therefore, the government had not violated his civil rights. The ACLU lost the Tatum case but, as a result of the negative publicity for the government, won the battle: The Army suspended all counterintelligence operations against domestic political groups in June 1970 and ordered the files and databases destroyed.[384]

Break-in at the FBI Field Office

On the night of 8 March 1971, a radical group broke into the FBI's field office in Media, Pennsylvania, and took more than 800 documents, many of them classified or sensitive. Among the stolen documents were files compiled on individuals and organizations, as well as memos directing active disruption of student groups and the incitement of conflict between violence-prone extremists.[385]

Over the next two months, the burglars sent copies of the stolen documents to newspapers and members of Congress; the first public airing of Bureau policies and activities relating to domestic intelligence programs.[386] Former FBI Special Agent Robert N. Wall confirmed the contents of the stolen files: information on Americans who were not suspected of any crime, but were subjects of interest based on their political activism.[387]

---

[382] Ben A. Franklin, "Spying: They've Probably Got You on the List," *New York Times*, 27 December 1970, A8.

[383] "A.C.L.U. Seeks to Curb Undercover Agents," *New York Times*, 18 January 1970, A25.

[384] Jensen, 249-255; *Laird v. Tatum* 408 U.S. 1, 22-23 (1972); L. Britt Snider, Counsel to the Subcommittee on Constitutional Rights of the Senate Judiciary Committee, 1972-1975, and Counsel to the Senate Select Committee on Intelligence, 1975-1976, interview by the author, 21 May 2003.

[385] Sanford J. Ungar, *FBI: An Uncensored Look Behind the Walls* (Boston: Little, Brown and Co., 1975), 484-492; and Frank J. Donner, *The Age of Surveillance: The Aims and Methods of America's Political Intelligence System* (New York: Alfred A. Knopf, 1980), 157.

[386] "Radicals: Ripping off the FBI," *Time*, 15 April 1971, 15; and Frank J. Donner, *The Age of Surveillance: The Aims and Methods of America's Political Intelligence System* (New York: Alfred A. Knopf, 1980), 108.

[387] "FBI in the Nude," *New Republic*, 29 January 1972, 11-12.

The "Family Jewels"

On 22 December 1974, while newspapers were still carrying stories on the investigations and accusations stemming from domestic intelligence activities, the largest disclosure yet made the front page of the *New York Times*.[388] It was based on an 800-page CIA document listing all Agency activities that could be considered illegal or questionable, or could possibly cause the CIA embarrassment with Congress, the press, or the public. These "Family Jewels" were leaked to the press and published, exposing a wide range of covert CIA programs and operations, including spying and collecting files on American citizens.[389]

EXECUTIVE REACTION

The Ford administration attempted to negotiate with Congress the creation of a joint commission to investigate intelligence activities, but the lawmakers were not interested in a cooperative effort. Instead, the Administration set up the Commission on CIA Activities within the United States, with Vice President Nelson Rockefeller as chairman.[390]

President Ford gave the commission a limited scope of responsibility: examine the CIA's activities within the U.S. and determine whether the Agency had exceeded its statutory authority, as established in the National Security Act of 1947.

The Rockefeller Commission completed its six-month investigation and published a 300-page report in June 1975, finding that intelligence operations had suffered a lack of guidance. The members of the commission found that clear and definitive limits to authority had not been drawn either in law or executive guidance. Because of the deference accorded national security activities, intelligence operations had been insulated from the constraints applied to law enforcement.[391]

CONGRESSIONAL INVESTIGATIONS

In the past, Congress had been content to let the executive branch police itself. That changed after 1974.

---

[388] Loch K. Johnson, *A Season of Inquiry: Congress and Intelligence* (Chicago: The Dorsey Press, 1985), 9-10.

[389] John Ranelagh, *The Agency* (New York: Simon and Schuster, 1986), 554; Johnson, 10; and Seymour Hersh, "Huge C.I.A. Operation Reported in U.S. Against Anti-War Forces," *New York Times*, 22 December 1974, A1+.

[390] Christopher Andrew, *For the President's Eyes Only* (New York: Harper Perennial, 1996), 404-405.

[391] John M. Oseth, *Regulating U.S. Intelligence Operations* (Lexington: The University Press of Kentucky, 1985), 72-79; and William R. Corson, *The Armies of Ignorance: The Rise of the American Intelligence Empire* (New York: The Dial Press-James Wade Books, 1977), 437-439.

Congressional Oversight Prior To 1974

Congressional oversight was formally established by the National Security Act of 1947. Title V of the Act provided for Congressional oversight of intelligence activities, under the authorizing jurisdiction of the Armed Services Committees. This was the first time Congress had taken upon itself a role in overseeing intelligence activities.[392]

Between 1947 and 1974, Congress performed little real oversight of intelligence activities. The CIA briefed intelligence operations to the Committees on a semiannual basis and issued annual reports. However, as Senator Leverett Saltonstall (R-MA) remarked in 1956, "It is not a question of reluctance on the part of CIA officials to speak to us. Instead, it is a question of our reluctance, if you will, to seek information and knowledge on subjects, which I personally, as a member of Congress and as a citizen, would rather not have."[393] A former CIA legislative counsel noted, "We allowed Congress to set the pace. We briefed in whatever detail they wanted. But one of the problems was you couldn't get Congress to get interested."[394]

Congressional Oversight After 1974

The initial Congressional reaction to disclosure of domestic surveillance was somewhat muted; but when the ACLU's *Tatum* case reached the Supreme Court, the involvement of other agencies (primarily the FBI) in Army surveillance was revealed.[395] This, along with the publishing of the "Family Jewels," greatly increased Congressional involvement in intelligence oversight. The view that the IC, and in particular the CIA, was a "rogue elephant" with no political control gained momentum on Capitol Hill. There was strong support for formal congressional hearings. It was also generally agreed that oversight by the Armed Services Committees had failed and that they could not be left to conduct the inquiries. The Senate created a select committee to conduct its investigation, as did the House.

Senate Select Committee on Intelligence Activities (Church Committee). The Senate was first to open an investigation into intelligence activities. Senator Frank Church (D-ID) was appointed chairman of the committee. The committee's mandate included questions of domestic operations by the CIA, the FBI, the NSA, the Army, the Defense Intelligence Agency, the National

---

[392] National Security Act of 1947, 55 U.S. Code § 102, 201 (1947); Katherine S. Olmsted, *Challenging the Secret Government: The Post-Watergate Investigation of the CIA and FBI* (Chapel Hill: University of North Carolina Press, 1996), 13; Mark M. Lowenthal, *Intelligence: From Secrets to Policy* (Washington: CQ Press, 2000), 141-142; and Oseth, 81.

[393] Roger H. Davidson, *The Postreform Congress* (New York: St. Martin's Press, Inc., 1992), 279-280.

[394] Frank J. Smist Jr., *Congress Oversees the United States Intelligence Community, 1947-1994*, 2nd ed. (Knoxville: The University of Tennessee Press, 1994), 5.

[395] Jensen, 248-252.

Security Council, the Department of State, and even the Internal Revenue Service. The committee questioned the relationships between these agencies, the policies and guidelines that governed them, and the extent to which they conformed to the law and Congressional intent.[396]

The committee found that the U.S. intelligence agencies investigated a vast number of American citizens and domestic organizations. Since the First World War, the FBI had developed over 500,000 domestic intelligence files, opening 65,000 files in 1972 alone. At one point the FBI had listed over 26,000 individuals to be rounded up in the event of a "national emergency." Between 1967 and 1973, during the course of its Operation CHAOS, the CIA listed some 300,000 individuals in a computer database and created separate files on approximately 7,200 Americans and over 100 domestic groups. Army Intelligence created files on over 150,000 Americans.[397] Even the IRS received information from the Army, Navy, and Air Force to support its investigations.[398]

The report identified the primary problem as a failure by the executive and legislative branches to oversee intelligence activities and by the IC to keep its masters informed. There had been "a clear and sustained failure by those responsible to control the IC and to ensure its accountability. There has been an equally clear and sustained failure by intelligence agencies to fully inform the proper authorities of their activities and to comply with directives from those authorities."[399]

House Select Committee on Intelligence (Pike Committee). After an abortive start, the House appointed Representative Otis Pike (D-NY) to head its investigation in parallel with that of the Church Committee. However, while the Church Committee centered its attention on the more sensational charges of illegal activities by the executive agencies, the Pike Committee examined the IC's effectiveness, its costs to taxpayers, and oversight of IC activities. Unfortunately, the Committee and its staff never developed a cooperative working relationship with the CIA or the Ford administration. Unlike the Church Committee, the Pike Committee had a predominantly young liberal staff with little experience either on the Hill or in the IC.[400] CIA

---

[396] Johnson, 10-27; and U.S. Congress, Senate, Select Committee to Study Governmental Operations with Respect to Intelligence Activities, Book 1, *Foreign and Military Intelligence*, 94th Cong., 2d sess., 1976, S. Rept no. 94-755, 6. Cited hereafter as U.S. Congress, Senate, Book 1, *Foreign Intelligence*.

[397] U.S. Congress, Senate, Book 1, *Foreign Intelligence*, 7; and Johnson, 223.

[398] U.S. Congress, Senate, Book 2, *Intelligence Activities*, 53, 93-94; and Donner, 323-336.

[399] U.S. Congress, Senate, Select Committee to Study Governmental Operations with Respect to Intelligence Activities, Book 2, *Intelligence Activities and the Rights of Americans*, 94th Cong., 2d sess., S. Report No. 94-755, 1976, 14-15. Cited hereafter as U.S. Congress, Senate, Book 2, *Intelligence Activities*.

[400] Smist, 154, 290.

officials came to detest the Committee and its efforts at investigation. DCI Colby came to consider Pike a "jackass" and his staff "a ragtag, immature and publicity-seeking group."[401]

On 19 January 1976, the committee turned over a copy of the 338-page report for Agency review and asked to have it back by the close of business the next day. This naturally drew a strong attack on both the report and the committee. The CIA criticized the extreme time constraints placed on its response and painted the report as an "unrelenting indictment couched in biased, pejorative and factually erroneous terms" that gave a distorted view of U.S. intelligence, thereby "severely limiting its impact, credibility, and the important work of your committee."[402]

Responding to the Agency's complaints, the House voted to suppress the report until it was approved by the administration. However, this decision was only a political formality: The *New York Times* had already printed large sections of the draft report and on 16 February *The Village Voice* published the full report.[403]

The Pike Committee had made some useful recommendations, but the uproar over the committee's internal disputes and the leak of the report made them politically unsupportable. The release of the report was voted down and the recommendations were ignored and soon forgotten.[404]

INSTITUTIONALIZING OVERSIGHT

In the wake of these committee reports, Congress established committees to oversee intelligence agencies and passed laws to more closely regulate those agencies' activities. The administration responded by promulgating new guidelines and regulations to conform to the new realities.

Congressional Oversight Committees

The Senate adopted the Church Committee's recommendation for a permanent committee to oversee intelligence operations: the Senate Select Committee on Intelligence (SSCI). The House followed suit, creating the House Permanent Select Committee on Intelligence (HPSCI).[405]

---

[401] Smist, 161.

[402] Johnson, 176.

[403] Olmsted, 158-159; Smist, 169-171.

[404] Gerald K. Haines, "Looking for a Rogue Elephant: The Pike Committee Investigation and the CIA," *Studies in Intelligence* (Winter 1998-1999): 89-90; Olmsted, 163; and *The Intelligence Community: History, Organization, and Issues*, eds. Tyrus G. Fain and others (New York: R. R. Bowker and Company, 1977), 104-105.

[405] U.S. Congress, Senate, Book 2, *Intelligence Activities*, 339; Oseth, 62; Smist, 82-85, 214-215; and Johnson, 238-254.

In addition to intelligence operations, these two Intelligence Committees were also given oversight responsibility for law enforcement operations and activities involving foreign connections; in particular, counternarcotics and counterterrorism operations. Oversight of domestic law enforcement remained with the House and Senate Judiciary Committees.[406]

Foreign Intelligence Surveillance Act

After the Church Committee report was released, Congress passed a sweeping reform of statutory oversight: The Foreign Intelligence Surveillance Act (FISA). It established guidelines and controls over domestic electronic surveillance for foreign intelligence purposes. It required judicial warrants for surveillance to be approved by a special FISA court established to consider classified evidence. It closed the loophole that had allowed the President to authorize wiretaps for national security purposes without obtaining a judicial warrant.[407]

Guidelines and Regulations

The Justice Department and the FBI revised internal policies based on the new statutes and policies. In March 1976, Attorney General Edward Levi issued new guidelines to the FBI for initiating domestic security investigations. These "Levi guidelines" clarified standards for the conduct and external review of investigations. The guidelines established three levels of investigation (preliminary, limited, and full) with strict standards and limitations. No investigation could progress beyond the preliminary stage without reasonable indication that a crime had been committed or was imminent. They also precluded the employment, recruitment, or placement of informants or technical surveillance, except in full investigations approved by FBI headquarters. Information derived from investigations could be disseminated to other federal agencies only if it fell within their jurisdiction, would prevent violence, or was approved by the Attorney General.[408]

Department of Defense Regulation 5240.1-R, based on the FISA, covered electronic surveillance, physical monitoring and searches, examination of mail, undisclosed participation in organizations, and provisions for assistance to law enforcement. A significant component of this regulation and the FISA was the provision for criminal sanctions and civil liability for any individual or organization found to be in violation of the law. The criminal sanction imposed a penalty of $10,000 or five years imprisonment, while the civil liability is $100 per day of the violation or $1,000, whichever is greater. These

---

[406] Athan G. Theoharis, *The FBI: A Comprehensive Reference Guide* (Phoenix, AZ: Oryx Press, 1999), 195.

[407] "Public Law 95-511: Bill Summary and Status for the 95th Congress," *Library of Congress*, URL: <thomas.loc.gov/cgi-bin/bdquery/D?d095:1:./temp/~bdU7wl:@@@L|/bss/d095query.html>, accessed 3 June 2003; and Theoharis, *The FBI*, 154.

[408] Theoharis, *The FBI*, 195; and Oseth, 100-101;

criminal and civil sanctions are applicable not only to the agency involved, but also to individual employees of those agencies who may actually conduct the collection. These sanctions are a strong deterrent to the collection of any information about which the collector might be in doubt.[409]

While these controls reduced the potential for domestic intelligence surveillance violations by the LE and IC, they also created a barrier between the two communities, reducing the level of communication and cooperation that had existed prior to 1975.

LE-IC COOPERATION AFTER 1975

Prior to 1975, there had been significant cooperation between intelligence and law enforcement on counterintelligence and counter-subversion. Coordination of counterintelligence operations continued after 1976, though at a reduced level. Most other coordination and information exchanges were discouraged by the vagueness of statutes and policies. Intelligence and law enforcement professionals became overly cautious after 1976, less concerned with information sharing than with responding to Congress.[410]

THE WALL

Throughout the 1970s, dedicated employees of the FBI and the intelligence agencies saw their organizations exposed and humiliated before Congress while being constantly derided in the press. In the aftermath of this ordeal, the intelligence agencies, the FBI, and Congress were all determined to ensure the affronting activities were not repeated. The resulting oversight was accompanied by policies that chilled both communities. Over the past 25 years, the two communities have reacted by limiting contact and the sharing of information.

As a result, a wall developed between the two communities. The wall is as much a product of perception as actual policy or law, but it is real nonetheless. As a House staff study explained,

> One of the unwritten but significant effects of these investigations was behavioral in nature. The years following the investigations were marked by some reluctance on the part of the two cultures to form interactive relationships. The over-caution was based more

---

[409] Foreign Intelligence Surveillance Act, 50 U.S. Code § 1809, 1810, 1827, 1828, (1978); and DoD Regulation 5240.1-R, *Procedures Governing the Activities of DoD Intelligence Components That Affect United States Persons* (Washington: Department of Defense, 1982).

[410] Jon Wiant, Visiting Professor and Department of State Chair, Joint Military Intelligence College, interview by author, 12 May 2003; and Merrill Kelly, former CIC officer and a Senior Executive for Intelligence Policy of the ACSI during the 1970s, interview by author, 11 and 21 May 2003.

[on] a perception that closer association meant increased political risk than [upon] having any basis in law. [411]

L. Britt Snider, a Congressional staffer during this period, agrees. Describing the wall in a 1993 paper on intelligence and law enforcement, Snider points out that the IC has a wealth of capability to gather information. The law enforcement community lacks but needs this information. Nevertheless, the IC is reluctant to share. Sharing information is done on a case-by-case basis. Few people understand the process, and many believe coordination between the communities is not allowed at all. The guidance is ambiguous and leaves professionals of both communities unwilling to test the apparatus.[412]

Barriers to Information Sharing

The regulations and guidelines promulgated in the 1970s were intended to ensure intelligence collection was done legally, not to inhibit cooperation with other agencies. However, the effect, following the publicity of the congressional investigations into intelligence activities, was to reduce interagency cooperation. The Levi guidelines' restrictions prevented coordination between intelligence officers and FBI agents in preliminary investigations, where it might be most needed. It also denied the FBI access to technical intelligence formerly available through the IC. The overall effect of the guidelines discouraged FBI interaction with the IC.[413]

The procedures for gaining authorization to exchange information between law enforcement and the IC were cumbersome and time consuming. The vulnerability of sources and applicability of oversight restrictions needed to be considered and the information then vetted through, and approved by, the appropriate General Counsel's office. Only at the end of this lengthy process could the information be exchanged. There were no liaison officers exchanged between the FBI and the intelligence agencies; thus, no human contact was available to facilitate cooperation. In the face of all these impediments, there was little incentive for improving information sharing.

Annual oversight briefings and inspections by the IG were a constant reminder of the sensitivity of the issue; unless there was a compelling need, interagency coordination and information sharing were best avoided.[414] For instance, in the late 1980s, a major money laundering scandal involving the Abu Dhabi-based Bank of Credit and Commerce International demonstrated

---

[411] Richard A. Best Jr., "Intelligence and Law Enforcement: Countering Transitional Threats to the U.S.," *CRS Report to Congress* RL30252 (Washington: Congressional Research Service, 16 January 2001), 9-10.

[412] L. Britt Snider, "Intelligence and Law Enforcement," in *U.S. Intelligence at the Crossroads*, eds. Roy Godson and others (Washington: Brassey's, 1995), 247-248.

[413] Theoharis, *The FBI*, 195; and Oseth, 100-101.

[414] Merrill Kelly, former CIC officer and a Senior Executive for Intelligence Policy of the ACSI during the 1970s, interview by author, 11 and 21 May 2003.

the poor exchange of information between the two communities. The IC had information on the scandal three years prior to its being uncovered by the Justice Department but, because of sensitivities about mixing intelligence information with LE's investigative materials, the IC did not notify the FBI or the Treasury Department. Similarly, information developed through FBI criminal investigations of terrorist acts was often not shared with the IC.[415]

Not only was there a wall between the two communities, but the Justice Department intentionally strengthened an internal barrier between criminal and intelligence investigations during the early 1990s. FBI agents involved in intelligence investigations were barred from contacting colleagues in the FBI criminal division about an investigation unless they had prior approval from the Justice Department's Office of Intelligence Policy and Review (OIPR). The OIPR was reportedly "super-hyper reluctant" to concede that an intelligence investigation might lead to a criminal prosecution; better to delay than risk contaminating a criminal proceeding with inadmissible intelligence material. Agents were warned that breaching this barrier without the OIPR's approval was a "career stopper."[416] When the FBI violated these restrictions, it led to an investigation and the censure of at least one agent. Other agents, fearing the same fate, became more careful about mixing intelligence with criminal investigations.

At times, this was carried to extremes by overcautious agents, inhibiting investigations (including the tracking of a 9/11 hijacker) that did not even fall under FISA. Unsure of the dividing line, agents erred on the side of caution. In August 2001, the CIA informed the FBI that two suspects in the attack on the USS *Cole* had entered the U.S. The FBI's New York field office requested authority from headquarters for a full investigation. The request was denied, however, because of reluctance to base a criminal investigation on intelligence information.[417]

FISA, in particular, had a negative influence on cooperation. Intended to protect Americans from unreasonable invasions, it has also served to discourage legitimate investigations. Legal affairs offices, fearful of being denied their requests by the FISA court, scrutinized agents' requests and demanded a level of evidence guaranteed to satisfy the court before they would request a warrant. Meeting such bureaucratic requirements prevented some applications for warrants from even being submitted.

---

[415] U.S. Congress, Senate, Committee on Foreign Relations, *Report on The BCCI Affair*, 102nd Cong., 2d sess., 1992, S. Report, 102-140, URL: <http://www.fas.org/irp/congress/1992_rpt/bcci/>, accessed 1 June 2003.

[416] George Lardner Jr., "Report Criticizes Stumbling Block Between FBI, Espionage Prosecutors," *Washington Post*, 13 December 2001, A3.

[417] U.S. Congress, Joint Inquiry, Select Committee on Intelligence, Senate, and Permanent Select Committee on Intelligence, House, *Hearing on the Intelligence Community's Response to Past Terrorist Attacks Against the United States from February 1993 to September 2001*, 107th Cong., 2d sess., 2002, *Joint Inquiry Staff Statement*, 24-25. Cited hereafter as U.S. Congress, *Joint Inquiry Staff Statement*

Little serious effort was made to coordinate efforts between the law enforcement and intelligence communities in investigating threats developing within the U.S. until after the September 2001 attacks. The FBI had a counterterrorism task force, as did the CIA and the DIA, but the different priorities and methods between the communities and the reluctance to communicate prevented them from combining their efforts against terrorism.[418]

In testimony before the Senate Committee on the Judiciary, Attorney General John Ashcroft discussed in detail the effects FISA had had on the FBI. He testified that FISA had created a wall between intelligence and law enforcement officials, dividing them into separate camps. This wall broke down cooperation. He said, "Information, once the best friend of law enforcement, became the enemy." He cited the difficulty a criminal investigator examining a terrorist attack had in coordinating with an intelligence officer investigating the same suspected terrorists. To illustrate this separation, he listed additional impediments:

> Reforms erected impenetrable walls between different government agencies, prohibiting them from cooperation in the nation's defense. The FBI and CIA were restricted from sharing information. And as limitations on information sharing tightened, cooperation decayed. FBI agents were forced to blind themselves to information readily available to the general public, including those who seek to harm us. Agents were barred from researching public information or visiting public places unless they were investigating a specific crime.[419]

The reservations about contacts even had a deadening effect on counterintelligence organizations, for whom coordination with law enforcement continued to be necessary. Merrill Kelly, civilian deputy to the Army Chief of Staff for Intelligence in the late 1970s, described the oversight education program as "designed to discourage cooperation." He also stated that the "people in the field got the message" that oversight meant not collecting on Americans and not working with law enforcement on intelligence issues.[420]

The FISA restrictions also played a role in the IC's restrictions on information sharing. The Director of NSA testified that historically his Agency had been able to share information more easily with the Department of Defense than with the Department of Justice. He commented that, while

---

[418] Gregg Prewitt, Senior Defense Intelligence expert for combating terrorism, DIA Counterterrorism Office, interview by author, February 2003.

[419] U.S. Congress, Senate, Committee on the Judiciary, *Oversight and the Department of Justice*, 107th Cong., 2d sess., 2002, S. Report 107-125.

[420] Kelly, interview.

the reasons for restrictions may be valid, Congress had erected barriers that made sharing with law enforcement more difficult.[421]

NSA placed restrictions on sharing information with law enforcement based on FISA policy concerns. NSA reporting for FBI intelligence investigations is based on FISA warrants. That information is essentially indistinguishable from non-FISA-warrant-derived foreign intelligence. Because of the difficulty in identifying FISA-derived information, NSA generally indicates that all information must be cleared by the FISA Court before it can be shared with law enforcement.[422]

Responding to Congress

In addition to ensuring intelligence operations were kept within legal constraints, strengthened intelligence oversight created a new set of problems within the IC. At the agency level, oversight requirements and constraints became a priority. The commitment to keep Congress informed of activities at times took precedence over keeping the administration informed.[423]

In his monograph *Sharing Intelligence with Lawmakers,* L. Britt Snider describes successive administrations' frustration with the intelligence agencies' reactions to oversight requirements, pointing out the negative effect of oversight on IC relationships within the executive branch. He found that, as requirements increased for reports and briefings to the intelligence oversight committees, the IC became more intent on satisfying them than on coordinating within the IC or with the administration. Administration officials became frustrated that intelligence professionals were so quick to take intelligence products to Congress that they sometimes failed to coordinate them with the executive.

Policymakers found that "the Intelligence Community is so anxious to please its oversight committees that it's hell-bent to get the intelligence up there, regardless of whether it's reliable and regardless of whether they've touched base with the rest of the executive branch." Mr. Snider quotes another former executive branch official:

> The real problem that results from this [failing to notify what they plan to brief the Hill] is that it isolates them [the intelligence agencies] from the policymakers who want to close them out from any involvement in the policy process, to keep them from knowing

---

[421] U.S. Congress, Joint Inquiry, Select Committee on Intelligence, Senate, and Permanent Select Committee on Intelligence, House, *Hearing on the Intelligence Community's Response to Past Terrorist Attacks Against the United States from February 1993 to September 2001,* 107th Cong., 2d sess., 2002, *Statement for the Record by Lieutenant General Michael V. Hayden,* 10. Cited hereafter as U.S. Congress, Hayden Statement.

[422] U.S. Congress, *Joint Inquiry Staff Statement,* 25.

[423] L. Britt Snider, *Sharing Intelligence with Lawmakers: Congress as a User of Intelligence* (Washington: GPO, 1997), 35.

where the policy is headed, and so forth. It becomes a "separate camps" mentality, very destructive of the overall relationship between producers and consumers.[424]

Snider, who served as counsel both to the Subcommittee on Constitutional Rights of the Senate Judiciary Committee and to the Church Committee, explained that it was not the intent of Congress to inhibit or prevent cooperation among intelligence agencies or between the IC and the FBI, but rather to establish statutory controls to ensure the rights of Americans were safeguarded.[425] A result, however, was that the agencies became more attentive to keeping the oversight committees well informed than to serving their real customers.[426]

CRACKS IN THE WALL

By 1980, the problems created by some of the reforms of the previous decade were becoming clear. When the Soviet Union invaded Afghanistan in December 1979, President Carter had been unable to initiate covert operations to support the Afghan freedom fighters. In his final State of the Union address, he argued for strengthening the intelligence agencies.[427] Accordingly, some initiatives chipped away at the wall that had developed between the law enforcement and intelligence communities.

Counter-Drug Operations

In 1981, the drug problem in America was made a federal issue. Congress passed the *Military Cooperation with Civilian Law Enforcement Statute* in December. This allowed military assistance to civilian law enforcement agencies in combating drug smuggling outside the U.S. Under this law, the military could provide support, including facilities, vessels, aircraft, intelligence, translation, and surveillance, to U.S. law enforcement entities operating abroad.[428]

The FBI and the Drug Enforcement Administration (DEA) were the lead agencies for the federal government's War on Drugs. The military gradually increased its support to counter-drug operations during the 1980s. This mission began to receive higher priority with the IC as support to military organizations demanded an increasing volume of counter-drug intelligence.[429]

---

[424] Snider, *Sharing Intelligence*, 36.

[425] L. Britt Snider, Counsel to the Subcommittee on Constitutional Rights of the Senate Judiciary Committee, 1972-1975, and Counsel to the Senate Select Committee on Intelligence, 1975-1976, interview by author, 21 May 2003.

[426] Snider, *Sharing Intelligence*, 36.

[427] Oseth, 138-139.

[428] Military Cooperation with Civilian Law Enforcement Statute, 10 U.S. Code, § 371-380 (1981).

[429] Chad Thevenot, "The 'Militarization' of the Anti-Drug Effort," July 1997, *National Drug Strategy Network*, URL: <www.ndsn.org/july97/military.html>, accessed 2 June 2003.

The creation of Joint Inter-Agency Task Forces (JIATF) in 1994 further increased cooperation with law enforcement. These JIATFs were staffed by personnel from the FBI, DEA, DoD, Customs Service, Coast Guard, and a number of other federal, state, and local agencies, along with IC representatives. The incorporation of military intelligence collection platforms into these JIATFs led to some improvement in communication and sharing with law enforcement agencies on counter-drug operations.[430]

Revised Levi Guidelines

The Justice Department updated its oversight procedures in 1983. Attorney General William French Smith revised the Levi guidelines, which had been criticized as too restrictive and cumbersome. The Smith guidelines made it clear that the FBI had the authority to investigate suspected terrorist groups and did not need to wait for a terrorist act to be committed. The guidelines expressly stated, "In its efforts to anticipate or prevent crimes, the FBI must at times initiate investigations in advance of criminal conduct."[431] The threshold for opening a full investigation was lowered to whenever "facts or circumstances reasonably indicate that two or more persons are engaged in an enterprise for the purpose of furthering political or social goals wholly or in part through activities that involve force or violence and are a violation of the criminal laws of the United States."[432] Even armed with these revised guidelines, however, the FBI remained reluctant to pursue investigations based on intelligence, as noted in the case of the USS *Cole* bombing suspects.

Counter-Terrorism Operations

Prior to the September 2001 attacks, terrorism was generally viewed as a law enforcement issue. The United States classified terrorists as criminals. This designation meant the Justice Department took the lead against terrorist threats.

Although these threats were real and continuing, the threat of foreign terrorists attacking targets in the U.S. was given little attention prior to 1993. That year, in the attack on the World Trade Center, Americans saw a foreign terrorist organization attack a target in the U.S. Nonetheless, the probe into the attack was an investigation of a criminal act; thus, it remained clearly a law enforcement issue.

---

[430] "The National Drug Intelligence Center," 28 May 2003, *U.S. Department of Justice*, URL: <www.usdoj.gov/ndic/>, accessed 7 June 2003; and Thevenot, "The 'Militarization' of the Anti-Drug Effort."

[431] "The FBI's Domestic Counterterrorism Program," 26 April 1995, *Center For National Security Studies*, URL: <www.cdt.org/policy/terrorism/cnss.FBI.auth.html>, accessed 22 June 2003.

[432] Theoharis, *The FBI*, 195; and Oseth, 100-101.

In subsequent years, both the IC and law enforcement acknowledged the terrorist threat and coordinated investigations of attacks, such as Khobar Towers in 1996, the embassies in Tanzania and Kenya in 1998, and the USS *Cole* in 2000. Coordination of IC intelligence with FBI investigations gradually improved and, with the cooperation of foreign intelligence services, captured a number of terrorists and disrupted attacks. The FBI increased its representation in embassies from 16 legal attachés in 1992 to 44 in 2001. It also increased the number of its Joint Terrorism Task Forces to 35, all located in major cities. Yet, only six of these task forces had CIA agents assigned.[433]

SINCE 9/11

Legal Changes

Following 9/11, further efforts to loosen constraints on intelligence and law enforcement cooperation moved quickly. Congress passed the *Patriot Act.* One intent of the law was to improve cooperation and open communications channels between the IC and law enforcement.[434] The law relaxed the FISA restrictions on the collection of electronic communications relating to terrorism. It authorized the sharing of information gleaned from grand jury investigations or from FISA-warranted technical means between criminal and intelligence investigators. The law specifies that

> it shall be lawful for foreign intelligence or counterintelligence …information obtained as part of a criminal investigation to be disclosed to any Federal law enforcement, intelligence, protective, immigration, national defense, or national security official in order to assist the official receiving that information in the performance of his official duties.[435]

Clearly, there was a recognition that the wall between law enforcement and intelligence was counterproductive, and efforts were underway to dismantle it.

Is There Still a Wall? The Barracuda Syndrome

In a well-known experiment, a barracuda was placed in a tank where it was separated from its prey by a pane of glass. After banging its head repeatedly against the pane, it finally quit trying to "make contact" with the fish on the

---

[433] U.S. Congress, *Joint Inquiry Staff Statement*, 5-12.

[434] *Uniting and Strengthening America by Providing Appropriate Tools Required to Intercept and Obstruct Terrorism (USA PATRIOT) Act of 2001*, 56 U.S. Code (2001). Cited hereafter as *USA Patriot Act of 2001*.

[435] *USA Patriot Act of 2001*, § 203.

other side of the tank. When the pane was removed, the barracuda acted as if it was still there, ignoring its prey and remaining on its side of the tank.[436]

Obviously, many bricks have fallen out of the Wall since 9/11. A vast amount of intelligence information is now routinely available to the FBI. Liaison officers from DIA's Joint Intelligence Task Force-Combatting Terrorism (JITF-CT) provide the FBI's watch desk with access to virtually all the IC's finished intelligence products, other than those controlled by special compartmentalized accesses.

Nevertheless, many employees of the intelligence and law enforcement agencies act as if the wall is still in place. Agents, analysts, and officers at lower echelons are not alone in this belief. Senior managers, agency directors, and members of Congress openly discuss the existence of the wall. Despite the legal changes in the wake of 9/11, the wall is real because it is believed to be real.[437]

After all, the wall was never built exclusively of laws, regulations, and policies. It is primarily cultural in nature, not statutory. The wall is the product of human nature; the reaction to a traumatic decade of inquiry bordering on inquest.

Representative Nancy Pelosi (D-CA), then the Ranking Minority Member of the HPSCI, made this point in an interview. Expressing concern about the restrictions placed on the IC and misconceptions about the law, Pelosi noted that agencies, particularly the FBI, felt they could not share information due to legal restrictions. She maintained, however, that the problem was a "cultural thing," and that the FBI (and other agencies) misread the law.[438]

Similarly, former SSCI Vice Chairman and Ranking Minority Member of the Judiciary Committee Patrick Leahy (D-VT) acknowledged "the FISA process is strapped by unnecessary layers of bureaucracy and riddled with inefficiencies." However, he went on to point out that some of these inefficiencies were "related to the same problems that [the] committee has seen time and again at the FBI—poor communication, inadequate training, a turf mentality, and an obsession with covering up mistakes." Clearly, Senator Leahy is convinced that the prevailing culture was more at fault than the statutes and policies governing information collection and sharing.[439]

If that is the case, the wall will not be breached simply by removing legal obstacles or clarifying a few sections in FISA. In 1981, when the

---

[436] Stevie Ray, "The Elephant and the Barracuda," *The Business Journal*, URL: <http://www. stevierays.org/bizjournal_166.html>, accessed 28 September 2006.

[437] Prewitt, interview.

[438] Findings of Failure," 26 September 2002, *PBS Online News Hour*, URL: <www.pbs.org/newshour/bb/terrorism/july-dec02/findings_9-26.html>, accessed 28 September 2002.

[439] U.S. Congress, Senate, Committee on the Judiciary, *Oversight and the Department of Justice*, 107th Cong., 2d sess., 2002, S. Report 107-243.

military was told to support law enforcement in counter-drug operations, cooperation between the communities had degraded to the point that it took years to reestablish formal coordination in this narrow field alone.[440] It will undoubtedly be an even lengthier process to re-acquaint the larger law enforcement and intelligence communities with one another.

It takes time for the new laws' provisions to trickle down into the regulations of the agencies affected. Philip Mudd, who recently left the CIA to become the deputy director of the FBI's new National Security Branch, believes that it will "take a while for what is a high-end national security program to sink down to every officer."[441] This, five years after 9/11: regulations will continue to be slow in altering institutional cultures. Improving cooperation between the two communities will require addressing the cultural differences and overcoming nearly three decades of cultural division.

---

[440] Thevenot, "The 'Militarization' of the Anti-Drug Effort."

[441] Scott Shane and Lowell Bergman, "F.B.I. Struggling to Reinvent Itself to Fight Terror," *New York Times*, 10 October 2006, URL: <http://www.nytimes.com/2006/10/10/us/10fbi.html>, accessed 10 October 2006.

PROBLEMS AND PROGRESS IN
INFORMATION SHARING

Robert B. Murphy
Fellow, Center for Strategic Intelligence Research

INTRODUCTION

While 9/11 highlighted them, the problems associated with information sharing between and among the intelligence and law enforcement communities were known for some time. The nature of those problems is outlined below, followed by an update on the structural and systemic improvements that have begun to improve the situation.

INFORMATION SHARING PRIOR TO 9/11

Americans have been slow to recognize the direct threat of terrorism over the past six decades. Indigenous national liberation groups, such as the Kenyan Mau Mau, were viewed with anti-colonialist sympathy. Groups like the IRA were viewed with nostalgic sympathy by many Americans. The number of American victims of terrorism was small and the incidents, like the 1970 PFLP (Popular Front for the Liberation of Palestine) hijacking of four jet aircraft bound for New York (including TWA Flt 74), were usually far from the United States. Then, on 23 October 1983, the United States suffered its worst loss of life to terrorism prior to 9/11 with the bombing of the U.S. Marine Corps barracks in Beirut, Lebanon; 241 Marines and other service members were killed by a Hezbollah suicide bomber.

Counter Terrorism Center

The incident led to the creation of a Vice Presidential Task Force under then-Vice President George H.W. Bush. It made its report in 1986, recommending the establishment of a consolidated intelligence center dealing with terrorism:

> Intelligence gathering, analysis and dissemination play a pivotal role in combatting terrorism. Currently, while several federal departments and agencies process intelligence within their own facilities, there is no consolidated center that collects and analyzes all-source information from those agencies participating in antiterrorist activities. The addition of such a central facility would improve our capability to understand and anticipate future terrorist threats, support national crisis management and provide a common database readily accessible to individual agencies. Potentially, this center could be the focus for developing a cadre

of interagency intelligence analysts specializing in the subject of terrorism.[442]

Established in 1986, the new Counter Terrorist Center (CTC) was described as a "bureaucratic revolution, cutting across established hierarchies in the CIA to create an integrated element unlike anything that had come before."[443] The CTC brought together analysts, reports officers, and operations officers—a one-stop counterterrorism shop. Eventually, more than a dozen agencies had full-time representation in the CTC. They came from the Intelligence Community, law enforcement, and regulatory agencies. The deputy director position was reserved for an FBI special agent; Immigration and Naturalization Service (INS) officers worked next to CIA analysts. A professional cadre of counterterrorism analysts developed during the 1990s. Five years before 9/11, a special Bin Laden unit was formed. Within an hour of the attack on the World Trade Center, before there was any claim of responsibility, CIA Director Tenet asserted, "This has Bin Laden all over it."[444]

Gilmore Commission

A mechanism and a desire to share national information and intelligence with law enforcement agencies outside the federal government were not forthcoming, however. The Congressionally mandated Advisory Panel to Assess Domestic Response Capabilities for Terrorism Involving Weapons of Mass Destruction (the Gilmore Commission) found that information sharing "up, down, and laterally, at all levels of government—to those who need the information to provide effective deterrence, interdiction, protection, or response"—was imperative but hampered by a lack of security clearances at the state and local level and the complex structure of the federal bureaucracy.[445] One year later, the second report of the Gilmore Commission called for a web-based system that could deliver "real time" threat warnings to state and local authorities over a secure transmission system.[446]

RESPONSE TO 9/11

All of these recommendations were made prior to 11 September 2001, but the problems persisted. The 9/11 Commission noted them in its report:

---

[442] Vice President's Task Force on Combatting Terrorism, *Public Report of the Vice President's Task Force on Combatting Terrorism* (Washington: GPO, 1986), URL: <http://www.population-security.org/bush_Report_on_terrorism_3.htm>, accessed 14 June 2006.

[443] *Attacking Terrorism: Elements of a Grand Strategy*, ed. Audrey Kurth Cronin and others (Washington: Georgetown University Press, 2004), 191.

[444] *Attacking Terrorism*, 122.

[445] Advisory Panel to Assess Domestic Response Capabilities for Terrorism Involving Weapons of Mass Destruction (Gilmore Commission), *First Annual Report to the President and Congress* (Arlington, VA: RAND Corporation, 15 December 1999), 57-58.

[446] Advisory Panel to Assess Domestic Response Capabilities for Terrorism Involving Weapons of Mass Destruction (Gilmore Commission), *Second Annual Report to the President and Congress*, (Arlington, VA: RAND Corporation, 15 December 2000), 191.

Problems within the Intelligence Community and 9/11.

The intelligence community struggled throughout the 1990s and up to 9/11 to collect intelligence on and analyze the phenomenon of transnational terrorism. The combination of an overwhelming number of priorities, flat budgets, outmoded structure, and bureaucratic rivalries resulted in an insufficient response to this new challenge.

Many dedicated officers worked day and night for years to piece together the growing body of evidence on al Qaeda and to understand the threats. Yet, while there were many reports on Bin Laden and his growing al Qaeda organization, there was no comprehensive review of what the intelligence community knew and what it did not know, and what that meant. There was no National Intelligence Estimate on terrorism between 1995 and 9/11.

Problems in the FBI, Law Enforcement and 9/11

The FBI's approach to investigations was case-specific, decentralized, and geared toward prosecution. Significant FBI resources were devoted to after-the-fact investigations of major terrorist attacks, resulting in several prosecutions.

The FBI attempted several reform efforts aimed at strengthening its ability to prevent such attacks, but these reform efforts failed to implement organization-wide institutional change. On September 11, 2001, the FBI was limited in several areas critical to an effective preventive counterterrorism strategy. Those working counterterrorism matters did so despite limited intelligence collection and strategic analysis capabilities, a limited capacity to share information both internally and externally, insufficient training, perceived legal barriers to sharing information, and inadequate resources.[447]

As a result of such limitations, on 9 September 2001, 9/11 hijacker Ziad Jarah was stopped and released by a Maryland state trooper, unaware that Jarah was an individual of concern to the Intelligence Community.[448]

Barriers to Cooperation

The Intelligence Committee of the Armed Forces Communications and Electronics Association (AFCEA) produced a white paper in which it made

---

[447] The National Commission on Terrorist Attacks upon the United States, *Staff Statement No. 9: Law Enforcement, Counterterrorism, and Intelligence Collection Prior to 9/11*, URL: <http://www.9-11commission.gov/staff_statements/staff_statement_9.pdf>, accessed 12 June 2006.

[448] Jonathan R. White, *Defending the Homeland* (Belmont, CA: Wadsworth, 2004), 2.

a plea for greater cooperation among the IC, private industry, and academia. AFCEA's approach is commendable, but the IC can reach out to other communities as well. In an age of global, non-state terrorist threats, the IC must redefine itself as a tool to protect both the domestic and international security of the United States.[449] The IC has been grappling with reform and issues relating to enhanced coordination and cooperation since 9/11. If there is any consensus from the many investigations and recriminations that followed the destruction of the World Trade Center, it is that a joint effort by the externally focused intelligence community and the internally focused law enforcement community would have offered the best chance to prevent the suffering and death that took place in New York, Washington, and Pennsylvania.

"The Wall" Between Intelligence and Law Enforcement. There is no epistemological reason to distinguish between external and internal intelligence gathering, analysis, and dissemination. However, there are reasons solidly grounded in our national values and in our commitment to establishing a balance between the exigencies of security and a commitment to preserving our civil liberties that require these distinctions. At the same time, it is appropriate that the externally focused and information-rich IC come to know, understand, and interact with the domestic law enforcement community as both communities are now integral parts of the Homeland Security community.

Because of restrictions on collecting intelligence within the United States and because of the traditional investigative secretiveness of many federal law enforcement agencies, the IC has neither been eager to establish close relationships with domestic law enforcement, nor has it often found these relationships fruitful. Law enforcement agencies, with a paramount concern for successful prosecutions, had little incentive to share and develop intelligence with the IC. Sharing is not in the nature of either police agencies or intelligence agencies. Intelligence professionals are trained to disclose information only to those with a "need to know" and then only within strict and elaborate guidelines that limit who may see and who may share. Sensitive material may be restricted to those with special security clearance, or dissemination may be limited by the organization that created the information. Rapid declassification and dissemination may not be possible, even in exigent circumstances, without putting the holder of information at risk of career and criminal penalties. Police agencies also have a culture of confidentiality. The protection of witnesses and grand jury testimony is often vital to prosecutorial success.

While information sharing may sometimes be desirable, it is not without risks. The more people that know any intelligence "fact," the greater the risk of unauthorized dissemination, including inadvertent electronic dissemination.

---

[449] AFCEA Intelligence Committee, "Strengthening our Nation's Intelligence Community: 'Action This Day,' " December 2005, *Intelligence: The Way Forward*, URL: <www.afcea.org/events/fallintel/ thewayforward.pdf>, accessed 16 January 2006.

Information may be leaked purposely or inadvertently to the press, criminals, or even terrorists. Sloppy security practices may lead to the unintentional disclosure of sensitive material. Corruption may lead to the marketing of classified information. Divided loyalties may lead to the compromise of clandestine efforts.[450]

But there are also human barriers that will not be overcome by merely improving electronic distribution systems. Information sharing works best when relationships of trust are established. These relationships can build on professional camaraderie (cop-to-cop or analyst-to-analyst) but are rarely developed in a purely electronic relationship.

An American consul stationed in Canada in the 1980s had been an appointed and sworn town constable prior to joining the U.S. Foreign Service. His term of office as a constable was for three years. It gave him police powers (which he had never had to exercise) in one American municipality. His constabulary appointment had not expired when he was posted to Canada, however. As a result, he was often called upon to act as an intermediary between Canadian and American police agencies. Although he was a federal official requiring Presidential nomination and Senate confirmation, American municipal police were often unwilling to share information with him. Instead, American police officers often asked for the name and phone number of a Canadian police officer they could contact directly. However, if the Consul volunteered that he was also a "sworn officer with police powers," or responded yes when asked if he had law enforcement authority, information flowed freely without any further need to verify his status. He was accepted as a member of the police community and presumed qualified and trustworthy to share law enforcement information. He had straddled a cultural divide.[451]

The IC has much to offer the law enforcement community; not just information, but analytic skills and methods that can hinder terrorists, serve more traditional law enforcement needs, and enhance the security of the United States. Intelligence analysts are members of the IC and also members of an analytic community. Analytic skills are essential to both the Intelligence Community and Law Enforcement. Intelligence failures rarely come from collection failures, but from analytic failures. The 9/11 Commission found that

> the FBI had little appreciation for the role of analysis. Analysts continued to be used primarily in a tactical fashion—providing support for existing cases. Compounding the problem was the

---

[450] Thomas J. Cowper and Michael E. Burger, "Improving Our View of the World: Police and Augmented Reality Technology," *Future's Working Group* PFI/FBI, 55, URL: <http://www.au.af.mil/au/ awc/awcgate/fbi/realitytech.pdf>, accessed 27 March 2006.

[451] For a move extensive discussion of camaraderie among law enforcement analysts, see Deborah Osborne, *Out of Bounds: Innovation and Change in Law Enforcement Intelligence Analysis* (Washington: Joint Military Intelligence College, 2006).

FBI's tradition of hiring analysts from within instead of recruiting individuals with the relevant educational background and expertise.

Moreover, analysts had difficulty getting access to the FBI and intelligence community information they were expected to analyze. The poor state of the FBI's information systems meant that such access depended in large part on an analyst's personal relationships with individuals in the operational units or squads where the information resided. For all of these reasons, prior to 9/11 relatively few strategic analytic reports about counterterrorism had been completed. Indeed, the FBI had never completed an assessment of the overall terrorist threat to the U.S. homeland.[452]

The sort of cooperation that is needed is built on a human relationship between intelligence analysts and law enforcement. There must be a sense of shared community membership.

As difficult as "horizontal" relationships were within the federal government, "vertical" boundaries between the federal intelligence agencies and the state and local governments were more restrictive.

Decentralized Organization. The American law enforcement community is made up of the following organizational and manpower resources:

---

[452] National Commission on Terrorist Attacks Upon the United States, *The 9/11 Commission Report*, 77, URL: <http://www.9-11commission.gov/report/911Report_Ch3.pdf>, accessed 27 March 2006.

Type of Agency	Number of Agencies	Number of Full-time Sworn Officers
Local Police	12,666	440,920
Sheriff	3,070	164,711
State Police	49	56,348
Special Jurisdiction	1,376	43,413
Texas constable	623	2,630
All State and Local	17,784	708,022
Federal		88,496
TOTAL		**796,518**

Figure 1. Law Enforcement Agencies and Officers
Source: U.S. Department of Justice, "Office of Justice Programs," *Bureau of Justice Statistics*, URL: <http://www.ojp.usdoj.gov/bjs/lawenf.htm>, accessed 27 March 2006.

If we are serious about preventing another 9/11, we cannot have these almost 800,000 trained professional information collectors and first responders working in isolation from the IC.

As the story below illustrates, vertical collaboration between law enforcement agencies is not just a one-way street. While local authorities can benefit from the national and international reach and intelligence information of federal agencies, a local police department, with its detailed knowledge of and contacts within its own jurisdiction, can often flush prey that has managed to stay off the radar of federal counterterrorism agencies.

> ### "An L.A. Police Bust Shows New Tactics for Fighting Terrorism"
> ### by Robert Block
>
> On 15 February 2006, "LAPD busted eight people for fraud…and issued arrest warrants for 11 others" on charges related to an auto theft and insurance fraud scheme. Unmentioned in the indictments was the fact that the scam was part of a Chechen terrorist financing arrangement.
>
> Concerned about the possibility of Chechen terrorist activity in Los Angeles, LAPD's Counterterrorism and Criminal Intelligence Bureau uncovered a charity, Global Human Services, that "claimed to be sending large shipments of humanitarian aid regularly to Russia, Armenia, Georgia and Jordan." But GHS had lost its business license the previous year for failing to file an income tax return and, in any case, was not a registered charity.
>
> In June 2005, after LAPD had informed the Department of Homeland Security of its investigation's findings, Immigration and Customs Enforcement inspected two GHS shipping containers in Houston that were bound for the Republic of Georgia. Inside were late-model SUVs that the owners had allowed GHS to "steal." The owners collected from their insurance companies, and GHS sold the vehicles overseas to finance Chechen rebels.
>
> LAPD then worked with the FBI and Georgian authorities to "seize another 14 stolen cars listed on customs manifests as 'aid.' " The detectives identified 200 similar shipments over the previous two years, worth at least $5 million. LAPD's Detective Severino summed up that "what we found didn't look like terrorism: it looked like regular criminal activity; but when we followed it long enough, it developed into what we believed was a nexus to terrorism."
>
> Paraphrased from the *Wall Street Journal,* 29 December 2006, A1+.

There are many barriers to effective intelligence sharing between the federal government and state and local authorities. Most state and local officials and law enforcement officers lack federal security clearances. They may lack approved repositories for storing classified information. They may not have access to approved means of transmitting classified material. They may not know what federal sources would be of assistance.

HOMELAND SECURITY ADVISORS

The IC cannot suddenly establish a relationship with almost 18,000 state and local law enforcement agencies. A conduit of communication between the federal government and each state government has been established by the appointment of a Homeland Security Advisor in every state and territory. Many homeland security advisors have established task forces and fusion centers where federal, state, and local representatives can share information and coordinate actions.

This section briefly introduces the concept of Homeland Security, the placement of homeland security offices in the various states, and highlights the professional background of homeland security advisors. It also outlines the early stages of the outreach by federal agencies to establish an improved Intelligence Community-Law Enforcement information sharing environment.

Improving Federal Information Sharing

In the wake of 9/11, the states have established homeland security departments to organize state-wide emergency response efforts and to coordinate with regional and federal counterparts. Each governor has appointed a homeland security advisor (HSA), who is the primary state point of contact for the federal Department of Homeland Security, corresponding agencies in other states, and local government. The HSAs' purposes vary somewhat. Alabama's Office of Homeland Security is designed primarily "to collect and analyze intelligence regarding terrorist threats and activities"; its counterpart in Juneau is working "to prevent terrorist attacks, reduce Alaska's vulnerability to terrorism, and minimize the loss of life or damage to critical infrastructure, and recover from attacks if they occur"; whereas the office in Arizona "develops comprehensive emergency plans to prevent or respond to natural, technological and terrorist events."[453] Granted, these differences are primarily matters of emphasis, but they reflect the diversity that makes coordination difficult at times.

The establishment of the state counterparts to the Department of Homeland Security has been an adventure in federalism. The states were given little guidance or direction in how to establish a state homeland security advisor. However, they had to move expeditiously to assure they were not excluded from a treasure trove of new federal grants. Some states merely added the duties and the title of homeland security advisor to existing office holders. In 10 states, the Adjutant General of the National Guard was declared the HSA.[454] In 11 states, the director of emergency management was declared the HSA. In 7 states (and DC), the Secretary for Public Safety was declared the HSA. In Michigan and South Carolina the head of the state police or state investigatory agency was declared the HSA. In Vermont, a captain in the State Police is HSA. In 6 states, the HSA was attached to the governor's

---

[453] "State Offices of Homeland Security," 24 February 2005, *National Conference of State Legislatures*, URL: <www.ncsl.org/programs/legismgt/nlssa/sthomelandoffcs.htm.>, accessed 13 January 2006.

[454] In Rhode Island, it is the Deputy Adjutant General, who is also head of the Emergency Management Office.

office or staff. In only 7 states was a separate homeland security department created. Paradoxically, the independent HSAs are often the weakest. They are frequently given coordinating, planning, and grant procurement functions but no line authority over either police or emergency management departments. In Nebraska, the lieutenant governor was given the added duties of the HSA.

Placement of Homeland Security Advisor by State		
Adjutant General of the National Guard	**Director of Emergency Management**	**Secretary of Public Safety**
Alaska	Alabama	Colorado
Hawaii	Arizona	Delaware
Idaho	Arkansas	District of Columbia
Iowa	Connecticut	Massachusetts
Kansas	Georgia	Minnesota
Louisiana	Montana	North Carolina
Maine	New Hampshire	Ohio
Rhode Island	North Dakota	North Dakota
Wisconsin	South Dakota	
Washington	Texas	
	Utah	
Governor's Staff	**State Police or State BI**	**Stand Alone Office**
California	Florida	Indiana
Illinois	Michigan	Kentucky
Maryland	South Carolina	Mississippi
Nevada	Vermont	New York
Virginia		Oregon
Wyoming		Pennsylvania
		Tennessee
Lieutenant Governor	**Within Public Safety Department**	
Nebraska	Missouri	
	New Jersey	
	New Mexico	
	Oklahoma	

Source: Compiled by author.

Placement of Homeland Security Advisor by Office	
Director of Emergency Services:	11
Adjutant-General of National Guard:	10
Secretary/Commissioner of Public Safety:	8
Stand Alone Office:	7
Governor's Staff:	6
State Police or State Bureau of Investigation:	4
Within Department of Public Safety:	4
Lieutenant Governor:	1

Source: Compiled by author.

No geographical pattern is evident in these assignments. In New England, for example, two states made the adjutants-general the HSA, another state the secretary of public safety, and another two the emergency management directors; still another gave the HSA function to a captain in the state police. The large states of California, New York, and Pennsylvania have each created new positions reporting to their respective state governor.

The positioning of the HSAs in the states reflects the structural ambivalence in the homeland security concept. Is the stress to be on prevention and protection or on mitigation?[455] In many states, the emergency management programs grew out of the civil defense activities of the National Guard, which would correspond with an emphasis on mitigation following an incident.

Of the 48 men and 3 women named HSAs, the overwhelming majority are from military and law enforcement backgrounds. Nineteen come from state and local law enforcement backgrounds. They include a sheriff, several police chiefs, and heads of state police organizations. Six come from federal law enforcement, including 5 retired FBI special agents and 1 Customs officer. Several have had extensive experience in law enforcement and counter-terrorism intelligence. One HSA was with the Joint Terrorism Task Force after 9/11, another was in military intelligence, and a third was formerly with the Defense Intelligence Agency. Eighteen came from military backgrounds, some with intelligence experience. Of the 2 lawyers, both have been prosecutors and one was the Department of Homeland Security Coordinator for Intelligence Sharing with the States.

One HSA has a PhD, 3 have MPAs, and 5 HSAs hold law degrees. Twenty-three HSAs have master's degrees (6 of these are in Criminal Justice), and 14 hold only bachelors' degrees. Several held degrees from accredited "credit bank" schools.[456]

---

[455] Throughout this work, state refers to the 50 states and the District of Columbia. Each commonwealth and territory also has a HSA but they were not considered.

[456] State higher education authorities typically grant an accredited bachelor's degree, usually in general studies, upon accumulation of credits representing four years of recognized university level work, regardless of the number of institutions attended.

Who are the HSAs?	
Professional Background of HSAs at Time of Appointment:	
Local Law Enforcement	19
Career Military or National Guard	18
Federal Law Enforcement	6
Lawyer	2
Politician	2
Emergency Management	2
City Manager	1

Source: Compiled by author.

Information Sharing Structures

During a February 2003 speech, President Bush recognized the importance of information sharing in thwarting terrorism and pledged, "All across our country we'll be able to tie our terrorist information to local information banks" so that local law enforcement will have the tools needed to serve as the "front line" in anti-terror efforts.[457] The U.S. Department of Justice, cognizant that 75 percent of the nation's almost 18,000 law enforcement agencies consisted of fewer than 24 sworn officers and had no intelligence specialists, established the Global Intelligence Working Group (GIWG) in 2003 with federal, local, state, and tribal law enforcement participation. It produced the National Criminal Intelligence Sharing Plan.[458] The GIWG also produced "Fusion Center Guidelines" that outlined the basic processes, products, and protocols that would allow the establishment of fusion centers in accordance with federal law and sound intelligence practices.[459]

When the HSA is in a non-law enforcement setting, a separate "fusion" or counter terrorism information center is often established to handle intelligence functions. Most of the HSAs have either founded a fusion center or designated someone within their office, or in a cooperating agency, to coordinate the intelligence function. A few states have staffed

---

[457] "President Speaks at FBI on New Terrorist Threat Integration Center," 14 February 2003, *White House*, URL: <www.whitehouse.gov/news/releases/2003/02/20030214-5.html>, accessed 16 January 2007.

[458] U.S. Department of Justice, "Annual Report to Congress: Fiscal Years 2003-2004," *Office of Justice Programs*, URL: www.ncjrs.gov/pdffiles1/ojp/215106.pdf>, accessed 16 January 2007; U.S. Department of Justice, "National Criminal Intelligence Sharing Plan," *Bureau of Justice Assistance*, rev. June 2005, iii, URL: <http://it.ojp.gov/documents/NCISP_Plan.pdf>, accessed 27 March 2006.

[459] U.S. Department of Justice, "Fusion Center Guidelines," *Bureau of Justice Assistance*, July 2005, URL: <http://it.ojp.gov/documents/fusion_center_guidelines_law_enforcement.pdf>, accessed 27 March 2006.

homeland security intelligence sections with analytical capability. In several states the HS function was given to the office charged with establishing 911 emergency police/fire telephone systems. Setting up fusion centers is often combined with the challenge of engineering coordinated, compatible communications programs.

In December 2004, the Department of Homeland Security called upon every state to establish at least one fusion center and urged additional centers for large urban areas and interstate regions with common interests. DHS promised the state HSAs that it would provide "current and actionable and unclassified information" that can be immediately disseminated to local law enforcement. DHS chose not to expand the legal definition of the Federal Intelligence Community to include state, tribal, and local entities, which would have imposed considerable costs on tribal, state, and local jurisdictions.[460] DHS continues to provide expedited security clearances, at DHS expense, for state and local officials, law enforcement officers, liaison officers, task force and fusion cell members, intelligence officers, analysts, and program managers preparing for chemical, biological, radiological/nuclear explosive incidents, based on a demonstrated need to know, usually upon the recommendation of the state HSA.[461] In March 2006, DHS announced plans to place DHS intelligence officers and analysts in selected JTTFs and fusion cells across the United States.[462] There are now 31 of these cells functioning, with about a dozen more in the planning stage.

On 17 August 2004, FBI Executive Assistant Director Maureen Baginski testified before the House Select Committee on Homeland Security to discuss progress on the information-sharing recommendations of the 9/11 Commission. She averred, "Our core guiding principle at the FBI is that intelligence and law enforcement operations must be integrated." Because operational coordination requires full and free exchange of information, "we have taken steps to establish unified FBI-wide policies for sharing information and intelligence both within the FBI and outside it. Vital information about those that would do us harm is not produced by the federal government alone. We are proud to be part of an 800,000 strong state, local, and tribal law enforcement community who are the first to encounter and defend against threats." The FBI has "placed reports officers in several Joint Terrorism Task Forces (JTTFs) to ensure vital information is flowing to those who need it. These reports officers are trained to produce intelligence reports that both

---

[460] Homeland Security Advisory Council, "Intelligence and Information Sharing Initiative: Final Report – December 2004," *Department of Homeland Security*, URL: <http://www.dhs.gov/interweb/ assetlibrary/HSAC_IntelInfoSharingReport_1204.pdf>, accessed 27 March 2006.

[461] "Fact Sheet: State & Local Security Clearance Program," *Department of Homeland Security*, URL: <http://www.scd.state.hi.us/upload/DHS/SL_Clearance_Fact_Sheet.doc>, accessed 27 March 2006.

[462] Dibya Sarkar, "DHS adds brainpower to intelligence centers," *Federal Computer Week*, 14 March 2006, URL: <http://www.fcw.com/article92600-03-14-06-Web>, accessed 27 March 2006.

protect sources and methods and maximize the amount of information that can be shared." There are now more than 100 JTTFs receiving both raw and finished intelligence. The FBI has also "established Field Intelligence Groups (FIGs) to integrate analysts, Agents, linguists, and surveillance personnel in the field to bring a dedicated team focus to intelligence operations. As of June 2004, there are 1,450 FIG personnel, including 382 Special Agents and 160 employees from other Government agencies." FIG officers have TS/SCI clearances. The FBI is now producing Intelligence Information Reports (IIRs), Intelligence Assessments, and Intelligence Bulletins that are shared within the intelligence and law enforcement communities.[463]

FIGS: INTELLIGENCE FOR LAW ENFORCEMENT

The Field Intelligence Groups (FIGs) are embedded intelligence entities in each of the FBI's 56 field offices in the U.S. FIGs are designed to integrate the intelligence cycle into field operations and manage the Intelligence Program in coordination with the Directorate of Intelligence at FBI Headquarters. The FIGs represent an integrated intelligence service, leveraging the core strengths of the law enforcement culture, including source reliability and fact-based analysis. FIGs are responsible for coordinating, managing, and executing all the functions of the intelligence cycle. Each FIG combines FBI specialists with officers and analysts from other agencies as appropriate.

FIG operations focus on locating and disseminating actionable intelligence. This intelligence is not focused on only one case or one division's needs, but rather on the entire Bureau and the Intelligence Community. FIGs are expected to:

- Develop expertise related to the FBI's priorities, based on the threats to the nation;
- Understand the local and national intelligence collection capabilities that can be applied to address intelligence requirements;
- Support the needs of the Special Agent in Charge and FBIHQ for intelligence products and services, based on the FBI's investigative and national intelligence priorities;
- Identify and report raw intelligence against requirements to FBIHQ in a timely manner; and
- Analyze and report regional developments to FBIHQ for further dissemination to the national security and law enforcement communities.[464]

---

[463] Maureen Baginski, "Statement Before the House of Representatives Committee on Homeland Security," 17 August 2004, *Federal Bureau of Investigation*, URL: <www.fbi.gov/congress/congress04/ baginski081704.htm>, accessed 12 January 2007.

[464] "FBI Professional Staff Field Intelligence Groups," *Federal Bureau of Investigation*, 2006, URL: <http://www.fbijobs.gov/12141.asp>, accessed 17 September 2006.

SYSTEMS FOR SHARING

These products are distributed over several systems. Intelink (sensitive highly classified material), SIPRNET (classified material), and LEO—"Law Enforcement Online (LEO), a virtual private network that reaches federal, state, and local law enforcement at the Sensitive but Unclassified (SBU) level." LEO includes tools that "assist law enforcement in intelligence-led policing," including "the National Crime Information Center, the Integrated Automatic Fingerprint Identification System, and the Interstate Identification Index."[465] LEO reaches over 17,000 state and local police agencies in the United States.

In March 2003, President Bush signed Executive Order 13292, providing a unified system for "classifying, safeguarding, and declassifying national security information."[466] In October 2005, the President issued Executive Order 13388, which ordered "the sharing of terrorism information to protect Americans." It set out the goals for what would become the IC and law enforcement information sharing environment, calling for the exchange of terrorist information among federal agencies and between federal agencies and state and local governments.[467]

Congress joined the discussion with Section 1016 of the Intelligence Reform and Terrorism Prevention Act of December 2004 (IRTPA). It requires the President to "create an information sharing environment (ISE)," to ensure that "there are facilities and means for the sharing of terrorism information" among "all appropriate Federal, State, local, and tribal entities."[468] The ISE includes all terrorism related "information, whether collected, produced, or distributed by intelligence, law enforcement, military, [or] homeland security." The Act designated the National Counterterrorism Center (NCTC) as the primary organization for integrating and analyzing all intelligence pertaining to terrorism and counterterrorism and for conducting strategic operational planning by integrating all instruments of national power.[469]

In 2005, the President established the Office of the Program Manager (PM) for ISE and placed it, with community-wide responsibilities, under the Director of National Intelligence (DNI).[470] A short time later, the Information

---

[465] Baginski, "Statement."

[466] U.S. President, Executive Order 13292, "Classified National Security Information," 25 March 2003, 1.

[467] U.S. President, Executive Order 13388, "Further Strengthening the Sharing of Terrorism Information to Protect Americans," 25 October 2005, 1.

[468] § 1016(b); PL 108-458; 118 Stat. 3638, Intelligence Reform and Prevention of Terrorism Act of 2004.

[469] *Intelligence Reform and Terrorism Prevention Act of 2004*, Sec. 1016(a)(4). The CIA's CTC (see above) gave way in September 2003 to the inter-agency Terrorist Threat Integration Center (TTIC), which was incorporated into the NCTC in 2004.

[470] "Presidential Memorandum on the Creation of the Office of Program Manager," 2 June 2005, *PM/ISE*, URL: <www.ise.gov/sitemap.html>, accessed 16 January 2007.

Sharing Council, under the chairmanship of the PM and with the heads of the major government departments and intelligence organizations, was established by the President.[471] In January 2006, the "Interim Implementation Plan" was announced.[472] The plan called for improving IC standards, revamping the use of SBU information, and effecting cultural change in federal agencies to encourage sharing.

In December 2005, the White House issued "Presidential Guidelines and Requirements in Support of the Information Sharing Environment."[473] They called for greater IC interagency coordination and common standards for the ISE of federal, state, tribal, and local officials. By May 2006, the NCTC was collecting intelligence information from 28 different government networks and posting it to a single website, accessible by individual agencies; Guidelines for Tearline Reporting were issued to maximize intelligence information sharing; and the IC's 40,000-member OSIS computer system and Law Enforcement's LEO system (35,000 terminals) had been linked.[474]

CONTINUING EVOLUTION

While no one would contend the transition is complete, many signs of progress dramatize the process of institutionalizing information sharing between and among the intelligence and law enforcement communities. Over 700 FBI linguists now hold Top Secret clearances. In October 2001, the FBI established a College of Analytic Studies at the FBI Academy in Quantico, Virginia. It has graduated 264 analysts from its six-week full-time introductory course. The FBI has begun a certification program for analysts. It has also produced an "Intelligence Dissemination Manual" to assist in the transmittal and dissemination of classified material to the law enforcement community. Senior FBI officials work with their IC counterparts on the NCTC to enable full integration of terrorist threat-related information and analysis. The National Joint Terrorism Task Force has interagency representation at FBIHQ. The FBI now contributes to the CIA-coordinated President's Terrorist Threat Report (PTTR).

These steps, coupled with the work toward full integration of systems outlined above, are symptoms of a changing culture in both the IC and law enforcement.

---

[471] E.O. 13288 of 25 October 2005.

[472] *Information Sharing Environment Interim Implementation Plan*, January 2006, URL: <www.ise.gov/ISE%20Interim%20Implementation%20Plan%20-%2020060109%20FINAL[1].pdf>, accessed 16 January 2007.

[473] "Presidential Guidelines and Requirements in Support of the Information Sharing Environment," 16 December 2005, *PM/ISE*, URL: <www.ise.gov/sitemap.html>, accessed 16 January 2007.

[474] Ambassador Thomas C. McNamara, Program Manager for the Information Sharing Environment, "Building on the Information Sharing Environment: Addressing Challenges of Implementation," statement before the Subcommittee on Intelligence Sharing, and Terrorism Risk Assessment, House Committee on Homeland Security, 10 May 2006, 6-7.

ADDRESSING THE DIFFICULTIES

This volume concludes with abstracts of other pertinent graduate studies by LE and IC professionals. They suggest ways of addressing the difficulties by changing attitudes, organizations, and technologies in ways that facilitate rapid dissemination of information, intelligence, and ideas from anywhere in the IC-LE community to the point of need.

For Law Enforcement and the IC to "get along" requires a series of adjustments. Several have already been legislated. Some are being implemented. These abstracts suggest others. They represent assessments of various IC and LE professionals whose experience has been supplemented by the luxury of time to stop and think about problems their agencies face. They provide a perspective from those who have been "out in the field," "down in the trenches," and "at the pointy end of the spear" in recent years—a perspective worth hearing.

PERCEPTIONS OF LAW ENFORCEMENT-INTELLIGENCE COMMUNITY INFORMATION SHARING

Captain Stacey Smith, USAF
Master of Science of Strategic Intelligence, 2003

Whatever the reality of LE-IC information sharing, the perception among law enforcement professionals at the local, state, and federal level is that much remains to be done. The anonymous interviews on which this author's conclusion is based give a "from the field" perspective on information sharing among law enforcement agencies and between law enforcement and the IC.

The Fear Factor

Fear is the driving factor for the recent improvements in information sharing. The motivation to share will recede once the fear has abated. Across the board—federal, state, and local—all the law enforcement personnel interviewed believed that recent improvements in information sharing were driven by fear. Most believed that over time information sharing would go back to the way it was prior to 11 September 2001. A smaller number felt that some degree of the current positive environment could be maintained.

Despite changes in procedure designed to make information sharing easier, most interviewees (7 of 9) named individual contacts as the most effective way to obtain information, rather than institutional connections or liaisons.

Sharing Among LE agencies

Law enforcement professionals have much more experience sharing information among themselves than with the IC, with which they have had a sometimes rocky relationship.

State and Local Police. All interview subjects had a good-to-excellent opinion about local and state information sharing. The comments were overwhelmingly positive. All the interviewees except one (8 of 9) believed that they received all the information available from local law enforcement. The majority of the interviewees (7 of 9) stated that the states shared information. Two federal agents, however, thought the information provided was not helpful.

The FBI. Every local and state law enforcement official interviewed during the research phase noted that overall information sharing had improved since 11 September 2001. However, everyone also gave unsolicited comments to the effect that the FBI had not really changed fundamentally and was still withholding information. The level of trust of the FBI by local law enforcement is still very low when it comes to information sharing.

Local law enforcement personnel did not give glowing reviews of the FBI. While the locals stated that generally the FBI was perceived as a good agency, the subjects believed that the FBI took on too much responsibility and was overwhelmed by its work load. Both Border Patrol subjects said it was easy to work with individual FBI agents, but the further one went up the organization, the more difficult it was to work with the FBI. The Customs subject stated that individual FBI agents were good, but that trust of field agents by FBI management was poor.

The overwhelming response was that the FBI's information sharing was poor. Although the Border Patrol subjects stated that the local FBI relationship was good, Customs interviewees noted the inefficiency in the FBI information sharing process. Obtaining information from the FBI simply takes a lot of time. Only one local law enforcement official believed that the FBI was doing a better job of sharing information. The same individual stated that the "old school FBI" might have sat on information in the past. The NYPD subjects viewed FBI information sharing as poor. One of these interviewees stated that the FBI never volunteered anything and contended that this was still true after 11 September 2001.

In the wake of 9/11, the FBI's New York Task Force had to plow through hundreds of leads but reportedly turned down NYPD officers who were not on the task force but offered to help. The FBI practice of taking information, while at the same time not revealing the full extent of the information it possesses, is seen as a cultural mind-set that negatively affects local police in the conduct of their duties. Local police do not have access to information that is of concern and that affects their jurisdictions. The FBI has a reputation of waiting until local police develop information and are getting close to making an arrest. Then the FBI moves in and takes over the case.

Both FBI agents gave almost identical answers to the question, "How do you define information sharing?" They stated that the information would be disseminated to only the appropriate jurisdictions. This definition was more restrictive than that given by others, even the other federal law enforcement agencies. The FBI agents interviewed mentioned the Robert Hanssen case as an example of why information has to be based on clearance and on a need to know. The betrayal factor felt among FBI agents is enormous and should not be underestimated.

One FBI official stated that there was a perception that the FBI has information that is withheld. He also said that there is a "mystique" assigned to the FBI, that they are all-knowing and wise. This is a factor in the FBI reluctance at times to share information for fear that it will be blown out of proportion or leaked prior to resolution of the case.

Other Federal LE Agencies. The majority of the subjects believed they were not receiving all the information available from federal law enforcement. The majority of those that believed they were receiving all the information (2 of 3) were themselves in federal law enforcement. A Customs agent stated there was a perception that federal agencies withhold information and do not share everything. The agent stated that this was a myth about federal agencies.

All subjects stated they had good impressions of federal law enforcement. Two NYPD officials made interesting comments. One stated that he believed federal law enforcement officers to be competent, but that their knowledge of local issues was limited. The other stated that uniformed federal law enforcement was pretty good, but the FBI was mainly focused on investigations and not as good at police work as the NYPD.

The majority of the subjects (6 of 9) opined that federal law enforcement sharing was good. A minority strongly believed that it was difficult to deal with federal law enforcement. This included one Border Patrol interviewee who stated that it was often the federal agencies that are the most difficult.

DoD/IC Information Sharing with LE. The majority (6 of 9) had a good opinion of DoD information sharing. One NYPD subject believed that DoD was too slow and bureaucratic. A Border Patrol interviewee believed that on a day-to-day basis, information from DoD was some of the most helpful.

All subjects had a good impression of the IC. Several were laudatory. One FBI official stated that he had no impression of the IC, and federal law enforcement subjects in general had little understanding and involvement with the IC.

The majority of local law enforcement believed that information was still being withheld by federal law enforcement and intelligence agencies. An interesting dichotomy was that all the subjects nevertheless stated that they trusted that critical information would be provided to them by other agencies when needed.

Approximately half (5 of 9) believed they received everything available from the IC. The majority of the local law enforcement officials believed that the IC withheld information due to classified sources. They all believed that the IC generally had good reason to restrict access due to classification. It seemed that the resources of the Intelligence Community are not clearly understood within law enforcement.

CHALLENGES AND OPPORTUNITIES OF INTELLIGENCE COMMUNITY MEMBERSHIP

Sallie Casto
Master of Science of Strategic Intelligence, 2005

The calculus of the pros and cons of IC membership for DEA presented here are generally applicable to other law enforcement agencies as well. While the hassle-factor of IC membership is a concern, there are clearly both real and intangible benefits to being inside the IC tent. In any case, most law enforcement agencies will remain outside the IC, while continuing to be producers and consumers of intelligence.

Weighing intangibles

DEA's ability to have a "seat at the table" through IC membership is a strong, intangible benefit that may very well outweigh the more practical—and arguably more numerous—negative considerations of IC membership. By being an IC member, DEA would be able to ensure that the drug issue was appropriately relayed to policymakers as the threat to national security that it is. In addition, DEA would raise its own awareness of the requirements of the IC and bring the Agency's unique resources to bear against national security threats such as terrorism. Thus, DEA could more effectively participate in the national security process through IC membership.

Funding Issues

DEA has an excellent working relationship with members of the IC. Once it joins the IC, however, the IC component of DEA would be in competition for funding with other IC members, possibly increasing tension between DEA and other IC agencies.

The IC component of DEA would likely receive some funding from National Intelligence Program (NIP) accounts to fulfill its IC obligations, potentially boosting DEA funding overall. But there is no guarantee that DEA would receive such increased funding or that the increase would not be offset by reductions in other DEA accounts. So DEA might have to fulfill its IC obligations with inadequate funding, which would negatively affect its law enforcement mission. And whatever the level of funding, there will certainly be increased requirements for justifying the budget to Congress.

Legal Requirements

Joining the IC will impose new legal requirements on the Agency as well. Executive Order 12333 on national intelligence activities requires that DEA members associated with the IC be trained on their responsibilities under the law. That training, as well as monitoring compliance with the Order, can be expected to generate new and on-going reporting requirements. Additional Congressional oversight by intelligence-associated committees will also be a condition of IC membership.

Tasking Authority

It is possible that DEA will not have complete control of its IC component, since the DCI (and now the DNI) has control over non-DoD NIP budget. Thus, DEA could have one set of goals for its Intelligence Component while the DNI, for example, could mandate different goals or objectives for DEA's IC component.

Handling IC-LE tensions

Concerns about appropriate handling and separation of intelligence and law enforcement information have been addressed as DEA and the IC have become increasingly skilled at successfully sharing information without jeopardizing cases or sources and methods.

Because of the natural tension between foreign intelligence collection and domestic law enforcement, membership in the IC poses unique challenges for any law enforcement agency. These challenges center on the need to separate IC information from law enforcement information so that criminal prosecutions are not contaminated by IC information, nor are IC sources and methods subjected to disclosure in U.S. courts of law. At the same time, effective collaboration between the IC and law enforcement functions must not be impeded. DEA is already successfully managing this "wall" in the way in which its Special Operations Division (SOD) translates IC information into actionable law enforcement leads. DEA success in its SOD operations can serve as a template for the structure and process of the IC component at DEA.

A Seat at the Table

DEA should not count on a significant influx of funds or information as a result of joining the IC. However, DEA would bring "to the table" a wealth of human intelligence not otherwise available to the IC. Moreover, DEA can expect to interact more directly with policymakers about the international drug problem and to expand DEA's "sphere of influence." Also, DEA can expect the opportunity both to identify and receive intelligence collection requirements as a result of IC membership. In addition, DEA can expect to be exposed to greater opportunities for training as a result of IC membership.

INTELLIGENCE FUSION IN THE FIELD: TRANSLATING NATIONAL STRATEGY INTO PRACTICE

Lieutenant Angelina Hidalgo, USCG
Master of Science of Strategic Intelligence, 2005

Since 9/11, the procedures and process by which federal, state, and local agencies share and exchange intelligence and information have come under considerable scrutiny. Until there are standard interagency information and intelligence sharing procedures, as well as routine collaboration for homeland security operations, the U.S. will remain vulnerable to terrorist attack.

Barriers to Sharing

According to this case study of intelligence and law enforcement operations along the Gulf Coast, there is still room for improvement when it comes to information fusion. While there has been progress in strengthening interagency partnerships, as well as advances in "sharing" technologies, intelligence and information sharing gaps still remain. They impede the kind of collaboration that is needed to counter emerging threats. These gaps are the result of several factors:

1. Intelligence/Information sharing procedures are still heavily dependent on person-to-person exchanges based on personal relationships.

2. Each agency has a different opinion concerning what they believe constitutes effective intelligence/information sharing.

3. A systematic intelligence/information sharing process is not in place, resulting in case by case sharing.

4. While various intelligence/information databases and networks help link agencies, many of these databases are still in the maturing process.

Characteristics of a Solution

A sharing framework that identifies the different centers and fusion initiatives and that describes the different databases available for sharing would help operators stay informed about resources available to them. Currently, agencies must identify initiatives and develop new sharing strategies on their own. This proposed interagency framework, whether created through a collective effort at the strategic level or in the newly created fusion centers at the tactical level, would help unify intelligence/information sharing efforts and create a common understanding of intelligence/information fusion concepts.

It would also help pinpoint additional sharing shortfalls and prevent agencies from duplicating efforts. At the very least, this framework should include:

- a plan for achieving newly identified strategic intelligence/information sharing objectives;

- the various intelligence/information sharing initiatives currently underway or planned for the future, starting with DHS Headquarters down to local levels, including scheduled completion dates for all projects;

- the available databases that facilitate interagency sharing; and

- a list of agency intelligence/information sharing representatives at DHS headquarters and among units at the tactical level.

SEMANTIC WEB: TECHNOLOGY FOR INTEGRATION

Captain Rachel Hingst, USAFR
Master of Science of Strategic Intelligence, 2005

The Semantic Web project seeks to enhance the World Wide Web's search and information exchange capabilities by creating "smarter" computer-processable documents. They would be compatible with a variety of disparate systems and would advertise their contents through the use of standards, markup languages, and related processing tools. If there's a will, this may be the way.

The real power of the Semantic Web (SW) approach is that it takes advantage of the distributed nature of the World Wide Web. Rather than assuming a one-size-fits-all approach, it recognizes that individual communities often have specific needs and languages. The SW vision recognizes that different groups have developed technologies tailored to their specific issues, and it only seeks to enhance current efforts, not replace them. The various forms of Extensible Markup Language (XML)[475] can all be easily exchanged between different types of computers using different operating systems and application languages. This would allow for a standard metadata definition such as Justice XML to be mapped to another standard such as IC XML, resolving differences in structure and language so that information could flow between these groups regardless of the source on which the information is based. In other words, the LE community could continue to use Justice XML (which has already been deployed in over 50 initiatives), the IC could continue to use IC XML, and the Department of Homeland Security could use their emerging National Information Exchange Model (NIEM). Using separate XML standards can be beneficial because each model is distinct and has been constructed by experts based on specific community needs.

In addition to leveraging current XML standards, the SW vision recommends tools to allow for automatic discovery, execution, and monitoring of services. With such tools, new sources can advertise their availability as soon as they are connected to the network; other methods of discovering data sources are not as dynamic and require maintenance to stay current. Such source discovery is a major challenge in distributed environments, and software agents designed to support LE and IC members would benefit greatly from this technology.

As new sources become available, information overload becomes an issue. Large amounts of data create "signal to noise" problems, and determining

---

[475] Extensible Markup Language facilitates the sharing of data across disparate systems.

what is really important becomes increasingly difficult. Metadata can be used to flag the more relevant and actionable information within the queue, indicating that Report Y supersedes Report X, for instance.

Below are several possible scenarios illustrating the potential benefits of a Semantic Web-enabled sharing environment.

- A counterterrorism analyst charged with evaluating terrorist financing submits an intelligent search on an organization suspected of having terrorist ties. The search not only goes to the Financial Crimes Enforcement Network (FinCEN) but also relevant IC and LE sources. The intelligent search capability is able to take some initial returns, such as names of the group members, and automatically run them against many of the same sources. This second search brings back information on investigations of several members for fraud. Currently, this would require multiple log-ins to multiple systems, multiple search requests, and the manual piecing together of relevant information returns. The technologies that make this a reality are data mediation among disparate systems, metadata tagging for more intelligent searches, and Public Key Infrastructure (PKI) digital certificates that rapidly authenticate users' credentials.

- An analyst submits an intelligent search to find the most recent image of a location prior to 21 January 2005 and the most recent image of the same location after 21 January 2005, both with N/S orientation and the same resolution. The search brings back photos from multiple sources for the analyst to review. Currently, many analysts spend a great deal of time just trying to find good images from multiple sources. The technologies that make this scenario a reality include data mediation, machine-understandable metadata on images (to include date taken, orientation, and resolution), and PKI digital certificates.

- An agent submits a search for information on suspected terrorist Jack Jones, who once lived at 1234 Skippy Lane. Her intelligent search includes LE databases that have Jack Jones at Skippy Lane using aliases Paul Simpson and Jake Johnson. The name Paul Simpson shows up as a traffic stop (driving without a license) in St. Louis. Jake Johnson comes back with a traffic stop in Clark, Missouri (expired license plate). These returns can then be automatically plotted on a map or graphed using XML-enabled analysis tools. The technologies that could be used to make this scenario a reality include data mediation, PKI certificates, and analysis tools that would use metadata such as geo-coordinates for a location to allow for automatic display on a map.

The Semantic Web has enormous potential for improving information sharing between communities such as LE and the IC. However, to implement the envisioned SW solution, a significant amount of change still needs to occur in IC and LE cultures; in effect, a move toward a "need to share" mentality. The SW concept hinges on machine-understandable metadata being added to information by its current "owners": analysts and agents who have been in the habit of playing things close to the vest.

ABOUT THE AUTHORS

Marilyn B. Peterson worked in state and local law enforcement as an intelligence analyst for 25 years. She has written on and taught basic, advanced, and strategic intelligence analysis. Her first work was as chief writer of *The 1980 Report: A Decade of Organized Crime* (Harrisburg, PA: Pennsylvania Crime Commission, 1980). Her latest is *Intelligence-Led Policing: The New Intelligence Architecture* (Washington: Bureau of Justice Assistance, 2005), URL: <www.ncjrs.gov/pdffiles1/bja/210681.pdf>. She now works for the Defense Intelligence Agency as an Instructor at the Joint Military Intelligence Training Center. She has received Lifetime Certification from the Society of Certified Criminal Analysts and from the Association of Certified Fraud Examiners, where she is also a Fellow.

Gloria Freund is a DIA civilian analyst with more than 20 years experience working military intelligence issues related to China, the Middle East, and the Persian Gulf. A retired commander in the Navy reserve, she served as an attaché, on Service operational and intelligence staffs, and in the Office of the Secretary of Defense.

Major (P) **Edward Gliot,** USA, is Chief of the Intelligence Operations Division at EUCOM's Joint Analysis Center, having previously served in PACOM's Joint Intelligence Center as a politico-military analyst for China and Southeast Asia. His prior assignments included command and staff billets in armor units overseas and the 82nd Airborne Division. In Washington, he provided direct support for the planning and execution of Operation IRAQI FREEDOM as a member of the Joint Staff/J2. He later deployed to Baghdad with the Iraq Survey Group (ISG), investigating the former regime's weapons of mass destruction programs.

Technical Sergeant **Lloyd E. Dabbs**, USAF, is the Non-Commissioned-Officer-in Charge of Training and Analysis for the 608th Air Intelligence Squadron, Barksdale AFB, Louisiana. He has spent the past 10 years in the intelligence analysis field, covering a wide spectrum of global issues, providing analytic and targeting support for Operations ALLIED FORCE and DESERT FOX, and deploying overseas for Operations SOUTHERN WATCH and IRAQI FREEDOM.

David W. Spencer has been an Intelligence Research Specialist with the Drug Enforcement Administration (DEA) since 1991, serving in South America's Andean region and at Headquarters. A veteran military intelligence officer, he served in the National Guard Counter-Drug Program in the Pennsylvania Attorney General's Bureau of Narcotics Investigations before joining DEA.

Captain **Devlin Kostal,** USAF, an Air Force security officer, is currently Chief of Security Forces for the 478th Expeditionary Operations Squadron's forward operating location in Ecuador. A graduate of the Air Force Academy, he deployed twice in support of Operation ENDURING FREEDOM, to Pakistan and Afghanistan. The 2004 thesis on which his article is based won the Joint History Office Fleet Admiral Chester W. Nimitz Award for Archival Research.

Chief Warrant Officer Five **Devin Rollis,** USA, is Chief of All-Source Intelligence and Warrant Officer Training Development at the U.S. Army Intelligence Center, Fort Huachuca, Arizona. He works with military police and the FBI to incorporate law enforcement investigative skills into intelligence training for counterinsurgency operations. A 30-year Army veteran, he was deployed for Operation DESERT STORM and with NATO's IFOR in Sarajevo.

Robert Murphy is a Foreign Service Officer who currently heads a Provincial Reconstruction Team in Iraq. In addition to working in the State Department's Bureau of Intelligence and Research, he previously served as Senator George Mitchell's assistant for the Northern Ireland peace process, as U.S. representative to the Angolan Peace Commission, as principal officer at the consulate in Jeddah in the aftermath of a major terrorist attack, and as a Camp David Treaty Observer in the Sinai. He holds undergraduate degrees from Harvard and the University of London, as well as graduate degrees from Suffolk University, University of Leicester, Trinity College of Dublin, and Syracuse University's Maxwell School. He is a candidate for the LL.D. degree from the University of South Africa.

Major **Stacey Smith**, USAF, is a Special Agent in the Air Force Office of Special Investigations. As security adviser to the Secretary of the Air Force, he maintains contact with senior government officials, as well as international, federal, state, and local law enforcement agencies. He served as a counter-intelligence agent with Iraq's Coalition Provisional Authority and was a Marine infantry NCO during Operation DESERT STORM.

Sallie Casto is a Supervisory Intelligence Research Specialist with DEA and has served in operational and strategic support functions within DEA for the past 23 years. Her area of specialization is drug trafficking in Mexico and Central America, as well as its impact on the United States.

Lieutenant **Angelina Hidalgo**, USCG, investigates terrorism threats to the maritime domain for the National Counterterrorism Center. A Coast Guard Academy graduate, she previously commanded the USCGC *Kingfisher* and served as Law Enforcement Officer aboard the USCGC *Dauntless*.

Captain **Rachel Hingst**, USAFR, is an Advanced Programs intelligence officer at the Air Force Intelligence Analysis Agency. She also works as a Domain Analyst for Lockheed Martin's Advanced Technology Laboratories and previously developed and tailored data mediation technologies for law enforcement and criminal justice clients.

BIBLIOGRAPHY

519th Military Intelligence Battalion. "Operation IRAQI FREEDOM HUMINT Lessons Learned." Fort Bragg, NC: 29 March 2004.

Andrew, Christopher. *Her Majesty's Secret Service: The Making of the British Intelligence Community.* New York: Elisabeth Sifton Books, 1986.

Anti-Defamation League. *Dangerous Convictions: An Introduction to Extremist Activities in Prisons,* March 2002. URL: <http://www.adl.org/learn/Ext_terr/Dangerous_Convictions.pdf>. Accessed 11 November 2005.

Attacking Terrorism: Elements of a Grand Strategy. Ed. Audrey Kurth Cronin and others. Washington: Georgetown University Press, 2004.

Best, Richard A. Jr. "Homeland Security: Intelligence Support." *Congressional Research Service Report for Congress* RS21283. Washington: Congressional Research Service, Library of Congress, 4 March 2003.

_____. "Intelligence and Law Enforcement: Countering Transnational Threats to the United States." *Congressional Research Service Report for Congress* RL30252. Washington: Congressional Research Service, 16 January 2001.

"Peace Keeping—Perils and Prospects: 'The Big Ten' Lessons Learned from Recent Operations in Somalia, Rwanda, Haiti and Bosnia," January 1996. *Business Executives for National Security.* URL: <http://www.bens.org/pubs_0196.html>. Accessed 30 November 2006.

Bodnar, John W. *Warning Analysis for the Information Age: Rethinking the Intelligence Process.* Washington: Joint Military Intelligence College, December 2003.

Bouza, Anthony V. *Police Intelligence: The Operations of an Investigative Unit.* New York: AMS Press, 1976.

British and American Approaches to Intelligence. Ed. K.G. Robertson. New York: St. Martin's Press, 1987.

Carter, David L. *Law Enforcement Intelligence: A Guide for State, Local, and Tribal Law Enforcement Agencies.* Washington: Department of Justice Office of Community Oriented Policing Services, November 2004.

Cassidy, Robert M., Major, USA. "Why Great Powers Fight Small Wars Badly." *Military Review,* September-October 2000, 41-53.

Casto, Sallie. *Challenges and Opportunities that Await DEA as It Considers Membership in the Intelligence Community*. MSSI Thesis chaired by Dr. Barry Zulauf. Washington: Joint Military Intelligence College, January 2005.

Central Intelligence Agency. *CIA Factbook on Intelligence 2002*. URL: <www.odci.gov/cia/publications/facttel/intelligence_cycle.html>. Accessed 27 November 2003.

_____. *A Consumer's Guide to Intelligence*. Washington: CIA Office of Public Affairs, 1999.

Chappelear, James W. *Department of Defense Intelligence Support to Civil Authorities*. MSSI Thesis. Washington: Joint Military Intelligence College, 5 September 2001.

Clark, Robert M. *Intelligence Analysis: A Target-Centric Approach*. Washington: CQ Press, 2004.

Coakley, Robert W. *The Role of Federal Forces in Domestic Disorders, 1789-1878*. Washington: GPO, 1988.

Community Model, The: A Basic Training Curriculum for Law Enforcement Analysts. Washington: Counterdrug Intelligence Executive Secretariat, March 2003.

Criminal Intelligence Analysis. Eds. Paul P. Andrews and Marilyn Peterson. Loomis, CA: The Palmer Press, 1990.

Cuthbertson, Ian. "Prisons and the Education of Terrorists." *World Policy Journal* 21, no. 3 (Fall 2004): 15-22.

Davidson, Kimber E. *Intelligence Community Support to Law Enforcement*. MSSI Thesis chaired by Dr. Mark V. Kauppi. Washington: Joint Military Intelligence College, August 2001.

Deacon, Richard. *A History of the British Secret Service*. London: Granada Publishing Ltd., 1980.

Decker, Scott, and others. "Gangs as Organized Crime Groups: A Tale of Two Cities." *Crime and Justice Quarterly* 15 (1998): 395-423.

_____. "The Problem of Gangs and Security Threat Groups (STG's) in American Prisons Today: Recent Findings From the 2004 Prison Gang Survey." *National Gang Crime Research Center,* December 2005. URL: <www.ngcrc.com/corr2004.html>. Accessed 8 December 2005.

Drug Enforcement Administration. *New Era of DEA Intelligence, Preliminary Action Plan*. Washington: N.p., February 2005.

Enzensberger, Hans M. *Civil Wars: From LA to Bosnia*. Trans. Piers Spence and Martin Chalmers. New York: New Press, 1997.

Etter, Gregg W. "Common Characteristics of Gangs: Examining the Cultures of the New Urban Tribes." *Journal of Gang Research* 5, no. 2 (Winter, 1998): 19-33.

FBI, The: A Comprehensive Reference Guide. Eds. Athens G. Theoharis and others. Phoenix: Orys Press, 1999.

Fritsch, Eric J., and others. "Gang Suppression Through Saturation Patrol, Aggressive Curfew, and Truancy Enforcement: A Quasi-Experimental Test of the Dallas Anti-Gang Initiative." *Crime & Delinquency* 45, no. 1 (January 1999): 122-139.

Gates, Robert M. *From the Shadows*. New York: Simon and Schuster, 1996.

Geraghty, Tony. *The Irish War: The Military History of a Domestic Conflict*. London: Harper Collins Publishers, 1998.

Gliot, Edward, Major, USA. *Bringing All the Guns to Bear: Employing Police Anti-Gang Intelligence Techniques in Support of Operations Other Than War*. MSSI Thesis chaired by Major Christopher Marshall, USA. Washington: Joint Military Intelligence College, July 1999.

Global Intelligence Working Group. *The National Criminal Intelligence Sharing Plan*, October 2003. URL: <it.ojp.gov/documents/NCISP_Plan.pdf>. Accessed 1 November 2006.

Godson, Roy. *Intelligence Requirements for the 1990s: Collection, Analysis, Counterintelligence, and Covert Action*. Lexington, MA: Lexington Books, 1989.

Gourley, Scott R. "Speaking the Same Language: Preparing Civilian and Military First-Responders to Work Together." *T&S Training and Simulation Journal*, August/September 2003, 24-26.

Grabo, Cynthia M. *Anticipating Surprise: Analysis for Strategic Warning*. Washington: Joint Military Intelligence College, 2002.

Halperin, Morton H., and others. *The Lawless State: The Crimes of the U.S. Intelligence Agencies*. Harmondsworth, UK: Penguin Books Ltd, 1976.

Heuer, Richards J. Jr. *Psychology of Intelligence Analysis*. Washington: Center for the Study of Intelligence, 1999.

Hidalgo, Angelina, Lieutenant, USCG. *Intelligence Fusion in the Field: Translating National Strategy into Practice*. MSSI Thesis chaired by Lieutenant Commander Eric Ensign, USCG. Washington: Joint Military Intelligence College, August 2005.

Hingst, Rachel G., Captain, USAFR. *Leveraging Technology to Enhance Information Sharing Between Law Enforcement and the Intelligence Community.* MSSI Thesis chaired by Dr. Barry Zulauf. Washington: Joint Military Intelligence College, March 2005.

Howell, James C. *Youth Gangs: An Overview.* Washington: Department of Justice, 1998.

"IC21: The Intelligence Community in the 21st Century." *Staff Study for the House of Representatives Permanent Select Committee on Intelligence,* 104th Congress. URL: <www.access.gpo.gov/congress/house/intel/ic21/ic21009.html>. Accessed 16 April 2004.

Intelligence 2000: Revising the Basic Elements. Ed. Marilyn B. Peterson and others. Sacramento, CA: LEIU and IALEIA, 2000.

International Association of Law Enforcement Intelligence Professionals (IALEIA). *Guidelines for Starting an Analytic Unit.* South Florida, FL: IALEIA, 1997.

Jeffrey, Keith. "Intelligence and Counterinsurgency Operations: Some reflections on the British Experience." *Intelligence and National Security* 2, no. 1 (January 1987): 118-149.

Johnson, Loch K. *A Season of Inquiry: Congress and Intelligence.* Chicago: The Dorsey Press, 1985.

Kostal, Devlin A., Captain, USAF. *Integration of Law Enforcement and Military Intelligence During the Tan War, 1920-21: Lessons Learned for the Global War on Terrorism.* MSSI Thesis chaired by Jon A. Wiant. Washington: Joint Military Intelligence College, July 2004.

Kretchik, Walter E. "Fielding the International Police Monitors for Operation Uphold Democracy." *Low Intensity Conflict & Law Enforcement* 7, no. 2 (Autumn 1998): 107-120.

Lowenthal, Mark M. *Intelligence: From Secrets to Policy.* Washington: CQ Press, 2000.

Meigs, Montgomery C. "Unorthodox Thoughts About Asymmetric Warfare." *Parameters* 33, no. 2 (Summer 2003): 4-18.

McClintock, Bruce H., Major, USAF. "Transformation Trinity: Vision, Culture, Assessment." *Joint Force Quarterly,* no. 26 (Autumn 2000): 27-31.

The Missing Dimension: Governments and Intelligence Communities in the Twentieth Century. Eds. Christopher Andrew and David Dilks. Urbana: University of Illinois Press, 1984.

Mockaitis, Thomas R. *British Counterinsurgency, 1919-1960: Studies in Military and Strategic History*. London: MacMillan, 1990.

Moore, David. *Critical Thinking and Intelligence Analysis*. Occasional Paper No. 14. Washington: Joint Military Intelligence College, 2006.

_____. *Creating Intelligence: Evidence and Inference in the Analysis Process*. MSSI Thesis chaired by Francis J. Hughes. Washington: Joint Military Intelligence College, July 2002.

National Commission on Terrorist Attacks Upon the United States. *The 9/11 Commission Report: Final Report of the National Commission on Terrorist Attacks Upon the United States*. New York: W.W. Norton & Co., 2004.

O'Hayon, Gregory. *Creating an Organized Crime SENTINEL: Development and Implementation of a Strategic Early Warning Methodology for Law Enforcement*. Ottawa: Criminal Intelligence Service Canada, April 2005.

Osborne, Deborah. *Out of Bounds: Innovation and Change in Law Enforcement Intelligence Analysis*. Washington: Joint Military Intelligence College, 2006.

Peterson, Marilyn B. *Intelligence-Led Policing: The New Intelligence Architecture*. Washington: Bureau of Justice Assistance, 2005. URL: <www.ncjrs.gov/pdffiles1/bja/210680.pdf>. Accessed 28 November 2006.

_____. "Product vs. Process." *IALEIA Journal* 11, no. 1 (Winter 1998): 1-13.

Perkins, David, Lieutenant Colonel, USA, CI and HUMINT Directorate, Office of the Deputy Chief of Staff for Intelligence. "HUMINT/CI." Case Study on HUMINT and CI conducted by the U.S. in Bosnia. URL: <www.fas.org/irp/ops/smo/docs/bosnia_humint/humint.htm>. Accessed 16 April 2004.

Polmar, Norman, and Thomas Allen. *The Spy Book: The Encyclopedia of Espionage*. New York: Random House, 1998.

Rollis, Devin C., Chief Warrant Officer Four, USA. *The Wall: The Creation of the Barrier between Intelligence and Law Enforcement*. MSSI Thesis chaired by Ronny B. Bragger, July 2003.

Schneider, Stephen R. "The Criminal Intelligence Function: Toward a Comprehensive and Normative Model," June 1995. *International Association of Law Enforcement Intelligence Analysts.* URL: <http://www.ialeia. org/09021.shtml>. Accessed 12 July 1999.

Smith, Stacey L., Captain, USAF. *Information Sharing: Between Law Enforcement and the Intelligence Community.* MSSI Thesis chaired by Dr. Pauletta Otis. Washington: Joint Military Intelligence College, August 2003.

Spencer, David W. *Predictive Intelligence: What the Drug Enforcement Administration Can Glean from the Intelligence Community.* MSSI Thesis chaired by Jan Goldman. Washington: Joint Military Intelligence College, July 2006.

Thompson, Clive. "Open Source Spying." *New York Times Magazine,* 3 December 2006. Accessed via Proquest, 4 December 2006.

Turbiville, Graham H. "The Organized Crime Dimension of Regional Conflict and 'Operations Other than War.'" *Special Warfare* 7, no. 2 (April 1994): 6-7.

Valentine, Bill. *Gang Intelligence Manual: Identifying and Understanding Modern-Day Violent Gangs in the United States.* Boulder, CO: Paladin Press, 1995.

White, Jonathan R. *Defending the Homeland.* Belmont, CA: Wadsworth, 2004.

INDEX

www.ingramcontent.com/pod-product-compliance
Lightning Source LLC
Chambersburg PA
CBHW072042280526
45788CB00006B/2153